On Realism

J. P. Stern

Professor of German,
University College, London

ROUTLEDGE & KEGAN PAUL

LONDON AND BOSTON

First published 1973
by Routledge & Kegan Paul Ltd
Broadway House, 68–74 Carter Lane,
London EC4V 5EL and
9 Park Street,
Boston, Mass. 02108, U.S.A.
Printed in Great Britain by
Cox & Wyman Ltd, London,
Fakenham and Reading

ISBN 0 7100 7379 8

PN
56
R 358

General Editor's Introduction

The study of literature has normally centred on the consideration of work, author, or historical period. But increasingly there is a demand for a more analytic approach, for investigation and explanation of literary concepts of crucial ideas and issues—topics which are of general importance to the critical consideration of particular works. This series undertakes to provide a clear description and critical evaluation of such important ideas as 'symbolism', 'realism', 'style' and other terms used in literary discussion. It also undertakes to define the relationship of literature to other intellectual disciplines: anthropology, philosophy, psychology, etc., for it is in connection with such related fields that much important recent critical work has been done. *Concepts of Literature* will both account for the methodology of literary study, and will define its dimensions by reference to the many activities that throw light upon it. Individual works will describe the fundamental outlines of particular problems and explore the frontiers that they suggest. The series as a whole will provide a survey of recent literary thought.

To Alan and Teresa Marter

Contents

Acknowledgments

My thanks are due to the Modern Humanities Research Association and its editors for permission to reprint my contribution to *A Garland of Essays Offered to Professor Elizabeth Mary Hill* (Cambridge 1970), which appears as §§ 4–11 of the present book; to the editors of the *Journal of European Studies*, for allowing me to reprint, as parts of Chapter 2, an article which appeared in their first (1971) number; and to Messrs Thames & Hudson, for allowing me to summarize in § 35 an argument from Chapter 1 of my *Re-Interpretations: Seven Studies in Nineteenth-Century German Literature* (London 1964).

It is an especial pleasure to acknowledge the helpful criticism made in the course of many discussions with three friends: Michael Beddow, Nicholas Boyle, and above all Graham Hough.

All translations, unless otherwise indicated, are my own.

Non iam desiderabam meliora, quia omnia cogitabam; et meliora quidem superiora, quam inferiora; sed meliora omnia, quam sola superiora, iudicia saniore pendebam. . . . Et omnia vera sunt, in quantum sunt; nec quidquam est falsitas, nisi cum putaretur esse, quod non est. Et vidi, quia non solum locis sua quaeque suis conveniunt, sed etiam temporibus.

S. Augustinus, *Confessiones*, VII, xiii–xv.

Because I contemplated all things, I now no longer desired the higher; reckoning in my better judgment that although the higher things are better than the lower, the sum of all things is better than the higher things alone. . . . All things are true in so far as they are; falsehood is nothing but the supposed being of that which is not. And I saw, too, that all things are fit and proper not only to their places but also to their times.

1

Three samples

i The riches of the world

§ 1

Chapter 33 of the *Pickwick Papers* is devoted to certain minor events which occurred on the thirteenth of February 1828, the day immediately preceding that appointed for the hearing of Mrs Bardell v. Mr Pickwick. We know what a traumatic subject the law-courts were for Dickens. In the very next chapter, and then again when describing Mr Pickwick's life in the Fleet, Dickens will break the serene flow of his narrative with harsh facts and acid comment. But here his tone is light, with occasional laconic understatements: 'People who go voluntarily to law, or are taken forcibly there for the first time, may be allowed to labour under some temporary irritation or anxiety.' Mr Pickwick, 'in a state of excitement and worry', is no exception to the rule. Not until we have been given 'a full and faithful Report of the memorable Trial' for breach of promise, and verdict has been passed against him, does Mr Pickwick regain that 'perfect cheerfulness and content of heart' which we know to be his usual mood.

However, our business is with Samuel Weller junior, his servant of 'imperturbable good humour and unrufflable composure'. Having said goodbye to his master, who is quite glad to be left alone with his worries, Sam sets out for a meeting with his father at the Blue Boar in Leadenhall Market. Walking past a stationer's window, he notices an especially picturesque and exotic Valentine:

> The particular picture on which Sam Weller's eyes were fixed . . .
> was a highly coloured representation of a couple of human hearts
> skewered together with an arrow, cooking before a cheerful fire,

while a male and female cannibal in modern attire: the gentleman
being clad in a blue coat and white trousers, and the lady in a
deep-red pelisse with a parasol of the same: were approaching
the meal with hungry eyes, up a serpentine gravel path leading
thereunto. A decidedly indelicate young gentleman, in a pair of
wings and nothing else, was depicted as superintending the
cooking; a representation of the spire of the church in Langham
Place, London, appeared in the distance; and the whole formed a
'valentine', of which, as a written inscription in the window
testified, there was a large assortment within, which the
shopkeeper pledged himself to dispose of, to his countrymen
generally, at the reduced rate of one and sixpence each.

[Nelson Classics edition]

The novelist's ostensible reason for this diversion is that the valentine
reminds Sam of 'Mary, Housemaid at Mr Nupkins's [the] Mayor's,
Ipswich', with whom he was smitten when attending on Mr Pickwick
in the course of his adventures in that town. Obviously, the whole
description is too elaborate to serve merely as a reminder, but what
other purpose does it serve?

Two very simple narrative lines are here combined. The homely
sentiment of a 'gentleman' and a 'lady' in love is contrasted with
luridly exotic and fanciful allegory. The people depicted are very
ordinary mortals, like Sam and Mary. This fact is established by their
dress, and the prosiness is underlined by such expressions as 'of the
same' 'leading thereunto', and 'decidedly indelicate'. The allegory
on the other hand takes us to distant lands, far away from 'the spire
of the church in Langham Place, London'. The mildly humorous
effect of the passage derives from this contrast between the prosy
and the romantic; and this contrast in turn—with the prosy side
dominant—is characteristic of Sam Weller. He *is* something of a
romantic, even though his main role in the novel is to be severely
practical and down-to-earth. Yet even this doesn't fully explain the
purpose of the scene, for by dwelling on it the narrator is not adding
much to our understanding of one of his main characters. Why
'Langham Place', why 'London'? Because here we all are—Sam
Weller, his creator, readers and all—friendly neighbours and in-
habitants of one world. The fullest purpose of the diversion is to add
and superadd to that sense of assurance and abundance and reality
that speaks to us from every page and every episode of the novel—

to add to that sense both by the fantasticality of the 'cannibals in modern attire' as well as by the quaint commercial flourish with which the passage ends.

Now Sam enters the shop and purchases 'a sheet of the best gilt-edged letter-paper, and a hard-nibbed pen, which could be warranted not to splutter' (which in due course it does), and proceeds to the Blue Boar where, on being told that his ancient parent isn't expected for a while yet, he orders a drink and settles down to his unwonted labour:

> The brandy and water luke, and the inkstand, having been carried into the little parlour, and the young lady having carefully flattened down the coals to prevent their blazing, and carried away the poker to preclude the possibility of the fire being stirred, without the full privity and concurrence of the Blue Boar being first had and obtained, Sam Weller sat himself down in a box near the stove, and pulled out the sheet of gilt-edged letter-paper and the hard-nibbed pen. Then, looking carefully at the pen to see that there were no hairs in it, and dusting down the table, so that there might be no crumbs of bread under the paper, Sam tucked up the cuffs of his coat, squared his elbows, and composed himself to write.
>
> To ladies and gentlemen who are not in the habit of devoting themselves practically to the science of penmanship, writing a letter is no very easy task; it being always considered necessary in such cases for the writer to recline his head on his left arm, so as to place his eyes as nearly as possible on a level with the paper, and while glancing sideways at the letters he is constructing, to form with his tongue imaginary characters to correspond. These motions, although unquestionably of the greatest assistance to original composition, retard in some degree the progress of the writer; and Sam had unconsciously been a full hour and a half writing words in small text, smearing out wrong letters with his little finger, and putting in new ones which required going over very often to render them visible through the old blots. . . .

§ 2

There are countless such scenes in the *Pickwick Papers*, such slightly shapeless lagoons of expatiation, where the flow of the narrative slackens almost to a standstill (not to mention the numerous *novelle*, whose connection with the main story is hardly discernible to the most partial eye). There are so many of them, in fact, that we are apt to regard them as signs of authorial self-indulgence. After all, the main function of Sam Weller in the structure of the whole story is quite clear. He provides the common-sense contact between the guileless, harmless, and awkward Mr Pickwick, a figure of almost angelic innocence but also of impractical righteousness, and a world which, if not outright evil, is at all events calculating and expedient, money-minded and 'sharp'. Sam provides a contact, and a defence. For he too is sharp, capable of ruses on his master's behalf, while he remains loving and loyal to him throughout. Sam's blandness can be deceptive, and there are many occasions when his endless anecdotal patter saves Mr Pickwick from disaster (though again these rescue operations don't justify nearly all the anecdotes he tells). At the same time there is about Sam—especially in matters of the heart—a naïvety and lack of sophistication, which are apparent in the passages I have quoted. These qualities explain his elaborate preparations for the epistolary task, the mention of 'ladies and gentlemen who are not in the habit of devoting themselves' to what after several more lines of banter will be described as 'original composition'; and it is this good-natured naïvety that speaks from the letter itself, which will be quoted, cockney spelling and all, albeit with many anxious interruptions from Sam Weller senior, later in the chapter.

Of the charm of this scene in the Blue Boar there is, I think, little doubt. Yet we feel that here again is a good deal that hasn't very much to do either with Sam, Mr Pickwick's naïve, kindly, and unlettered servant who is having a crush on a housemaid, or with Sam, Mr Pickwick's wily protector and extricator from awkward situations. The brandy-and-water, the inkstand, the mild ploy about the fire, even perhaps the details of Sam's painful penmanship, seem a little in excess of what may be needed to establish the appropriate mood. What is it that Dickens is indulging?

§ 3

I chose these scenes because there is nothing grand or passionate about them. They are set in the modest regions of life, of social and emotional life alike. The scenes are, if you like, 'typical Dickens', but they aren't typical of anything much else (to the social historian they will say something, but not very much). They offer us physical details, some of the 'bric à brac' of the age, but not from very close by, and with no emphasis on their symbolical quality. Many of the details ('Leadenhall Market') point to the whole of which they are a part, yet they do so perfunctorily, in the most casual way. For this is no more than a tiny corner of that England which Dickens will never tire of evoking: sometimes humorously (as here), sometimes nostalgically and sentimentally (as in *David Copperfield*), sometimes satirically (as in the Eatanswill scenes), sometimes with deepest indignation at its barbaric ugliness (*The Old Curiosity Shop*), with scathing comments on its social injustice and heartlessness (*Hard Times*), on its hideous poverty (*Barnaby Rudge*), and again and again with violent invective against its petrified and inhuman legal system.

Yet, however different the moods, what informs his evocations is always an unabating *interest* in this world and in this society as a thing real and, as to its reality, wholly unproblematic. *This* is the indulgence of the narrator's self, and the acknowledged condition of his muse. Brandy-and-water, inkstand and mean coal-fire in the little parlour at the Blue Boar are the signs of this acknowledgment, of the *eros* that binds him to this world. They are the signs not of a deprivation, not of a want of reassurance, but the emblems of plenty.

On the other hand these abundant scenes from the social and physical world are not very carefully arranged, not 'highly structured', and only in the later novels will they be informed by a critical consciousness. But even then the delight in the elaboration of the circumstances of living situations and encounters, of jobs and houses and rivers, of clothes and bodies and faces, will often get the better of the narrative line. Franz Kafka, who saw his own unfinished *Amerika* as 'sheer [imitation of] *Copperfield*', is critical yet full of admiration mixed with envy. It is all *so* unlike what he himself can ever hope to do, he writes in his diary (8. x. 1917), for 'Dickens is all richness and heedless overflowing'.

ii *The testing of the prince*

§ 4

'The meek shall inherit the earth': what would it be like, a novel on that theme?* It is difficult to think of a biblical text that would lend itself more readily to fantasy, utopia, and spiritual extravaganzas, yet from *Don Quixote* through the *Pickwick Papers* to Dostoevsky's *The Idiot* it has been the inspiration of some of the greatest works of modern fiction. Here is a text which offers a paramount challenge to the writer who makes it his task 'to bring into being . . . an instance of the feeling of what life is about';[1] to the novelist who, with this task before him, chooses to restrict his imaginative and creative resources to a specific set of conditions in the worldly world. It is the accomplishment of this task in its most rigorous and most exacting form—the very palpable problem it poses—that interests us here.

§ 5

'Of course, all that happened tonight was ephemeral, fantastic, unseemly—and yet, don't you agree, it was full of colour, full of originality': the character who, at the end of part I of *The Idiot*, thus describes his impression of that first evening at Nastasia Filipovna's, might be describing our first impression of the novel itself. 'Ephemeral, fantastic [or perhaps we had better stick closer to the text: romantic], unseemly': the novel is placed at the farthest remove from those middle regions of life in which Mr Pickwick has his benign being. There is something extreme about the regions of experience that are here charted. The ambience is heavy with every kind of passion and desire, rank with an assortment of crimes and sins (and some, for which there is no room in the action, are added by way of anecdote); it is full of ineptitudes and *faux pas*, of monstrous betrayals, heedless avowals and accusations and, again and again, absurd because pointless 'declarations' and confessions. An attempted suicide, two strokes of apoplexy, two epileptic fits, an attempted murder and, finally, a successful one seem amply to bear out the narrator's claim that 'it is better for the writer to content himself with a bare statement of events' because 'the motives of human actions are as a rule infinitely more complicated and diverse than our subsequent explanation of them' (IV. iii). However, unless

* 'By theme we mean that whose representation contains the sufficient reason of other representations supplied in the discourse [= the literary work], but which does not have sufficient reason in them' (A. G. Baumgarten, *Reflections on Poetry* [1735], § 66, transl. K. Aschenbrenner & W. B. Holther, Berkeley, 1954, p. 62).

we include conversations under the heading of 'events', we had better not hold the narrator too strictly to his word. For of course we must add to our list all those long and frequently absurd and always inconclusive discussions about Mother Russia, Russian and Roman Christianity, love and beauty, the 'social question', the 'woman question', the present and future standing of the aristocracy, the. . . . It is far from easy to complete this patently unprepossessing catalogue of the novel's dramatic data. Are those critics right who charge Dostoevsky with a lack of narrative discipline? Or those others, who see his work smothered in a syrup of sensational spirituality?

§ 6

The novel opens breathlessly, with Prince Lev Nikolaevitch Myshkin's arrival at St Petersburg Station at the end of a long journey from Switzerland. The Prince's guilelessness and innocence, his sweet temper and inability to see other people's motives except in a good light, in brief his other-worldliness, are established before the train has come to a stop; and so is the fact that he was, and perhaps still is, an epileptic. His last two sleepless nights in the third-class compartment are followed by an even more exhausting day, which occupies the whole of part I. (Small wonder that Yevgeni Radomsky, whom Dostoevsky wished to present as the last gentleman of the old style,[2] suggests caustically at the end of the novel that a good night's sleep might have saved the Prince a lot of trouble.) Myshkin is twenty-six or twenty-seven years old. Having left Russia as a child, he comes as a complete stranger, yet within a few hours he will be fully involved in an intricate network of relationships.

Almost all the characters of the drama are presented in the course of that first day and the following night, and all the convolutions of plot and ideas will develop from these early encounters. On the train Myshkin meets the ghastly Lebedev, lowly clerk, money-lender and cat's-paw, the Uriah Heep of the piece, and Parfen Rogozhin, who has just come into a fortune and who will soon see Myshkin as his rival for the love of Nastasia Filipovna, the Mary Magdalen of the story. Myshkin as yet knows nobody, but his ancient family name and its snob appeal (of which he is at first unaware) secure him admission to the family of General Yepanchin, whose wife, Lizaveta Prokofievna, is a distant relation of his. Almost instantly he falls in love with Aglaia, the youngest and most charming of the three Yepanchin girls. From the Yepanchins he moves to other circles, all interrelated, each more questionable in its social standing, intersecting again at Nastasia Filipovna. She is much admired by old General Yepanchin, she is wooed by Gania (Gavrila Ardalionovitch), the General's impecunious secretary, and for her Rogozhin will stake his all. Gania, who has just unsuccessfully proposed to Aglaia, offers Myshkin lodgings in his family's flat, where he meets the 'nihilist' Ferdishenko, and Gania's brother, the boy Kolia, who will be Myshkin's dearest and only friend and who is the hope (if there is a hope) for a better Russia. All these people will in due course move to their residences at Pavlovsk, the summer resort of Petersburg society, under the watchful eye of the ubiquitous Lebedev. They will be followed by that *Lumpenproletariat* of drop-out students and retired sub-lieutenants who call themselves 'socialists' and 'nihilists', of whom Ferdishenko is one and whom Rogozhin has 'introduced' to Myshkin during that first astonishing evening ('ephemeral, fantastic, unseemly'); and they will accompany Myshkin like a hideous chorus, like a band of marauders, almost to the end. They in turn . . . but enough has been said to indicate *how close* are the interconnections between the respectable and the scurrilous, how claustrophobic is the social network in which the Prince is caught up, *how substantial* is the world he enters. How does Dostoevsky evoke this substantiality?

§ 7

Each of the four parts of the novel is centred on a house in the city or at Pavlovsk, and each part culminates in a dramatic showdown. The houses and their furniture don't matter very much. There are, to be sure, some obvious 'symbolical' parallels between the settings and the dominant moods of the various scenes. A dying youth's eyes are focused on a spring-green tree. Rogozhin's huge and gloomy city house figures repeatedly in the last part: here he murders Nastasia Filipovna, and here the Prince's mind suffers its final trauma. Something is made of the fact that the first of Myshkin's epileptic seizures, and the murder, take place in the sultry heat of approaching summer storms. A collision with a chair, a shattered Chinese vase, a shower of pearls and diamonds after an abandoned wedding; the Prince's outlandish cloak and gaiters; a huge diamond pin that fastens a filthy cravat; a dirty boot on the lace skirt of a lady's dress—all this detritus of life is in the novel, but it merely supports meanings, it doesn't significantly contribute to them. The reader becomes familiar with Dostoevsky's interiors, but in an off-hand, almost mechanical way; he feels that the author attends to them impatiently and by way of a concession. It would be a foolish undertaking to apply to the physical details of the novel the same 'technique of analysis' developed for the purpose of scrutinizing Vronsky's shirts before the steeplechase, let alone Emma Bovary's slippers or Charles's hideous cap.

The focus of Dostoevsky's creative attention is on the conversations. On that most inexact and impermanent of human pastimes he expends his greatest exactitude. He excels at bizarre openings—as when Myshkin has just entered a room:

> 'Why are you staring at me?' [Rogozhin] muttered.
> 'Sit down.'
> The Prince sat down.
> 'Parfen', he said, 'tell me honestly, did you know I was coming to Petersburg or no?'
> 'Oh, I supposed you were coming, and, you see, I was quite right', the other replied with a grin, 'but how was I to know that you would come today?'

There are strangely inconsequential snatches of words:

> 'She asked me what I should do if I found that she deceived me. I said, "You know well enough".'
> 'What did she know?' replied the Prince.
> 'How do I know?' replied Rogozhin with an angry laugh.
>
> [II. iii]

There are brilliant vignettes of the sort of semi-educated moonshine that passes for 'philosophizing', as when Lebedev bores everyone with the story of the man who was sentenced for eating sixty fat monks in an age—the twelfth century—when the laity was lean:

> 'A brilliant idea! And most true!' cried Lebedev. 'He never took a bite of the laity. Sixty monks and not a single layman! It is a terrible idea, a *historic* idea, a *statistic* idea! Indeed, from such facts an intelligent man constructs history, because from it may be inferred with numerical accuracy that the clergy in those days were sixty times happier....'
>
> [III. iv]

And there is of course a good deal of sheer sententiousness, as when Madame Yepanchin concludes her sermon to Kolia's father, who is an alcoholic: 'Go away! I speak seriously to you. There is nothing better for repentance than to remember the past with remorse' (II. vi).

From such elements as these Dostoevsky assembles those huge far-ranging conversations where everybody is playing 'Truth', some more truthfully than others. These conversations follow almost always the same pattern: intimate confessions and blush-making self-disclosures widen into huge generalities and encyclopedic statements of the human condition. Some of these statements are no doubt intended satirically, others come very close to Dostoevsky's innermost beliefs. All of them are in a sense futile, since they all contribute to the final doom. They are all a comment on that particular social situation—that Russian situation—in which talk and yet more talk is a substitute for purposeful action; that situation which is Goncharov's concern in *Oblomov* and Gogol's in *Dead Souls*; which is endlessly enacted in Chekhov's plays; which Thomas Mann understood so well that he built *The Magic Mountain* from it; which is the exasperation of superficial Western readers and the peculiar glory of nineteenth-century Russian literature. These conversations are here driven forward by a restless, at times hysterical energy. Their verbal texture is obviously that of the ordinary vernacular, but unselfconsciously so: the colloquial dimension of the language is used to reveal something of the social status and personal characteristics of each speaker, but all within a relatively narrow range of variations and effects. Colloquialisms, verbal repetitions, syntactic deformations for the purpose of emphasis offer difficulties to the translator; but since all these devices are wholly in the service of the conversational argument, since they aren't lingered over in the restless narrative flow, the translator's difficulties are not insurmountable. The language is wholly devoid of verbal play. The paradoxes of the novel are not entrusted to aphorism but take on an extended form, the form of action and conversation—in short, Dostoevsky's language displays no 'poetic creativeness', is essentially unpoetic. The stylistic devices, like the physical settings, are in the service of the overall structure and idea of the novel.

But of course there is another sense, in which these conversations are the opposite of futile. They as well as the deeds they analyse and the deeds that proceed from them contain the challenge to Myshkin's saintliness, to that utterly problematic *imitatio Christi* which is enacted in 'the idiot's' life in the world. To put it briefly and obscurely: the substantial challenge to the Prince—*to meet the world*—is identical with the formal challenge to the Prince's creator —*to create a world*.

§ 8

'If Don Quixote and Pickwick as philanthropists are charming to the reader, it is because they are comical', Dostoevsky writes in his notes. And again: 'The hero of this novel, the Prince, is not comical but does have another charming quality: he is innocent!' And triumphantly, at last (after eight drafts) in perfect possession of what he calls 'the idea of the book': '*He is a prince*'.[3] Yes—but how is such a character to be made convincing? How in Dostoevsky's day and ours, is innocence to be made credible? There is, as he says, the humorous solution: Mr Pickwick (and humour in its purest form, Mr Wodehouse's Bertie Wooster). But humour depends upon an omission of one part of the substantial world, namely its weightiness, and a corresponding exaggeration of another part, namely its inconsequentiality;[4] neither of these is to Dostoevsky's present purpose. There is the device of coupling humour with more or less satirical indirection: *Don Quixote*, *Candide*, Hašek's *The Good Soldier Schweik*—there are a good many devices of this kind in *The Idiot*. The story of the big party in honour of Myshkin's and Aglaia's engagement, and of the priceless vase that breaks in the course of that party, is splendid if sombre social comedy, especially since it is preceded by her anxious warning: 'Look here, once for all', cried Aglaia, boiling over, 'if you start talking about capital punishment, or the economic condition of Russia, or about Beauty redeeming the World, I'll . . .' (IV. vi).

And there is, as we shall see, the grim, mortifying humour of disillusionment. But humour and satire alike are incidental to Dostoevsky's purpose (like the furniture, like the houses, like the colloquialisms). Humour is part of the wider meaning, not an end in itself. Occasionally events are presented in a comic light, but to see the whole novel in *that* perspective is to see it from a point too distant to make out its details. There are several occasions, notably the opening of part IV, where the narrator very deliberately adopts something like this distant perspective, interposing arch devices of authorial self-consciousness ('There were rumours to the effect that . . .', 'we can't be sure what happened . . .') between the reader and the fictitious world. It may be that they are intended as moments of respite from the almost heedless flow of the narrative. But Dostoevsky cannot keep to this mode for long. These devices are only successful to the extent that they offer a contrast to those other, more numerous passages where we are much closer to the scene of the action, and more fully involved in Dostoevsky's central undertaking: which is, to oppose to Myshkin's innocence *the weight of worldly experience*.

How much closer? He engages in very little psychological analysis. The interior monologues he gives us are couched in the same language as the language he uses when his characters are playing 'Truth', when they are articulating for the benefit of others what goes on inside their minds. The *public* nature of all those declarations and confessions and acts of repentance is essential to Dostoevsky's purpose, because Myshkin has come among men. Meekness, to survive, must be armed. If the meekness and forgiveness Myshkin has to offer is to be armed with wisdom and strength, these qualities must be tested in contact and conflict with those who now encompass his horizon, who are now his world. This is how the testing is done.

§ 9

The scene (II. vi–x) is Lebedev's countryhouse at Pavlovsk (it might, incidentally, be the Dean of Students' room on any 'revolting' campus). There are present: the Prince, all the Yepanchins, the host, and that motley crew of protesters I have mentioned (as well as several other people). They are not just nihilists, Lebedev explains to the General, 'they go further, they are men of action'. One of them has composed and published an article, which he now reads to the assembled company and which turns out to be a slanderous attack on Myshkin. For Myshkin has meanwhile inherited a small fortune to which (so the newspaper article claims) he has no *moral* right. Whatever the legal niceties of the case, the author of the article asserts, the rightful heir is Burdovsky, one of their own lot, his *moral* right being based on a complicated tale in which he claims to be the illegitimate son of Myshkin's late guardian. (Myshkin meanwhile has been supporting Burdovsky's mother.) The reading of the article and the subsequent heated discussion are accompanied by the chorus, 'We demand, we don't beg!'[5] However, with Gania's help the article is proved to be a complete fabrication, all the details connected with the 'rightful claim' turn out to be false (most of them, incidentally, were supplied by Lebedev for a small fee)—nevertheless, the Prince is prepared to honour the 'rightful moral claim'. For every act of meanness and betrayal he finds a more or less plausible explanation, exonerating the claimant, the writer of the article, exonerating even Lebedev. Now the claimant, who does have a spark of honour in him, refuses Myshkin's offer, which enables one of the gang to assail him: 'Well, Prince, to do you justice, you certainly know how to make the best of your—let's call it infirmity, for the sake of politeness. You have made your offer of friendship and money in such a way that no honourable man could possibly accept it' (II. ix).

And so the verbal battle rages on, the ever more incontinent attacks on the Prince being met with the sweetness and equanimity of—a saint? No, of a man whose seemingly endless compassion enables him to understand the misery, the deprivations, and the feelings of inferiority to which these wretched young men (the noisiest of them is dying of consumption) are prey. An astonishing combination of insights—political, social, moral, and psychological —is embodied in this scene. And when it is at its noisiest, at its most intense, when, short of physical violence, there is apparently no insult left for them to hurl at Myshkin and each invective has been encountered by his generous understanding and forgiveness, then it is Madame Yepanchin's turn. And in her outburst (II. ix)—of which the following dismembered quotation gives no more than a suggestion—every single theme of the novel makes its appearance, every aspect of reality is given its full weight:

'Enough!' Lizaveta Prokofievna cried suddenly, trembling with anger, 'we've had enough of this balderdash!'
In a state of terrible excitement she threw back her head, casting flaming looks of contempt and defiance round the room, in which she could hardly distinguish friend and foe. . . .
'Enough, Ivan Fedorovitch! Leave me alone. Why do you offer me your arm now? You didn't have enough sense to take me away before. . . . Wait a moment, I've still got to thank the Prince. Thank you, Prince, for the entertainment. I was most amused to listen to

these young people. It's vile, vile. This is chaos, infamy, worse than a nightmare. Are there many like them?' ...

'So you, my dear man', she continued, turning to the Prince, 'you are even asking their forgiveness! "Forgive me!" he says, "Forgive me for offering you a fortune." And you, you mountebank, what are you laughing at?' she pounced suddenly on Lebedev's nephew. ' "We refuse the fortune", he says, "we demand, we don't beg!" As though he didn't know that this idiot will come to them tomorrow, and will offer them his friendship and his money all over again. You will, won't you? Come now—will you or won't you?'

'I shall', said the Prince, quietly and humbly.

'You hear him. That's what you are counting on', she continued, turning on Doktorenko. 'The money is as good as in your pocket, while you're playing the mountebank to throw dust in our eyes. No, sir, you may take in other fools, I can see through you! ... And this stutterer—won't he murder?' (she was pointing at Burdovsky, who was looking at her in utter stupefaction). 'I bet he will. Maybe he won't take your money, your ten thousand, maybe his conscience won't let him, but he'll come at night and murder you and take it from your cashbox. He'll take it with a clear conscience! He doesn't call it dishonest! He calls it "the impulse of noble despair", "negation", or the devil knows what!' ...

... 'Why did you come here tonight full of insolence? "Don't dare to come near us. Give us our rights, but don't dare to open your mouth in our presence. Show us your deepest respect, and we'll treat you like the lowest of the low." They seek absolute truth, they stand on their rights, and yet they slander him in their article like a lot of heathen miscreants. "We demand, we don't beg, you will get no thanks from us because you're acting to satisfy your own conscience." What morality! But, don't you know, if you say you offer no gratitude, why then shouldn't the Prince answer that he feels no gratitude to [his guardian] either, because his guardian was also only satisfying his own conscience. But you counted on the Prince's gratitude, didn't you, you never lent him money, he owes you nothing—so what were you counting on if not his gratitude? Why do you yourself deny it to him? ... They don't believe in God, they don't believe in Christ! Why, you are so eaten up by vanity and pride that you'll end up by eating up each other—that's my prophecy. Isn't this chaos, disgraceful confusion

and chaos? Isn't that infamy. . . .' (She turned on Ipolit.) 'He's at
his last gasp yet he corrupts others. You've corrupted this boy'
(she pointed to Kolia), 'he just raves about you, you teach him
atheism, you don't believe in God, but you're not too old to be
flogged, sir! A plague on you! . . . And so you will go to them
tomorrow, Prince Lev Nikolaevitch, won't you?' she asked the
Prince breathlessly, for the second time.
   'Yes. I'll go.'

Translators are apt to want to 'improve' such passages, shortening
a bit here, avoiding a repetition there, making them more 'readable'.
Nothing much goes wrong when they do this (the result will still be
entirely characteristic of Madame Yepanchin), but the improve-
ments don't really matter. There is so much worldly substance, so
much material in this tirade that its verbal quality (its lexis, the
order of the argument, the nature of the connections) becomes
secondary. For here, as I have said, every major concern of the novel
is touched on.
   This is an outburst of profound indignation, therefore the question of who is right, Mme Yepanchin or the Prince, receives no
simple answer. As to that, we are witnessing four violent *volte-
faces*: the original accusation (Burdovsky's slanderous article) sounds
entirely convincing, until the Prince, with Gania's help, refutes it, bit
by bit; his refutation spills over into explanations of motives and (so
help us) 'forgiveness' which in turn sound perfectly convincing;
until Mme Yepanchin, informed by a worldly common sense that has
nothing trivial or expedient about it, shows the pointlessness and
indeed the immorality of such 'idiotic' forgiveness; all of which is
refuted once more by the human, all too-human facts of the case—
Ipolit is at death's door, Burdovsky is really a 'decent fellow' and
terribly poor, &c. The question is not who is right but whether the
Prince's innocence and sweetness can stand up before the 'facts of
the case'. And the answer is that the greater the number of these facts
presented, and the more fully they are presented, the less adequate
he proves. As the novel proceeds, his *saying*, 'I forgive you', even
though it is backed by a truthful *feeling* of forgiveness, leads to deeds
which are beyond the scope of his forgiveness because they involve
the lives and deaths of other people. The authority he wields is an
existential authority, based on what he is as a person and a man, and
thus limited. He can say, with perfect sincerity, 'Thou art forgiven',

but he hasn't the authority to add, 'Go and sin no more'. When the conflict between the ideal and the real (as Schiller, whom Dostoevsky so greatly admired, would have called it) reaches its highest pitch, the Prince's moral will collapses. What my long quotation was intended to show is how varied are the possibilities of sin, how weighty and dire is the conflict he faces.

§ 10

But then: who is Myshkin, why does he fail? Dostoevsky leaves his innocence defenceless, infinitely vulnerable. We gather that during his epileptic fits Myshkin experiences moments of elation and mystic insight ('a strange *inner* light illuminated his soul'). Yet Dostoevsky doesn't omit what he himself calls 'the dialectical part of the argument' (II. v), for he unsparingly connects these 'moments of supreme awareness, unbounded joy, ecstatic prayer and fullest life' with the state of 'stupefaction, mental darkness and idiocy' which follow in their wake. On his long walk through the sultry town (II. v) Myshkin is presented in a visionary state that heightens his sensibility and gives him prophetic insight (Dostoevsky, himself an epileptic, believed that Mohammed was one too). And the seizure which occurs at the end of that walk, at the moment when Rogozhin is about to knife him, saves Myshkin's life. Then again, Myshkin's strange *eros* and impaired sexuality are quite explicitly connected with the disease; and this strange *eros* in turn accounts for his inability to choose between Aglaia and Nastasia, or rather for his inability to choose Aglaia when he thinks Nastasia is doomed. But all this isn't saying any more than that his illness is an inseparable, incurable *part* of Myshkin, part of the strangeness and the charm of the man he is. We don't know whether Dostoevsky wished us to see the illness as divinely inspired. It certainly doesn't make Myshkin a wiser man, or one better able to help others. (In the Christian Orthodox tradition a lack of worldly wisdom is often said to be a condition of divine inspiration.) Yet even though neither the novel nor the notebooks contain a single word in affirmation of a divine origin of Myshkin's *illness*, there can be no doubt that his total *person* is intended as something like an *imitatio Christi*. We come to the borderline of theology. Yet even here—or rather, here especially—Dostoevsky doesn't abandon the perspective to which he has committed himself throughout the novel: what he shows is the defective nature of

Myshkin's *imitatio*, a defectiveness measured not in terms of transcendent spirituality but in terms of the world.

The issue is raised early on in the novel (II. v), in connection with the Holbein Deposition, a copy of which hangs in Rogozhin's house. That terrible picture is not described, but the portrayal of the dead body of Jesus makes Myshkin exclaim (as did Dostoevsky), 'Why, by this picture a man's faith might be ruined'. The thought is not pursued here (as it is in *The Brothers Karamazov*), the testing of Myshkin's faith takes another form. Or rather, what is being tested is not his faith only but his total personality, faith and *eros* and moral will all together. To the woes of the world Myshkin knows only one answer: 'Compassion', he argues with himself, 'will teach and give understanding even to Rogozhin. Compassion is the chief, perhaps the only, law of life' (II. v). But it isn't—not of the life that is here unfolded, and incidentally not of the life we know.

The irony of the denouement challenges any facile assumption about the nature of Dostoevsky's spirituality. It is the enlightened rationalist, the 'last gentleman-landowner', Yevgeny Radomsky who, just before the final tragedy, shows up the inadequacy of the 'chief law' of Myshkin's life. The explanations of the Prince's conduct (partly psychological, partly medical, partly social) to which Radomsky treats him may be ridiculously inadequate—rationalists generally are among Dostoevsky's *bêtes noires*. What Radomsky says (IV. ix) isn't 'the truth' but a partial truth about the world of the novel and the Prince's role in it. Some of the psychological vocabulary Radomsky chooses (especially where he suggests that Myshkin was moved by 'a cerebral enthusiasm, an enthusiasm of the head') is clearly questionable. Nevertheless, at the point where he explicitly draws the parallel between Nastasia Filipovna and Mary Magdalen, and thus between Myshkin and Christ, Radomsky comes as close to the truth about Myshkin as anyone can come to the truth within the formal limits that Dostoevsky has imposed upon himself.

Long before Myshkin first met her, Nastasia had been a kept woman; it is Myshkin's reaction to this fact that Radomsky singles out as the source of the weakness and confusion of his (Myshkin's) feelings, a confusion which is about to plunge all the main characters into disaster:

'... it is clear that you, in the rapture of your enthusiasm, so to speak, should jump at the chance to demonstrate publicly your

c

magnanimous idea that you, a prince and a pure man, did not consider a woman dishonoured if she was disgraced by a sin not her own but that of a disgusting socialite and libertine. Heavens, dear sir, it's comprehensible enough! But that's not the question, my dear Prince. The question is, was there truth, was there real truth in your feeling? was it nature, or only an intellectual enthusiasm? What do you think: a woman was forgiven in the temple—what a woman!—*but surely it doesn't say that she had done well*, that she was worthy of all honour and respect! Didn't your own commonsense tell you, in all those months, what the true position was?' [my italics].

The forgiveness which that other woman received was in confirmation of a law, the law of the New Covenant, which Myshkin hasn't the strength to uphold.

§ 11

Radomsky's 'commonsense' may distort some things, fail to account for others; all the same, while questioning its adequacy we mustn't exaggerate Myshkin's oddness. If we accept his illness, meekness, innocence, and gentleness as related aspects of his character (as I think we must), there emerges a personality that, throughout the bulk of the novel, is distinct and unified—unified but by no means immutable. In the course of his brief venture into the world—a venture out of the solitude of madness into relative health and sanity, and thus into a community and communion of sorts—Myshkin comes to make a few concessions to the ways of that world: concessions of tact and manners, though not of his essential truthfulness. And in the end the world proves to be too much for him. Its sins and sorrows lie too heavily on it—too heavily *for him* to redeem them. His *imitatio* is defective, not because it is merely human—given the limits of the convention Dostoevsky has chosen, the re-enacting of Christ could not be anything else. The *imitatio* is defective, because at the crucial moment Myshkin's meekness is unsupported by an equal spiritual strength: it would have to be the strength required for the acknowledgment of love, for the choices implied in that acknowledgment, and for the responsibility it involves. And his weakness is all the more terrible in its consequences since they all—the men and women whose life he shares—looked up to him, since for a while he held them all under the spell of his as yet untested strength. For a while: before more was asked of him than forgiveness. Nietzsche, not such a strange witness as it might seem, writes: 'This, ah, this is least pardonable in you; that you have power but will not rule!'[6]

In the end, then, Myshkin will have added to the suffering of many and brought permanent comfort to none. Of course, he isn't guilty of the murder of Nastasia, certainly not in any simple moral sense. Yet what drives Rogozhin first to his attempt on Myshkin's life and then to that murder is not merely his insane jealousy of Myshkin but also the fact that his jealousy is met by that mixture of compassion and weakness and love, that sad confusion which makes Myshkin the 'idiot' he is. As for his innocence, that has long since ceased to matter, has long since been swallowed up by the sad confusion.

The last pages, the Prince's return to the now irremediable darkness of insanity, are brief and laconic. Aglaia's moment of glory has gone, only vanity and foolishness (a last dig against Catholicism and the Poles, another set of Dostoevsky's *bêtes noires*) remain. Kolia and Radomsky 'the rationalist' will look after the Prince in his darkness. In Radomsky, Lebedev's gentle daughter will perhaps find a husband. Perhaps Kolia, the white hope for the future, will be richer for having known the Prince and cared for him. However that may be, the world has had no triumph, its burden is unlightened, it only goes on. The meek shall not inherit it. At all events, not this meek one.

iii The logic of a fiction

§ 12

Here, then, are two strands in the pattern of nineteenth-century fiction: the richness and variety of Dickens's London and England, the emotional and spiritual weightiness of Dostoevsky's St Petersburg and Russia. The novels in which we traced these strands were complex and, as to their achieved forms, opaque. For Dickens this doesn't present much of a problem. The flow of anecdotes and associations is basic to his design, the fiction of the *Pickwick Papers* is more or less adhered to throughout, and it is in harmony with 'the idea' of the book—the innocent abroad in a world that is relatively unresistant to his innocence, serenity, and goodness of heart.

To Dostoevsky the purposeful organizing of the narrative whole offers a major challenge (witness the eight separate drafts of the novel). What he has written are certainly not mere 'Papers'. The overall form of *The Idiot* is simple. It is given by the Prince's entry into and exit from the common world of men. The experienced life Dostoevsky presents within this framework is such that the details of the form in which it is organized don't readily emerge. The fusion of spiritual substance and narrative structure is achieved at a deep level, a level that is determined by the spiritual substance. The events of the story are dovetailed into a complex and consequential plot, as in *Hamlet*, rather than drawn up in a single line of action and thought, as in *Phèdre*. Our present purpose is to illustrate the logic, the consequential nature of fiction, and for that we must turn elsewhere, to a simpler, more open structure.

At its simplest it occurs in almost any detective story. Whatever the involutions of its intrigue, the typical 'whodunit' consists of a straight logical line that runs from palpable event (the murder) to the unravelling of causes. What makes such stories unsatisfactory as literature is a lack of that weightiness of living experience which Dostoevsky conveyed—is the fact that the murder doesn't matter enough. Enough for what? Of course, to show a murder in its full gravity is not the purpose of the genre. To go to detective fiction with that expectation is ridiculous—such stories aren't meant to provide occasions for brooding over spilled blood. The *pesanteur* of which I spoke is certainly not a necessary attribute of all literature; but in a situation that naturally calls for it (when our whole nature revolts against the double scandal of man-inflicted death) the question arises: since *that* expectation isn't satisfied, what is offered instead? And the reader who finds the intellectual riddle—the ingenuities and technicalities of detection—a poor compensation for the lack of importance attached to the crude fact of murder had better stay away from such stories.

§ 13

William Golding's *Lord of the Flies* (1954) is a work that destroys several preconceptions. Among them is the view that there is something falsely 'aesthetic' and 'literary' about novels which are built on the ruins of other novels. Golding's story is related to *Coral Island* in something like the critical way that *Don Quixote* is related to the chivalresque literature of its immediate past, or *Madame Bovary* is related to the romantic fiction of *its* yesteryear, or Thomas Mann's *The Magic Mountain* is to the tradition of the *Bildungsroman*, and his *Doctor Faustus* to Goethe's and earlier treatments of the Faustian theme. Here the critique takes the form of an anti-romance of boyhood and its 'heroic' adventures (and, incidentally, an attack on the cliché 'It couldn't happen here'). However, the fictional parallel and the critique remain implied, they provide merely an unemphatic *basso continuo* below the level of the action, and below the level of meanings encompassed by the action; yet the critique of the earlier fictional mode and its outlook is there throughout, part of the achieved whole that remains in the reader's mind. It is, I suppose, this implicitness that keeps the novel clear of any 'literariness'— this, and the fact that it has a splendid adventure story to tell, which even on the level of interesting action and suspense is a match for Ballantyne's romance of boyhood.

The adventures of a group of English boys marooned on a South Sea island after the plane in which they were being evacuated from wartime England has crash-landed in the sea, killing all its adult occupants—what could be more utopian, more romantic? The story has a built-in unity of action and narrative point of view. The island, as in any utopia, is the boys' world, and it is a complete world. The fiction has a transparent, classical simplicity about it, for it consists in no more (yet how much *that* is we shall see) than a purposeful and unsparing exploration of the consequences of that initial situation. The question, 'How will these boys behave in this situation?' receives a complete answer—an answer, that is, given in terms of the fictional analogue of 'completeness' as we understand the word outside fiction. Our imagination being inferior to Golding's, the achieved form of his novel answers our expectations in unexpected ways: his form answers our questions.

The boys' behaviour—the substance of the story—will of course be determined by what they are, by their reactions to the terror the island hides, and by the various ways they avail themselves of the resources of their material situation, the odds and ends the tropical island provides for their survival. What they are is in turn determined by their ages, their physical stamina and mental resourcefulness, their qualities of leadership and discipline; and again by the social backgrounds, all diverse yet all English, from which they come. England, their wartime England, is alive in them: in the

lower-middle-class Piggy with his asthma and spectacles, and his
memories of Auntie who kept a sweet-shop; in Ralph, the naval
officer's son, with his handsome face and fine physique, his Boy
Scout resourcefulness and decency, his courage in moments of
physical danger and lack of self-assurance at the crucial point where
his leadership is challenged. But also in Jack Merridew, head-boy of a
choir school, a 'born' leader where Ralph is only an elected leader,
Jack, for whom the ultimately unlimited exercise of the power he has
usurped becomes an end in itself.

Only one other boy, Simon, shares the foreground of the action.
His social past is not mentioned; his age places him somewhere
between the two 'natural' groups into which the boys split up—the
'biguns' in their early 'teens and the 'littluns' aged six and below—
and so do his epileptic fits. He alone will confront Beelzebub, the
Lord of the Flies, and learn the dreadful secret of the island, he alone
will live and die in the realm of truth. The other 'biguns' are less fully
individualized. Their first days on the island are idyllic, they and
their leaders rejoice in its exotic beauty and charm, and in the apparently limitless freedom it offers. But soon they move, one by one,
under the threat and then the reality of terror, from the decent
democratic leadership of Ralph who presides over the assembly, to
the savage tribal régime of Jack and his chorus of hunters, whose
symbol is the pig's head on a stick and the war-dance ('Kill the
beast! Cut his throat! Spill his blood!'). And finally, at the lowest
level of individualization, all but indistinct in their reactions to
what goes on around them, there are the 'littluns': wretched and
helpless almost from the beginning, their numbers horribly depleted
at each successive stage of the adventure, a prey to nightmares and
diarrhoea and unending terror: '[His] wail rose, remote and un-
earthly, and turned to an inarticulate gibbering. Percival Wemyss
Madison of the Vicarage, Harcourt St Anthony, lying in the long
grass, was living through circumstances in which the incantation of
his name was powerless to help him' (chap. v). And in the end their
very names are blotted out from their memory.

§ 14

Here, then, is an emblem of the changing reality of freedom. The
freedom the island offers at the beginning is unlimited: 'Merridew
turned to Ralph. "Aren't there any grown-ups?" "No." Merridew sat

down on a trunk and looked round the circle. "Then we'll have to look after ourselves" ' (chap. i). The conflict opens as soon as the two leaders become conscious of their conflicting aims. The ends for which Ralph (with the help of Piggy) is striving are survival and rescue, his concern is to keep the fire going that has been lit with the help of Piggy's spectacles. Jack's first appearance, at the head of his choir that is moving in close military formation, is ominous: his purpose is the war-game and the power that goes with it. It is he, not Ralph, who has managed to save a sheath-knife and bring it to the island; he and his gang of chorister-hunters provide the meat; to keep his fire going he robs Piggy of his spectacles; and to perpetuate his rule Jack turns the unlimited, idyllic freedom of the beginning into the absolute licence and anarchy of the end.

Both sides love games. But we have only to compare the orderly ritual of the conch, which convenes and regulates the conduct at general assembly, with the savage ritual of the war-dance, in the course of which not only the pigs are slaughtered—we have only to compare the ceremony of the Woolsack with the ritual of the Jew hunt—to see which game is the more attractive and exciting; and to see why, over and above the threat of terror and the promise of meat, Jack will gradually get everybody except Ralph and Piggy to join him in his camp, his mountain citadel.

Ralph, with Piggy's fine intelligence behind him, is concerned to preserve the social and moral certainties of their common past, their England. Jack's progress is away from that past, towards a barbarism where (as Nietzsche puts it) 'everything is permitted'; all the way to destruction, murder, and holocaust. As the story comes to its climax, the structure that originally determined the behaviour of 'the biguns'—individual self, social past, material present—recedes. A new morality, that of the pig-hunters who are the master-race—the morality of the will to power—takes over. In this lethal conflict between Apolline order and Dionysian frenzy, what hope is there for tubby, asthmatic Piggy, the Socrates of the story?

At this point the reader may feel that Mr Golding has made things too easy for himself, that he is able to present this conflict with such transparent directness precisely because these are only boys, with relatively simple motives and reactions, and because this is an island, with resources that elicit relatively simple social reactions; that the symbolical dimension of the story—the world at war in the midst of plenty—is achieved at the price of reducing the complexity of the

problems of adult life to the infighting of 'a bunch of kids'. Or is it
the critic who is at fault for having pressed his point too far—his
point about the story's classical simplicity?

What Mr Golding has done is to take the boys and their situation
absolutely seriously. This is what enables him 'to see the thing
through, all the way to the end' (as Henry James would say), to
create a world composed of nothing but the consequences of their
given situation. Are the boys' motives and reactions simpler than
those of an adult world at war? Relative to their conflicting goals,
their individual and collective reactions are as varied in form and
effectiveness as those of adults. Only at the end (chap. xii) when the
survivors of the 'adventure' are rescued by a naval officer ('On the
beach behind him was a cutter, her bows hauled up and held by two
ratings. In the stern sheets another rating held a sub-machine gun.'),
are the boys reduced to their 'real size', the size they have in the
adult world. Now Ralph, mere quarry before the kill, 'tensed for
more terror . . . looked at a huge peaked cap. It was a white-topped
cap, and above the green shade of the peak was a crown, an anchor,
gold foliage. He saw white drill, epaulettes, a revolver . . .' And only
now does the terrible Jack become 'a little boy who wore the remains
of an extraordinary black cap on his red hair [the square cap of the
choir he led] and who carried the remains of a pair of spectacles at
his waist'. The officer is no rescuing god. After all, the size and the
complexities of the adult world, too, are relative. As Mr Golding adds
in a later note, 'The officer, having interrupted a man-hunt, prepares
to take the children off the island in a cruiser which will presently
be hunting its enemy in the same implacable way. And who will
rescue the adult and his cruiser?'[7]

§ 15

No god, and no redeemer. The deity of the once beautiful island is
Beelzebub, the head of a pig black with flies, their buzz drowning out
the senses of that strange and solitary boy, Simon, who alone among
them all dares to approach his presence: what Simon discovers is a
mere dead thing, man-made in its hideousness, a sacrifice offered by
Jack Merridew and his hunters to 'the Beast' they all saw and from
whose unendurable presence they all fled. And this too is no god but
merely another thing, made and destroyed by man—the corpse of an
airman, swaying in its harness as the wind catches its billowing

parachute. This too, this harbinger from the 'adult' world, Simon endures in his agony:

> He crawled forward and soon he understood. The tangle of lines showed him the mechanics of the parody; he examined the white nasal bones, the teeth, the colours of corruption. He saw how pitilessly the layers of rubber and canvas held together the poor body that should be rotting away. Then the wind blew again and the figure lifted, bowed, and breathed foully at him. Simon knelt on all fours and was sick till his stomach was empty. Then he took the lines in his hands; he freed them from the rocks and the figure from the wind's indignity. [chap. ix]

His fellows in the 'adventure' Simon cannot free. He is slaughtered in the frenzy of the war-dance just before he is able to tell them the liberating truth about 'the Beast' that is now gently carried by the wind over the lagoon, the reef, and out to sea.

They are not worthy of the truth. And the deity they will continue to fear is as real and as evil as their deeds. The boys and their adventure are indeed taken seriously. The lineaments of their story are drawn together in a judgment that is not pronounced but remains wholly implicit, wholly intimated through the story. They have destroyed truth and beauty, Simon and the island. In their world God is dead. 'The Beast' is the deity they deserve, an incarnation and a last implacable consequence of what, under Jack Merridew's leadership, they have become.

§ 16

And they destroy Piggy too, the 'true and wise friend' for whom Ralph mourns, weeping for the first time on the island as he stands before the officer who has come to take them off. Of all the examples of Mr Golding's 'method', the portrait of Piggy is surely the finest. To get a clearer view of this dominant aspect of the fiction it may help to consider it as it were horizontally, out of the dimension of narrated time, by tracing out Piggy's physical and mental traits as if they were strands in a pictorial pattern.

Piggy is asthmatic and tubby, physically untrained (he can't swim) and awkward, and therefore ridiculed. His awkwardness is compensated for by his superior intelligence, which the biguns appreciate but which turns their ridicule into resentment and suspicion. He has an unbounded faith in thinking things out, and therefore in discussion and in the democratic 'assembly'. Yet, being awkward, he lacks the presence to address the boys confidently and has to leave it to Ralph to preside; but he has to prompt him, which Ralph in turn resents. Piggy's intelligence leads him to do more than merely bemoan the absence of adults (as most of the other boys do), and to try to think as purposefully as they would. He is therefore contemptuous of 'kids' games'; among these he includes Jack's ritual killings, whose true nature he fails to understand. His aim is to organize the boys for survival and to devise the means for their rescue—not to play games but to keep the fire going. Yet his appeal to reason is bound to be ineffective since it is not backed by the only things the biguns recognize—physical strength and skill. Moreover, Piggy's vision is badly impaired. With his spectacles—the symbol of his intelligence as well as of his physical inferiority—the fire is kindled: the fire on which the pigs are roasted, the fire that will attract the attention of the rescuers, the fire that will destroy the island. When his spectacles are stolen, the last vestige of order and restraint is gone. Mr Golding describes him as myopic:* Piggy never quite saw what happened when Simon was murdered, and in this way he too, the Socratic man of reason, was involved in that death; he doesn't quite see the boulder that Jack's hunters hurl down on him and Ralph as they stand pleading under Jack's citadel—the boulder that kills him and shatters the conch in his hands into a thousand fragments. In a situation where

* This description, at the opening of chapter 2, is inaccurate, except in the loose sense of 'defective vision'. It has been pointed out to me (by Graham Hough, who came by this knowledge in the realistic setting of Japanese captivity) that a concave lens required to correct myopia doesn't concentrate light but on the contrary scatters it over a wider area, and would therefore be useless for lighting a fire. If Piggy's spectacles are to be used for this purpose and he is to have the importance ascribed to him in the story, the lenses must be convex, which means that he must be hypermetropic. That this is the case is confirmed by his inability to see clearly both at a distance (e.g. he doesn't see the tree-tops or the boulder above him) and close up (he complains that without his glasses he sees his hand as a mere blur). Moreover, this hypermetropism (which is different from the organic long-sightedness of middle-aged people whose vision is otherwise normal) is part of Piggy's medical history. It goes together with his obesity, asthma, and underdeveloped physique (e.g. his hair hardly grows during the time on the island, so that he always looks civilized and never acquires the savage aspect of the other boys). The point of this Shandyan excursus is to show once more the compelling logic set in train by Mr Golding's fiction: even in this trivial matter of defective sight the author is tied to the consequences of his choice, which must correspond to our expectation.

his reasonableness is unheeded, Piggy is lost; and since his reasonableness is his all, he must die.

If we now ask ourselves why *Lord of the Flies*, telling a story of disenchantment, lost innocence, and violence, is not a depressing novel but on the contrary a fiction of beauty and delight, the answer lies where Aristotle[8] puts it: in 'the finish of the workmanship, or the colouring, or some such other cause'—which we here identify as the inexorable logic of the whole.

2

Aims, methods, metaphors

§ 17

The riches of the represented world; its weightiness and resistance
to ideals; its consequential logic and circumstantiality—these I take
to be among the attributes one would expect to find in realistic
literature. This is not to suggest that these attributes are always
present in equal measure, for in that case there would have been no
point in examining more than one work to establish them. Nor do
they amount to an inventory of the qualities relevant to realism. Any
attempt to 'define' realism (or tragedy, or whatever) by enumerating
'all its qualities', or by confining it to specific situations or character
types or material things, or again to particular verbal ploys or formal
structures, seems to me doomed to failure. I take it for granted that
the whole business of 'defining one's terms' has undergone a radical
revision in Wittgenstein's work, and that the results of this revision
are fundamental to any literary enquiry of this kind. Wittgenstein's
theory of family resemblances, it seems to me, resolves a host of
problems that have bedevilled literary criticism from Aristotle
onwards, and I shall do no more here than quote one of the versions
of the theory[1] and adapt it to our present purpose:

> The tendency to look for something common to all the entities
> which we commonly subsume under a general term.—We are
> inclined to think that there must be something common to all
> examples of realism, and that this common property is the
> justification for applying the general term 'realism' to the various
> writings; whereas 'realistic writings' form a *family* the members
> of which have family likenesses. Some of them have the same nose,
> others the same eyebrows and others again the same way of
> walking; and these likenesses overlap. The idea of a general

28

concept being a common property of its particular instances ... is comparable to the idea that *properties* are *ingredients* of the things which have the properties; e.g. that beauty is an ingredient of all beautiful things as alcohol is of beer and wine, and that we therefore could have pure beauty, unadulterated by anything that is beautiful.

The purposefully anti-scientific character of this theory alone must commend it to any critic who hasn't fallen victim to our current infatuation with the methods of science. What is in doubt is neither the validity of the procedure nor its relevance to criticism but one's ability to apply it, consistently and in the face of that 'craving for generality' with its Procrustean consequences, which every other theory seems to encourage.

§ 18

The analyses which yielded those attributes or richness, resistance, and consequentiality I mentioned were merely intended as examples of the kind of literary criticism relevant to our enquiry, and as variations on the kinds of undertaking we find in Auerbach's *Mimesis*.[2]

Auerbach's exemplary work requires no lengthy introduction. The material on which it is based consists of felicitously chosen texts from Homer, the Old and New Testaments, through Latin and Medieval French authors, Cervantes, Shakespeare and Schiller, to the French novels of the eighteenth and nineteenth centuries, all the way to Virginia Woolf. Each of these potsherds of text is subjected to a more or less close linguistic scrutiny; and the results are shown to contribute to a coherent argument which describes the changes in 'the serious representation of everyday reality' over that immense stretch of European literature. Without being in the least mechanical, Auerbach's method is roughly the same in each chapter. From an analytical comment on the quoted passage he moves outward, to wider, social and historical as well as stylistic observations, and hence to that literary-historical continuity which is his over-all concern. ('My purpose is always to write history', he says elsewhere.[3]) What finally emerges is not quite a history but a historical picture-album of one richly varied kind of literary imagination.

Only a scholar of Auerbach's discrimination and erudition could apply himself to the minutiae of linguistic usage (one thinks of the astonishing insights into Dante's work and world he is able to coax out of a mere conjunction used in the tenth canto of *The Inferno*[4]) without ever losing sight of the wider literary and social issues hidden in those minutiae.

Given Auerbach's scrupulous attention to linguistic details, given also the liveliness of his mind, it may well be inevitable that at times his method should have something of the rabbit-out-of-hat procedure about it. There is no harm in that. The mixture of patient induction and imaginative deduction he has hit on makes *Mimesis* one of the few masterpieces of modern criticism.

§ 19

'Fools rush in. . . .' In the course of his analyses and interpretations Auerbach has a good deal to say about those two terms, 'realistic' and 'realism', which his texts are chosen to illustrate and illuminate. And what he says is always related to a particular work or literary period. To reproach him (as some critics have done) for not providing a full-scale 'definition of his terms' is to misunderstand the nature of his undertaking, which is practical criticism in the service of an historical design. (To insist that the literary critic mustn't say anything until he has 'defined his terms' is like insisting that Monsieur Jourdain had no right to open his mouth until he had made his remarkable discovery—to which I shall return in § 106—that what he had been speaking all his life was prose.)

Some of Auerbach's observations on the subject of realism are obviously intended to carry wider meanings—unless they did that, his book would be no more than a series of independent essays. But these wider meanings again serve a purpose in practical criticism— they aim at establishing the coherence of a literary and cultural development, a story in time. What they do not provide—what Auerbach wasn't interested in providing—is something like a theoretical basis, abstracted from the works of literature, for an extended discussion of the problem of realism itself: a discussion, that is, which would address itself more directly to the question of what is, and what is not, 'realism' and 'realistic'. Not much that will here be said is likely to challenge Auerbach's insights and conclusions; my intention is rather to throw some light on the premises of his undertaking (which I think worth doing precisely because it is exemplary); to see, more fully than he had any need to see, what he and a host of other critics like him would be at.

Not only critics, of course. My enquiry is to be guided by the fact that the word 'realism' as well as being part of our literary and aesthetic vocabulary, is after all a part of our common everyday language. This double life of the word, which critics have either taken for granted or ignored or sought to extirpate by technicalities, seems to me both puzzling and illuminating. I have found it to be illuminating above all in respect of the connection between life and literature, and of the involvement of language in both.

§ 20

'When I am formulated, sprawling on a pin—', says the poet. We shall see that there are good reasons why every attempt at formally defining our terms—treating them as though they were technical terms—must fail. But to say this is very different from saying that no direct description of realism is possible either; that every such description is involved in 'the Fallacy of Realism',[5] or that it leads to the disheartening conclusion that 'the realistic theory is bad aesthetics'.[6] The present aim at all events is to show what is entailed, in literature and outside it, as we use these words; to show, occasionally in a philosophical way, the irrelevance to realism of philosophical enquiries into the nature of reality; to avoid the specious and the esoteric on the one hand, and the contradictory on the other; and in the process to find out something about the more reassuring areas of our world. I hope to show that realistic fictions are erected on firm ground which reveals no epistemological cracks, and that when such cracks appear, they are not explored but transformed into the psychology of characters: realism doesn't ask whether the world is real, but it occasionally asks what happens to persons who think it isn't.

More than most other literary critics, the writer on realism is apt to be told that his undertaking is impossible: 'How can you say anything sensible about realism unless you have first defined what reality is—and to do that, surely, is the business of a philosopher, not a literary critic!' It is an irrelevant objection. What we require for our present undertaking is not a 'definition of reality' at all but a certain kind of description of the world. Such a description, moreover, is not antecedent to or a condition of realism, it is the thing itself. That is what realism is.

Of course, anyone who has given thought to the meaning hidden in or emerging from a word in common usage is likely to have felt from time to time a sense of disenchantment, when his whole enterprise seemed little more than an elaborate exercise in pedantry. He will do well, at such times, to remember that his enquiry is taking him to the point where the distinction between words and things is questioned. Engaged in a search for an understanding of the words we use and the way things are, his motto must be 'Say what you choose, so long as this doesn't prevent you from seeing the way things are. (And when you see that, there will be a good deal that you will not say.)'[7] If, as I shall argue, realism and the realistic attitude in literature and outside it designate a perennial mode of representing the world and coming to terms with it, it follows that the words themselves, whose history is after all brief and subject to the fluctuations of critical fashion, don't matter very much. But before we are ready to dispense with them they remain useful enough— like that gnomic ladder which we are enjoined to throw away, though not before we have climbed it.[8] The words are useful in an attempt to orient ourselves in our thinking about literature and about the world of which literature is a part. And if, in spite of being conscious of many a booby-trap on the way, I take this to be a perfectly realistic enterprise, it is because I see realism as no more, and no less, than an undertaking to look all the relevant facts of a situation in the face—a situation which in literature tends to be chosen and in life is apt to be given. But as between the chosen and the given —who would boast of categorical differences?

§ 21

A contradiction remains in my evaluation of realism as a mode of writing. Sometimes I have presented it as a liberation and an emblem of the riches of the world, at other times as a restriction and a prison-house. But then, its greatest practitioners, too, have occasionally been in two minds about their art. Flaubert's disparaging remarks about *L'Education sentimentale* are well known:

> Ce qui me désole au fond, c'est la conviction où je suis de faire une chose inutile, je veux dire contraire au but de l'Art, qui est

l'exaltation vague. Or avec les exigences scientifiques que l'on a
maintenant et un sujet bourgeois, la chose me semble radicalement
impossible. La beauté n'est pas compatible avec la vie moderne.
Aussi est-ce la dernière fois que je m'en mêle; j'en ai assez.

And yet, on another occasion, he can say à propos of the same novel:
'Je ne connais rien de plus noble que la contemplation ardente des
choses de ce monde'.[9]

But in the end perhaps such ambivalences are no more to be
resolved than the question whether or not one likes Frédéric Moreau,
the hero of that novel: whether, in spite of and through the hero's
hesitations and breaches of faith and betrayals, his existence as
flâneur and dandy and social climber, his political fecklessness
and his apparently infinite capacity for squandering the gift of
life, one does or does not acknowledge the deep charm of that
figure in the carpet—the richest that nineteenth-century realism has
to show.

§ 22

What kind of a word is 'realism'? In answering this question I take it
for granted[10] that literature is distinct from other kinds of human
activity; that one language serves the purposes of both literature and
'life'; and that the overriding end of the study of literature is to
illuminate a given literary work and its connections not only with
other works but with something like the whole of 'life' in any one
era and culture. It follows that the language of the study of literature
(of literary history, interpretation, and criticism, from the cryptic
'Silly!!' in the margins of a public library copy to Roland Barthes)
will have to reflect these connections. And since it must do this with
the same resources, from within that single language which serves
the purposes of both 'life' and literature, the language of literary
scholarship can hardly lay claim to anything so distinct as a 'terminology'. It will depend for its resources partly on a fixed vocabulary
of its own, but more often on transferences and translations from
one sphere to another. (The vocabulary of all humanistic pursuits is
organized in this way; however, the vocabulary of criticism displays
its derivativeness more clearly and richly than others.) It may well be
that in respect of their status as borrowings and metaphors the words
of this vocabulary form something like an unbroken spectrum

D

between the two poles of 'life' and literature, but it is more to my
purpose to consider them under four headings, in four fairly distinct
groups. All four are equally necessary and relevant to the tasks of
criticism. Moreover, all four are part of our cultural vocabulary, and
therefore liable to changes of time and place. We shall see that some
of the words in the language of criticism may move from one group
to another, and there are sure to be borderline cases—all of which
should help us to see what kind of *technè* is involved, and what kind
of precision we may expect in literary criticism.

<h2 style="text-align:center">§ 23</h2>

First, and most obviously, literary terminology is derived from the
language of everyday life. A novel is said to be 'boring', a style
'lively', a drama 'exciting' in much the same way as my friend's
conversation, his manner of acting or reacting, are said to have these
qualities. At a slightly more sophisticated level: the ending of a novel
or a play is described as 'sudden' or 'unforeseen' or 'predictable', as
a death is; again, a poem is described as 'melodious', a tragedy as
'well constructed' or even 'highly structured', in something like the
way that music, or a house, or a political argument is described. And
again: when we speak of 'the high polish', 'the bad finish', or 'the
fragmentariness' of a literary work, we appeal to properties that
have their primary, non-metaphorical meanings (what I. A. Richards
calls 'the tenor' of a metaphor[11]) in the world at large. To this kind
of vocabulary, too, belongs that vast range of affective judgements
which we lavish on the personages of drama and fiction and on the
moods transfixed in lyrical poetry: as when we say that Mr Pickwick is 'jolly and innocent', Smerdyakov 'the epitome of baseness
and craftiness', Werther 'sentimental'. Indeed, when we refer to
them as 'people' or 'characters' we mean these words too to be
understood in a more or less metaphorical sense ('characters' less
metaphorically than 'people')—a sense that is transferred from daily
life into literature (Richards's 'vehicle'). And when we speak not of
'literature' but of 'the world of literature', we are on the way to being
conscious of the transference, for the phrase connotes a distinction
(as against another 'world') and thus stresses its own metaphorical
nature. Similarly, current objections to the 'How many children had
Lady Macbeth' kind of criticism; refusals to enquire what happens

once the happy couple of comedy is safely married—all these are really reminders that literary works are not the continuum that life is, and that one of the kinds of language in which we describe them is merely borrowed from real-life situations and encounters. This common-or-garden vocabulary doesn't seem to make for any great precision in describing the effects of a given literary work. The language of what one might call the 'top-of-the-bus kind of criticism' (e.g. 'Well, he really was rather a foolish old man, I mean, giving away his kingdom to those two ghastly women . . .') consists very largely of such a transferred vocabulary, and clearly literary criticism can do better than that. But when it does better, this isn't necessarily due to its choosing a different terminology. However limited and limiting *this* vocabulary may be, criticism cannot do without it any more than it can do without natural language itself. 'The view that metaphor is omnipresent in speech'[12] is self-evident.

§ 24

The second kind of vocabulary, diametrically opposed to the first, is technical and non-metaphorical, being devised (often in an historically documented way) for a literary-critical and scholarly purpose only. Its part of the spectrum spans all the way from mere imitations of technicality, like 'rhythmic prose' or 'low mimetic style', to the hard and fast terms of prosody. When we speak of 'tetra-dactylic verse' we have no notion (etymological or otherwise) of a 'four-fingered' or 'four-toed' anything in mind. The metaphorical origin of such terms as 'verse' or 'novel' is blocked out. Their relatively firm outline and definition, their relative lack of ambivalence and ambiguity, at least within one national culture, are concomitant with the fact that these terms have no full value or meaning outside literature. True, at a stretch they may provide the wherewithal for illustration and simile: 'She told me her life-story: it's as good as a novel.' 'A novel' here derives not from life but from literature, and whatever meaning it may have in a real-life, non-literary context it must borrow from its meaning as a technicality; but the word is awkward in this context, it isn't fully domesticated outside the study of literature.

Intellectual pursuits generally, and academic pursuits in particular, are apt to seek reassurance for their respectability from such specialized technical terms. The kind of precision[13] that this technical vocabulary invokes is different from the kind of precision of which the transferred vocabulary of our first group is capable—different but not necessarily greater. Its technical terminology removes the language of criticism from the language of the market-place, as far away (this side of quantification) as possible. French and German critics continue to be much concerned with the defining of genres and the creating of special critical vocabularies, and they regard English critics, who tend to ignore such procedures, as moralizing and impressionistic dilettantes. But whether vocabulary of the 'pastoral-comical' type makes criticism more precise and illuminating or less will depend on its appropriateness to the literary work at hand, not on any inherent superiority. It is difficult to *understand* French classical drama without appreciating the special emotive and intellectual function of the alexandrine, in a sense in which it isn't difficult to understand *Don Juan* without enlarging on the informality of Byron's verse. Technical vocabulary and analysis are indispensable, but no more so than other kinds of critical language.

§ 25

'She told me her life-story: it's a tragedy.' Here we have, thirdly, a vocabulary which is technical in its origin and still displays something of that origin, but is used metaphorically by way of transference from the literary sphere into life; moreover, unlike the term 'novel' in our second group, it is now fully domesticated in its non-technical, real-life context. The amount of consciousness involved in such usages is impossible to determine. ('What a tragedy!' has perhaps still some slight regard for one or another formal quality of the genre—as long as not every death reported in the newspapers is called 'a tragedy'; 'an epic statement' is an empty Madison Avenue cliché.) But leaving to one side this indeterminable question of the consciousness involved, it is clear that this kind of vocabulary is both part and parcel of literary criticism, and as such part and parcel of our common, non-literary language. As such: for it imports a certain literary quality into common language. True, it diminishes the isolation that the special vocabulary of criticism (our group 2) is apt to create round itself—it brings life and literature closer together. But only in the sense of bringing life closer to literature, of making life into a peculiarly literary affair. The language of our age is especially enamoured of this kind of vocabulary, we are all too prone to refer to living situations as though they were literary ones. (The only connotations words like 'tragedy' 'or 'the drama—or the lyrical sense —of life' can have, if they are to be more than synonyms for 'sad', 'exciting', 'serene' or whatever, are literary.) The result of this kind of transference—the direction, from literature to life, in which it moves—is not helpful to the critic. He must reclaim such words for his undertaking, usually by way of definition. And he must define *against* the usages of common speech, thus inviting the charge of pedantry: 'They don't really mean—they cannot possibly mean— "his death was a tragedy", because "tragedy" really means . . .', and so all the way to rigid definitions. However that may be, here again is an area of vocabulary which the critic cannot afford to lose. 'Irony' too belongs to this group, at least if we take its primary meaning to be literary or at any rate quotational, in the sense of 'artfully dissimulating that which is not the case'. However, the more independent its 'real-life' use becomes of its literary function, the closer 'irony' moves to the next section on our spectrum.

§ 26

'Realism' is a term that belongs to a fourth group, which is different from all these; and even in that group it has a somewhat special place. Clearly it is neither a simple metaphorical borrowing (like 'the *liveliness* of X's prose') nor a technicality (like 'the liveliness of X's *prose*'), yet it derives some connotations from each: in its meta-phorical aspect the word harks back to '*res*' and '*realia*'[14] in the sense of the given material fixtures of life, as an '-*ism*' it invites some sort of technical and systematic exposition.[15] What it shares with certain other terms (like 'naturalism', 'impressionism', 'symbolism', but also 'gothic' and 'baroque') is that they all lead a double existence, inside literature and out of it. But only of 'realism' can it be said that its meaning as a literary term has its parallel in 'life' rather than in one or more specialized pursuits (as 'baroque' has in architecture and music). Its 'grammar'[16] is in many ways similar to the grammar of such words as 'image' or 'style' or 'form', all of which lead a sort of amphibian existence in literature and in 'life': and it is this double existence which, it seems to me, must have a central place in any discussion of realism. But whereas the statement 'This novel has a form' is almost meaningless in its generality except as an invitation to a further discussion in which narrower descriptive terms will be involved, 'This is a realistic novel' is an invitation to such a discussion *and* a first move in it.

§ 27

An historical note. We have, it so happens, a good deal of evidence to show that the earliest uses of 'realism' and 'realistic' were non-literary (and the same is true, in a more restricted sense, of 'naturalism'). 'Realism' was first used to designate one of the two branches of medieval philosophy, the other being nominalism. How 'realism', once the doctrine concerned with the reality of ideal essences or universals, came to take on meanings of an opposite kind is obscure to me; such attempts to establish the connection as I have seen (on the lines of *lucus a non lucendo*) seem wholly unconvincing, and I will leave them to one side. (Nor shall I be concerned with 'philosophical realism' in its modern forms, as professed by Thomas Reid in his *Principles of Common Sense* of 1764, G. E. Moore, Bertrand Russell and others; except incidentally, to the extent that the views of professional philosophers may help us to find our literary bearings.)

The change from the medieval to the modern term, René Wellek observes,[17] occurred sometime in the eighteenth century. In 1790 Kant in his *Critique of Judgement* opposed 'realism' to 'idealism', and all subsequent discussions of the problem have been based on this or similar antitheses. By 1798 Schiller uses the contrasting terms quite freely in a literary context: the French, he writes in a letter to Goethe (27. ii.), are 'better realists than idealists', which to him is convincing proof 'that realism cannot make a poet'. Schiller's doubts about the poetic value of realism, perhaps surprising to readers unfamiliar with the temper of Weimar Idealism, are characteristic of the subsequent literary discussion in Germany. From Schiller's day to ours the most radical critiques of literary realism have come from German theoretical writers and philosophers; at the same time it is true to say that German literature in the nineteenth century has little to contribute to that wide spectrum of prose fiction which we now call 'European Realism'. By 1826 the *Mercure de France* refers to 'that literary doctrine which gains more ground every day and which leads to the faithful imitation not of the masterpieces of art but of those originals which nature offers us; [such a doctrine] could well be called realism. Such, to judge by several signs, will be the literature of the nineteenth century, the literature of the true.'[18] At this point, then, the term is appropriated for literature—mainly in France—and the protracted (and far from helpful) literary debate begins.[19] But has the term been wholly appropriated? Here as well as at most other points in that debate we notice that the word has not been converted into a technical term. In those phrases, *la littérature du XIXe siècle, la littérature du vrai*, it is programmatically connected with the world outside literature. It is for this reason that, unlike any other literary term, the word has a political as well as a literary history.[20]

It may well be possible to consider a given poem, even a novel or a drama, 'immanently', that is in terms of a narrowly conceived verbal analysis and without reference to the world outside (though to judge by some recent attempts it is hardly the gayest or most interesting way of doing things). The moment we single out the realistic aspect of a work, we are bound to be carried beyond the restriction of literary technicalities. For this, this presence of a full meaning of the term in both spheres, is what distinguishes it from all other literary terms.

§ 28

Yet while 'realism' and 'realistic' are different from the other kinds of vocabulary I mentioned, they also share some of the properties of each. Like our group 1 they are also real-life terms, used in wholly unliterary contexts: 'It was a realistic consideration that determined his choice', we say; or, 'It was his realism that made him choose'. What the words share with some of the vocabulary of group 1 (and distinguish it from group 2) is that they are capable of carrying a *relative* meaning: instead of 'a realistic consideration' we might have said, 'it was perfectly [or hardly] realistic, when you consider what the problem was'. And I shall also argue that our terms have certain *qualitative* connotations, which are inseparable from them; though to say this is not to say that the presence or absence of realism can ever be the sole, or need necessarily be the main, criterion of quality. In determining the relation of realism to values we shall have to make our way between two opposing views, both of them attempts to short-circuit an argument which the realistic writer solves intuitively but which, to anyone concerned with literary theory, is necessarily complex: I mean the one view that equates 'realism' with 'the truth about the world' and that in turn with excellence in literature, denying it to all other modes of writing; and its opposite, the view which proposes to reduce realism to a definable technicality, in order then to claim that (like 'drama' or 'structure' or 'rhymed couplets') it is, in and by itself, wholly neutral and free from all value judgments.

As to these qualitative connotations, the curious thing is that common usage seems to bring out a different set of values in each sphere. In literature nowadays the terms are used ordinarily as terms of praise—seeing that Schiller wanted to express his disparagement, we might have expected him to criticize the French for practising 'mere realism' or what nowadays is called 'photographic realism' (§ 39). In real-life situations, on the other hand ('It was a perfectly realistic consideration . . .'), the term has often something defensive or defiant about it, as though we wished to say that such-and-such a consideration was all right, and perhaps rather clever, but not exactly magnanimous, etc.

§ 29

With that (far from exact) notion of a difference in mind we are able to draw up a tentative list of meanings under each heading:

(1) *Realism 'in life'* connotes a way of estimating, evaluating, or assessing a situation; having 'an eye for the main chance', making a fair or comprehensive and adequate judgment; but *'realistic'* is also synonymous with clever, sharp, expedient, all the way to cynical and unscrupulous.

(2) *Realism in literature* connotes a way of depicting, describing a situation in a faithful, accurate, 'life-like' manner; or richly, abundantly, colourfully; or again mechanically, photographically, imitatively.

The meanings are certainly not always distributed in this way. Our list shows signs of overlapping and suggests possibilities of interchange. But this apparent untidiness is precisely what makes the term so indispensable in common and literary discourse alike. My aim is not to reduce it to some order unrelated to actual usage, but on the contrary to preserve and exploit its variety. All the same, this rough-and-ready distribution of connotations into two groups reflects a duality which will help us (§ 90) to focus on the meaning of 'realism' in literary discourse.

§ 30

Discussions of realism have often failed to preserve, or have denied, its relative and qualitative character, and have accordingly treated it as a technical term of the kind described in group 2. This has been especially true of the many attempts (exemplified by our quotation from the *Mercure de France*) to designate it exclusively as a period term, usually for the mid-nineteenth century. This in turn has involved critics in rigid formal definitions which could only be achieved at the price of denying the perennial nature of some aspects of what was being defined.[21] The moment we accept the statement 'Shakespeare is more realistic than Ben Jonson' as meaningful, the case for realism as a strict period term is lost. And what is gained is what every relevant projection into history—that is, every relevant comparison—gains for criticism: a better insight, a fuller understanding, even of the works that were written in conscious adherence to 'the tenets of the realistic school' of the nineteenth century.

The self-definition of a given literary school may well be of some importance for our understanding of its authors' achievement, but seeing that manifestos proclaim what should be rather than describe what is, such self-definitions can be no more than one element in our description. None of this renders the terminology of literary periods meaningless. Of fiction in the nineteenth century—of what we readily call *European Realism*—we may say that it contains *more* realistic elements than earlier literatures had done—that here certain tendencies of earlier literary works come to a head; though in evaluating this increase we shall obviously have to bear in mind that our own judgement of what is and what is not realistic is closer to the judgment of the nineteenth century than to that of earlier ages. And these, of course, are the kinds of observations we are bound to make when speaking of any other literary 'school' or 'movement'. Whatever else they are, period terms are not technicalities of the 'elegiac distich' kind.

§ 31

The affinities of our terms with those in group 1 (metaphors from life) should now be clear enough. Yet when the terms are used in literary contexts, 'realism' and 'realistic' give us no impression at all of being used metaphorically. They *are* literary terms, inasmuch as they occur in contexts, and especially in contrasts, where their description will involve us in certain technicalities (group 2), but these technicalities will never yield as adequate a description as they will for words like 'sonnet' or 'elegiac'. Like the vocabulary of group 3 (where every death is a 'tragedy' and every encounter is 'dramatic' and life has 'its little ironies'), the terms seem to bring life and literature together, but on the opposite side, on the side of life not literature, or anyway on some middle ground. Moreover, this is a one-way process. When in order to illustrate the real-life meaning of the term we spoke of a 'realistic consideration', we did not have in mind a way of thinking and making decisions that has its counterpart in literature; the fact that it has such a counterpart was irrelevant to our understanding; we certainly didn't need a literary definition to discover what was meant by the phrase. When, on the other hand, we speak of Balzac's 'realistic prose', the phrase as such, as part of our literary description, says something about Balzac's way of writing *and at the same time* brings it into a certain relation with its author's world, society, and life.

What unites the two areas of meaning—the real-life and the literary meanings—is their representational quality, is the fact that they both designate a 'standing-for-something', and a process of selection: they designate not a content but a condition, or at least an outlook, *and* a form. They refer to a way of thinking (in the one case) and to a way of writing (in the other), each of which is positively related to the real world. But of course what the second meaning designates is not only a way of *writing*. It refers to all the representational arts, though not to everything that happens in those arts. If further proof is needed that this representational quality is really inseparable from realism, we need only consider the restriction that common usage imposes on the word. For while we speak of 'realistic painting or sculpture' as readily as we speak of 'realistic literature', we don't use the term (at least not as readily, not without a good deal of explanation) in connection with music—an art whose representational status (*pace* Schopenhauer) is problematic and opaque; nor in connection with architecture (at the other end of Schopenhauer's scale of the arts), whose relation to life is so close that its representational nature is all but inseparable from its function as a part of life. Once again, then, we come to the point where realism emerges as a representational term with its fullest meaning at a middle distance from life.

3
Transcendent matters . . .

§ 32

The peculiar position 'realism' occupies in the language of criticism and in the economy of literature may be further illustrated by a comparison with its traditional opposite. 'Idealism' clearly carries no overt literary meaning but belongs to the metaphorical language of group 1; though, unlike most terms in that group, it is a metaphor not from 'life in general' but from philosophy. The phrase 'Schiller's idealistic drama' differs from the phrase 'Balzac's realistic prose' in as much as it denotes no literary technicalities whatever; it resembles the latter phrase in as much as it requires for its explanation some reference to a scheme of things outside Schiller's plays. But as soon as we begin to specify this reference we come upon a contrast which is as fundamental as any in this entire enquiry. In realism the relation that obtains between a work of literature and the world outside is positive, expressive of a fundamental assent, whereas in idealism it is negative, expressive of a problematic attitude towards the world. What the idealistic aspect of Schiller's plays refers to are not the *données* of life but a certain epistemological and moral system (in Kantian and perhaps in all other forms of idealism, epistemology and morality are linked). And what such a system requires for its elaboration is a radical alienation and distancing from those given realities of life: a distancing which, though ultimately not irrelevant to realism in life and literature, runs counter to and challenges the practice of realism in both. This focusing at a distance is what Schiller[1] had in mind when he praised Kant for 'the high value of a philosophy of life which by its constant *reference to universal laws* weakens the feeling we harbour for our individuality, teaches us to lose our petty self in the comprehensive order of the great

Whole, and thus enables us to treat our own self as we would a stranger'.

Schiller of course would argue that this is a case of *reculer pour mieux sauter*. Most forms of idealism pursue moral ends, aiming at a firmer philosophical foundation for their scheme of values than 'the world of mere appearances' can provide; and to this extent at any rate most forms of idealism will confess to a care for the worldly world. There is thus a point where idealism re-enters the world as realism knows it and becomes an element in a portrayal of that world (it becomes relevant to Schiller the dramatist). At this point idealism ceases to be a philosopher's abstract scheme of 'universal laws' and takes on the form of a (fictional or dramatic) character's concrete beliefs. It becomes a guide to his actions, and thus submits itself to a testing (a severe beating, it may be) in the real world. All testing is a form of conflict. And the conflict between the real and the ideal, presented from the vantage point of the real, provides literature with some of its most enduring themes. In this applied form, then, idealism becomes an object of realism's insatiable interest in the real world.

Not every idealism is founded in a complex philosophical doctrine, nor is my argument confined to some recondite or marginal area of literature. All that has here been said applies with equal force to *Don Quixote*, the one text that is at the back of any discussion of realism in literature. And it is no accident that here too epistemology and morality are linked: the world in which the Don practises his high ideals is not the world as others see it.

§ 33

Critics have frequently spoken of realism as being implacably hostile to any form of transcendence. It is certainly true that nineteenth-century realism is predominantly anti-religious in outlook, and concerned with showing up the bigotry, self-delusion, and general nastiness of the Christian faithful. As for the realistic literature of our own age, the bulk of it—at least in the West—seems to be written on the assumption that the tenets of the Christian religion are no longer at issue, that ours is an age without God and transcendence. Whether this assumption is true, whether it merely reflects the peculiar shallowness of much of contemporary fiction, or whether the fiction contributes to making the assumption true, are questions

I shall not attempt to answer. The claim, however, that realism is *necessarily* incompatible with a religious view of the world is, as I hope to show, based on a blatant anachronism. My present point is that any such claim is liable to challenge by the same critical argument as that which showed the relevance of idealism to a realistic account of the world.

The Platonic doctrine of a Reality outside the shadowy world of the cave resembles the Christian belief in a transcendent God in this respect, that in both cases it is given to man to glimpse that which is outside his cave (or the valley of death), and therefore in some way to be affected by it. (In the Christian doctrine it is more than an unsteady glimpse.) That other world isn't wholly remote from this. True, we cannot have any reliable knowledge of it, even though many a realist would gladly 'give a part of [his] life to know what was the average barometric pressure in Paradise'.[2] But even if we renounce such knowledge, our belief in that other Reality as an absolute perfecting of our relative virtues is capable of affecting our exercise of these virtues, our conduct in the cave.

Now if the Platonic doctrine were taken to assert (as it sometimes is) a complete separation of the two spheres (or Christianity were interpreted in the most Manichaean, world-contemning terms), the literary side of the matter would be straightforward enough. Realism would then be concerned with descriptions of what is happening inside the cave, and would assess those happenings by the dim light available to it—the situation, presumably, of contemporary realistic literature. The existence of another realm, informed by a greater reality, would not affect it; indeed it wouldn't be a question of a greater or smaller 'reality' at all but of two radically different kinds.

A part of this argument applies to the more common interpretation of Platonism (and to a more orthodox understanding of Christianity). For even if we accept that the Reality outside acts upon life in the cave, and is therefore intimated in it, what realism is concerned with is precisely that life inside the cave as it is acted upon and reacts to the intimations of the Reality outside; and *not* with that Reality, nor with the ways in which it directly reveals itself to some of the more favoured dwellers inside the cave. As to those revelations, a realist is apt to suspect that 'If an angel were to tell us what is in his philosophy, I dare say many of his propositions would sound like $2 \times 2 = 13 \ldots$'[3]

§ 34

No content or image of transcendence and no object of religious faith can be the concern of realism; but the often disillusioning search for transcendence, like the testing of faith against the weighty obstacles of the real world, these certainly have their appropriate place in realistic literature. *The Idiot* is a realistic novel because it is confined to the world Dostoevsky knew and shared, and it is a Christian novel because without his Christian faith Myshkin would have been another man (his story would have been another story), and his faith too is part of the world Dostoevsky is retracing. Myshkin's *imitatio* fails, for himself and for those around him. His compassion is overwhelmed by suffering because in the situation in which Myshkin is placed compassion without love is not enough, and because his love is inadequate. Yet it is only just inadequate: informed by a greater love he might have succeeded. But seeing that a greater love is continuous with the lesser, is conceivable within the same terms as those in which we accept the novel as it stands, a happier ending need not have been less realistic: the condition of its realism lies in the testing, not in the defeat.

The story of Myshkin is a bridge—the building of bridges between the visible and the invisible, we shall see (§§ 35, 113), is a prerogative of realism. Christ's incarnation too is inseparable from the worldly reality of suffering; which is why the account of Christ's death, of a life of supreme value destroyed for the most abject reasons (the value of the reasons being such as we are familiar with), is among the most realistic stories of all. True, it is more and other things: but it is that too; if only because the testing, which retraces the ways of the world (e.g. Matthew xxvii : 41 ff.) is so complete. The love that is here being tested is not inadequate, and as such it is continuous with the love that was defeated in Dostoevsky's novel. The Resurrection, which is the full consequence of Christ's victory, belongs to another sphere, beyond the reach of realism; but the life that led up to it and the lives of those who act on their faith in it do not.

§ 35

Medieval literature abounds in scenes which show the unembarrassed coexistence of realism with religious transcendence. My example should also indicate where to look for signs of realism as a perennial mode once we have rejected it as a period term.

The *chanson de geste* which tells the story of Charlemagne's war with the Saracens and Roland's death in the battle of Roncevaux survives in a French version written around 1100; this was done into German, with significant adaptions, by a Bavarian monk, Konrad, some fifty or more years later.[4] Almost all the changes and voluminous additions which Konrad made are concerned with the religious aspect of the epic. Where the *Chanson* plunges *in medias res*—'Charles the King, our great emperor, has been all full seven years in Spain . . .'—the first thousand lines of the German version are largely devoted to a lengthy theological placing of the warlike action. Again and again biblical parallels are invoked as prefigurations of the religious significance and aims of the war against the heathen Saracens, and countless liturgical phrases and pious exhortations reinforce a didactic moral intention which is wholly absent from the French original; in the national aspect of the war, on the other hand, the Bavarian monk is hardly interested at all. What Konrad has done is to turn a French national heroic epic into a German spiritual one.

The absence of liturgical allusions and of an explicit religious motivation doesn't mean that the French lay is lacking in religious content. On the contrary: the worldly actions of the battlefield are so unproblematically set in a mode of pious heroism that they don't require a theological placing. The religious, Christianizing aspect of Charles's war is the *donnée* of the narrative mode in which all is ensconced. There is no hiatus between the secular and the religious. Feudal loyalty, love of *la dulce France*, knightly valour and regard for posthumous renown, love of the companions-in-arms and hatred of the Saracen enemy—each of these secular motives has a religious value associated with it. So unambiguous and inconspicuous—so self-evident—is this association of the spiritual with the worldly that it requires emphasis only in moments of extremity, when it is quite natural to speak of a man's final rewards for his worldly deeds— deeds whose meaning and value are not determined but merely increased by those rewards that await him in Eternity. As in Anglo-Saxon poetry, God is invoked only when 'a man's time is no more'. There is never any doubt that Roland's valour is Christian, Oliver's loyalty pleasing in the sight of the Emperor and God, and that Guenulun (Roland's stepfather) is a traitor condemned by both;

Turpin is a 'gentle man' and archbishop, absolving the warriors and
settling their quarrels, yet he is also among the bravest of warriors,
distinguished *par granz batailles e par mult bels sermons*; and Charles
is Emperor, God's viceroy on earth, and valiant defender of the
faith. All these assessments are conventional rather than individual,
they belong to the ethos of the cycle of *chansons* round Charlemagne.
The characterizations are rudimentary, largely conventional, un-
probing. The good Christians are beautiful, the heathen almost
always ugly, black, fantastic. The characters are statuesque, arche-
typal; and yet, since the piety of the French and the wickedness
of the infidels are largely taken for granted, there is room for
individual characterizations which give rise to a remarkable play
of affinities and differences, for the characters to acquire a 'human
interest'.

The two great battle-scenes, for instance, which have often been
criticized for their length and goriness (though they are a good deal
shorter than in Konrad), are enacted in a formalized, dance-like and
preordained fashion. Yet the action is also shown to be determined
by the personal qualities (rather than the theologically significant
roles) of the combatants. This is primarily a war over the possession
of Spain and for the glory of France (and only implicitly a religious
conflict). This worldly concern provides the action with its scheme
of values and its dramatic impetus. And where Turold the narrator
lets his story be guided by this impetus, there he must depict the
heathen warriors as capable, at least on occasion, of the same
knightly virtues of valour and loyalty and warlike circumspection as
the Christians. There is no doubt that the infidels are doomed to
defeat and eternal damnation, and yet Baligant, their leader, is depicted as a man who has often proved his fealty: 'God, what a baron,
had he had the Christian faith!'; and the traitor Guenelun, too, soon
to be condemned to a horrible death, stands before Charles, 'his body
strong, his face the colour of a good man: / Had he been true, he
would have had the look of a baron'. And the same is true of the
settings: most of them are perfunctory, conventional, lacking in
physical detail, but this is not true at all. Describing the moments
before the opening of the last battle, a modern author might speak of
a tension that lies over the brooding landscape, of the ominous silence
of expectancy. Turold's way is slightly different but no less effective:
'Between them is neither hill nor vale nor mound / Nor even wood.
Hiding there is none. / They see each other clearly across the plain

E

land.' In all such details of characterization and description we recognize a poetic imagination whose concern is with the human meanings and worldly contours of the warlike action, with a rudimentary realism.

The German monk writes for a different audience in another country, and at almost twice the length. The chivalrous convention of the *Chanson* is suspect and unacceptable to him. The warriors are praised not for their valour but for their Christian humility. Their goal now is not renown and conquest *and* salvation, but salvation through obedience to the Divine Will and martyrdom. Earlier in the twelfth century these had been the monastic ideals of the Cluniac tradition, and it is Konrad's aim to recommend these ideals to his patron and to the knights at his patron's court. Kinrad's *Lied* has been called a 'supremely conservative anachronism' because its author, caring little for the contemporary courtly ideals beyond the Rhine, is intent on subduing the turbulent passions of his Germanic warriors by Christian virtues of humility, constancy, and spiritual devotion (seven hundred years later Heine was to complain that the task was never completed). There is nothing half-hearted about Konrad's didacticism. All virtues, including honour, are now worldly virtues,[5] and as such they are all attributed to the heathens. Feudal loyalty is changed to the steadfastness of Christian martyrs, *la dulce France* becomes *rîche*, the Empire, which in turn is identified with *himilrîche*, the Kingdom of Heaven. Only one Christian shows the worldly virtues and praises them in others—Guenelun, who is on the side of the heathens and whose portrayal lacks the pathos of the *Chanson*. His conflict is less with Roland his stepson than with the Emperor, and the pattern of *that* relationship is not that of a treacherous vassal to his lord but of Judas the vassal of Satan to Christ. And Charlemagne himself is not that human, all too human ruler who, at the end of the *Chanson*, faced with the prospect of yet another crusade, exclaims in bitterness and sadness, 'Oh God, how heavy [*si penuse*] is my life', but merely a shadowy figure of transcendent piety.

'Death is not an event in life. Death is not experienced.'[6] There is a sense, familiar to any lawyer, in which this apparent commonplace is quite untrue. Literature at all events can present it: either in its worldly dimension by describing its effects on the living, or in its full bitterness by contrasting it with the sweetness of life. Similarly, the

one way literature can intimate the kingdom to come is by attribut-
ing to it perfections in some way related to what is perfectible in our
world. Hence the more purposeful and precise—the more realistic—
the portrayal of men and things in the world, the more poignant the
evocation of death.

Turpin has been slain. In the *Chanson*, Roland weeps over his dead
body and lays him to rest, 'Upon his breast, where the keybone
divides, / He has crossed his hands white and beautiful', and then
commends him, archbishop and knight, to God: 'Never will there
be a man more willing to serve Him.' Konrad on the other hand,
opening the scene with the same gruesome details of Turpin's wounds
as does the *Chanson*, follows this with a descent of the angels who
take Turpin, now a martyr, into heaven where he is received by
God. And it is not Roland's act of homage to the dead warrior and
priest nor the voice of Roland, its prayer *rising* from this world into
the other, but God's voice that *descends* from on high with the words
of the antiphon, *procede et regna*, that concludes Konrad's version
of the scene. Attending to the details of this scene—the description
of the archbishop's hands, the prayer that speaks of the human
meaning of Turpin's qualities—we understand something of the way
in which the *Chanson* succeeds in fusing valour with spirituality;
how it comes to be more poignant in the evocation of what we shall
soon be leaving; why, in brief, it is the more realistic of the two
epics.

4

... and ideologies

It was my earlier claim that 'realism' has a wider meaning than a period-term like 'Greek drama', whereas now it looks as though I were proposing for it the status of a *Weltanschauung*. In fact it isn't confined either to an historical or an ideological dimension, though it is involved in both. The realistic mode is present *in* Greek drama as it is in many other kinds of literature (only thus, incidentally, can a work such as Auerbach's make sense), and we should be able to recognize its presence; though our historical situation, which here figures as the source of our ignorance, will limit the scope and assurance of our recognition. But if realism is perennial it cannot be identical with any one coherent ideology either, though it does stand in a significant and positive relationship with each prevailing ideology in turn. With each, that is, except those that proscribe its practice and have the power to enforce their proscription.

Realism is thus not a single style and has no specific vocabulary of its own, except in contrast to styles and vocabularies employed by other modes of writing in any given age. It is not a *genre*, nor a *Weltanschauung*, but rather a disposition of mind and pen, something like a humour—in brief *a mode of writing*. As a mode it makes its appearance in all kinds of cultural situations yet is identical with none. Thus an historian—Johan Huizinga—may see it as 'a fairly subsidiary cultural growth that springs up now here and now there, often quite unexpectedly, to disappear just as unexpectedly'.[1] It is at home in all literary periods and most fully in the nineteenth century —yet no sooner has it reached its fullest fruition than it begins to wane again, and to undergo radical transformations. Huizinga observes this process in the Middle Ages: 'at the point of its highest perfection [realism] swings over to its antipode: the word is no longer applicable to the sculptures on Bamberg Cathedral'; Brecht sees the same process at work in the 1930s and attacks it polemically: 'A bracing artistry turns into stinking aestheticism, brilliant fantasy into dreary miasmas . . . realism decays into mechanical naturalism'.[2]

Brecht's remarks on our topic may serve to point to the conflict between ideology and the creative imagination. Part of the time he argues in favour of the widest possible meaning and against a narrowly formalistic conception of realism. He quotes 'The Mask of Anarchy' at length, in order to counter the view that 'Shelley's great ballad doesn't correspond to the usual descriptions of the realistic mode of writing: if this is so [Brecht adds], it is our business to change, enlarge and complete that description'. What the poem proves, he tells us, is that 'Shelley is a better realist than Balzac'. Why? 'Because [Shelley] makes abstraction easier' for the reader; and because, unlike Balzac, 'Shelley is not an enemy of the lower classes but their friend'. By 'abstraction' Brecht means that distancing from the actualities of a given society which he, like Marx, regards as the prerequisite of the revolutionary consciousness and action. And he ends accordingly by asserting that 'we derive our aesthetics like our morality from *the needs of our struggle*', which is hardly more than a gloss on Lenin's 'Literature must become a component part of the organized, planned, unified Socialist party work'.[3] The argument that began as a plea for criticism without prepossession ends in that ideological mousetrap which Brecht's own finest plays happily avoid.

The notion of a pre-established harmony between realism and the proletarian cause is as blatantly unhistorical as is the notion of a realism that is necessarily anti-religious. But in rejecting it we mustn't fall into the opposite error of excluding politics from realism. The fact is that it simply cannot help being interested in the political scene—the extent of its interest being determined not by 'the needs of our struggle' but by the needs of the literary work at hand. The very simple distinction we must observe—and which all talk about *littérature engagée* sets out to obliterate—is the distinction between advocacy and interest (§ 67). Realism has no consistent political 'line' to advocate, being now subversive now conservative, now partisan now again indifferent in its *views* concerning the specific issues that affect the society in whose portrayal it happens to be involved. However, the passionate *interest* with which it is committed to these issues has no equal anywhere in literature.

§ 37

Realism courts oblivion ('He was Deputy Governor in the Province of N., and in 18. . received the Eagle of St Vladimir Second Class'), and conquers oblivion by its unashamed assumption that yesterday's ephemera are more alive than today's generalities. Realism (unlike a discussion of what it is) is philosophically incurious and epistemologically naïve: the idealists' claim that we can have no reliable proof of external reality strikes the realist as egregious, just as G. E. Moore's famous refutation of that claim ('Here is one hand, and here is another') would strike him as supererogatory. The realistic writer (again, unlike one who sets out to describe realism) has no contribution to make to any discussion about 'models of reality', for he has no doubt about the singularity of the world in which realism lives, in which we all live.

Which is the world of care: of scrounging and getting and being concerned over the possession of things; but also the world of giving and freeing and loving: the world of movement and change which knows no arrest. Of the fact that reality changes realism is more fully, more intelligently aware than any other literary mode: what it implicitly denies is that in this world there is more than one reality, and that this denial is in need of proof.

The Marxists' claim that this world of care is identical with 'the bad—or unhappy—consciousness',[4] and capable of radical alteration and improvement here-and-now (or rather here-and-very-soon), realism views with a sceptical interest which the party man is bound to condemn as subversive. But then, realism is altogether too scrupulous and too much concerned over what the ideologists call 'means', to wax enthusiastic about the 'ends' they propose to erect on the ruins of those 'means'. To realism any such 'ends' appear as ideological petrifacts filling a desert it excels at describing[5]—and that desert too is not its habitation but an object of its consummate interest.

The object of its interest is the real world, which is neither the world seen as the Absolute Spirit in one of its temporal-relative manifestations, nor the world as Will and Idea, nor the mindless 'world of praxis and pseudo-concreteness' waiting for ideological thinking to stamp it with a meaning.[6] It refuses to regard all thinking that is not ideological as non-thought. Being concerned with the affinities and differences between men, it certainly displays a vivid and perennial curiosity in all questions of social causation, and for this very reason regards statements like 'men are the products of social life' or 'the institutions of a society are the products of its economic base' as metaphors run wild. To all reductivist theories, to all literary arguments beginning with 'The only difference is . . .'[7] it responds with the utmost suspicion. 'They give me no joy', wrote a premature anti-ideologist about the laws scientists impose upon the living world, 'close by it's all not true.'[8]

How close by? It will be remembered that the place assigned to the term 'realism' in an earlier part of this discussion was 'somewhere between life and literature' (§ 26). That conclusion about its formal status may now be seen to correspond to its actual literary practice. In order to retrace the differences and similarities in the real world, realism must stand back from it at a certain distance—neither too far away nor too close by. In other words, it is neither philosophy nor history, neither naturalism nor *chosisme*: it focuses on the world neither from the far point where only the broad movements and skeleton structures of the world are discernible, nor as through a microscope, where each discrete object looms so large that it assumes a totality and a meaning of its own. This middle distance, this 'delicate meeting place between imagination and knowledge',[9] varies from age to age. Indeed, what else is an age, what else could it possibly be, than a bundle of experiences whose affinities are perceived from a more or less common vantage point? But though it varies from age to age, this middle ground is at all times the determining condition of the realistic artist's choices and thus of his real and relative freedom. Our own real freedom, too, is never other than relative. And in any given situation our realistic assessment of that freedom, somewhere between the absurdity of instant attainment and the absurdity of chiliastic perfectibility, is formulated at some remove, at a middle distance from the situation itself.

§ 38

To say all this, however, is not to say that, because it is 'merely interested' in the world and because it looks at it from a little way off, realism 'leaves things as they are'. No human activity pursued with any degree of intentness and intelligence does that. Realism thrives on change and excels at registering it—literature and life know no better instrument for the intimating of change in all its meaningful detail than the realistic novel, nor a better safeguard against the petrification of the real world into static image and number. And realism also produces change, though (as J.-P. Sartre discovered after writing *What is Literature?*) it isn't, at any rate on the socio-political plane, a particularly effective instrument for that. Focusing and portraying change at a certain distance from reality, that is, in a certain complex relation to it, realism has this in common with the ideologies, that it too exaggerates and omits, that is, distorts. The radical difference between the two kinds of distortions is dictated by their different ends. Since the major end of realism (as of all literature) is to delight, and to delight especially by a showing within an achieved form, whereas the end of every ideology is to effect or retard change, the exaggerations and omissions of realism are dictated and validated by the convention and form of the work in which they occur—at least to the extent to which the end of literature is achieved; whereas the distortions of ideologies are dictated by a will to power and validated by purges, forced labour, or less dramatic forms of suffering and deprivation. And whereas ideological systems view the 'distortions' which are a part of realism as, quite literally, crimes, realism views the distortions which are a part of the ideologies with the same interest with which it looks on all things that affect and are a part of the real world. Moreover, realism has at its disposal that relatively disinterested form of insight known as irony (necessarily and notoriously lacking in the ideologies), which enables it to enlist the critical awareness of its own distortions in the portrayal of life in the real world. (This is what Dostoevsky does in *The Idiot* when, in the course of his extended analyses of human motives, he tells us that such analyses are beyond the powers of any writer.)

Now the democratic ideology pays for the distortions in its account of the real world with deprivations rather than blood-baths. It not only shows no hostility towards the insights into its own life that realism secures for it but on occasion is willing to learn from them; moreover, democracy is not necessarily lacking in disinterested self-awareness. All this makes it singularly vulnerable in any contest with the more 'committed' and doctrinaire ideologies. It also

makes it more realistic—at least in the sense of its taking more
notice of what things *are* than of what they should be or shall be;
and also in the sense of making the democratic ideology a more
natural habitation for the practice of literary realism than any other
ideology I know.

§ 39

Before attempting to substantiate some of the claims made on behalf
of realism in the preceding pages, let me turn once more to the
double nature—the literary and the non-literary meanings—of our
terms, in order to show how they may dovetail and support each
other. In a recent enquiry into the nature of Good we read: 'If
quality of consciousness matters, then anything which alters consciousness in the direction of unselfishness, objectivity, and realism
is connected with virtue.'[10] We readily recognize that words like
'unselfishness, objectivity and realism' are part of a moral not a
literary vocabulary; that a literary meaning of realism is here
irrelevant; and that there is a sense (established in the course of that
enquiry) in which these three words—unselfishness, objectivity, and
realism—complement each other. About the last in particular we
feel that it comprehends a wider attitude than the others, designating
not only *the way* (unselfishly and objectively) a man looks at and
acts in the world, but also his relation to *the object* (the world) he
looks at and acts in: 'realism' here connotes a positive relation to that
world (distorted it may be, but only to the extent that no man's
knowledge of the world can be complete). And when, a few pages
later, we read: 'The realism of a great artist is not a photographic
realism, it is essentially both pity and justice',[11] our mind is already
attuned to the non-literary meaning of the word from the earlier
passage. Though it now refers us to a view of art, it does so in a
complementary, not in an exclusive way (for that exclusiveness the
phrase 'photographic realism' is reserved). On the contrary: the
sentence asserts that 'pity and justice', the products of the imagination and of stable knowledge respectively, exist in the real
world and are of the essence of realism. We may consider this
specific definition to be too restrictive; indeed any simple statement
of the kind 'realism $= x + y$' is likely to be unsatisfactory, for
what we seek is description rather than definition. But we shall have
no difficulty in acknowledging the reference to 'pity and justice' as

one of many legitimate attempts to elucidate the true nature of the term, its dovetailing involvement in literature and in life.

§ 40

But is there really anything that entitles us to claim that we are speaking of 'the true nature of the term'? Haven't we also claimed that its meaning changes? Didn't the literary men of the *fin de siècle* take delight in asserting that they would have nothing to do with 'realism' because it was merely the last and most absurd delusion of the gullible bourgeois, the *'fable convenue* of the philistines'?[12] Doesn't there exist in our own time a theory and practice of 'realism' (§ 111) which seems to contradict almost everything that is claimed for it here?

All words, the most recondite as well as the most common, are apt to petrify into clichés. Both the *fin de siècle* and the *nouveau roman* undertook to get literature out of the rut of received opinion; to make it and its terminology 'relevant' (to use one of our clichés) to what was or is felt to be a new sense of life, a new reality of the world. The *fin de siècle* (with Hofmannsthal and Rilke, and Oscar Wilde) may be denying that the great literature of the past had ever anything to do with realism, while the *nouveau roman* (with Butor and Robbe-Grillet and Nathalie Sarraute, and its theoretician, Roland Barthes) may be asserting a continuity with realism where we cannot see it; or again, both groups may be speaking on behalf of literatures whose connections with realism as we generally understand the term may be tenuous; and they are likely to be doing this for polemical reasons that have to do with the politics of their respective literary movements. But in order to decide whether the denial of a continuity in the one case, or its assertion in the other, are justified we must of course go to the works about which these judgments are made, not to the propaganda made on their behalf. And this in turn means going to them with a mind that is not, and in a sense never has been, wholly innocent of the pleasures of literature. (To keep alive the dialectic between the unique and the typical, between the appreciation of original genius and the *déjà vu*, between literature as monument and literature as stepping-stones [§ 118] is one of the nicest aspects of the critic's task.) The question we shall have to address to these works, which are said either to be exempt from the considerations of realism or to offer a total reappraisal of it, will be no different from the question we ask of all literature under this heading: do these works *add* to and enrich our notion or feeling for what *elsewhere* we take to be realistic (add by being continuous with it), do they fulfil and refine our expectation of what is realism, or do they flatly contradict it? And if the latter, is the contradiction such as to force a *complete* and *meaningful* revision of 'realism' on us? By a complete revision I mean one that would do better justice not only to the literary qualities that we have hitherto associated with the term, but also to its dual nature in literature and in life. And by a meaningful revision I have in mind a new description that would result in a fuller and clearer understanding not merely of the works that have forced that revision on us (the house that Jack built is meant for others also), but of all that we have hitherto called realistic. And if such a revision is not possible, we would surely be better advised to explain the different kinds of anti-realistic bias of the *fin de siècle* and of the *nouveau roman*, and to design for them another terminology altogether. After all, realistic literature isn't the only literature there is.

The 'true nature' of a term in criticism, then, is not *une idée qui se promène dans l'espace*. To say it is historically determined is not to say it is arbitrary. It is to be found where, at any one time, the greatest number of meaningful, non-contradictory insights is to be found. The fact that different authors at different times have described realism in different, perhaps mutually exclusive terms, may be of interest to the historian of literary criticism. But this doesn't invalidate the attempt to see what 'realism' must mean if the fullest consequences of these uses are to be drawn without contradicting each other and the rest of our experience of literature.

No word is proof against petrifying into a cliché. Similarly, no word is proof against changes of its meaning—and change may on occasion be for the worse, in the sense of confusing what hitherto was free, or relatively free, from confusion. It may be that nothing can stop people calling one thing by the name of another thing which is its opposite (certainly nothing can stop them being deluded about themselves and the world except their unhappiness). But at least it may be said that to recognize such procedures for what they are is a better undertaking than by acquiescence to further them. Better, that is, always assuming that 'reality is not whatever I happen to think; it is what I am obliged to think';[13] and that realism, too, is not whatever we happen to say, but what we are obliged to say.

5

A conversation

§ 41

A fairly crude—certainly an unexamined—contrast between 'life' or 'the world' on the one hand and 'literature' or 'art' on the other has had to serve as the basis of our argument so far. In one form or another the dichotomy is to be found in all critical and aesthetic discussions which are concerned with literature in its mimetic function. And from Plato's time onwards it has frequently led to the peculiar notion that, in so far as it is 'mimesis' or 'imitation', literature is inferior to 'life', its ontological status is that of a lower kind of 'reality'; this inferior or derivative status of literature is implied in the word 'imitation' itself, since one of its meanings, in Greek too, points in the direction of 'counterfeit', 'sham', and 'not the real thing'. The aim of the present chapter is to show that, outside a given metaphysical system, there is nothing to be said in favour of such an evaluation; and—more central to my overall argument—that the dichotomy from which it derives is very far from being commonplace or self-evident. The point to be argued is not that there is no difference between 'life' and 'art', but that there is no single summary way of distinguishing between them. Instead, what is involved is a whole set of distinctions and affinities, an enumeration of which should help us to determine the place of realistic (= 'mimetic') literature in its relation to 'life'; and to determine what use may be made for our purpose of the 'imitation' theory of literature, on which so much criticism has been based in the past.

We readily agree that the statue of Colleoni is not Colleoni himself; that 'a man painted in colours is not a human being but a portrait'; that a character in a novel is not the same as a man in the street. But (to quote from a recent contribution to the ancient con-

troversy) is the difference between them correctly described by
saying that 'a literary figure, however precisely observed and however discriminatingly described, is not *a living reality* but part and
function of a literary whole'?[1] Is it really meaningful to say that
the activity or the product of writing is divided by some unbridge-
able gulf from 'life' or 'nature' or 'reality'? That 'literature, however
"realistic", must fail if it wishes to represent what *is*'?[2]

There are many occasions when the distinction between art and
other kinds of experience is self-evidently valid—'a man painted in
colours, &c.' is one of them; just as there are many everyday occasions when 'realism' is in no need of a description. But an argument
such as that from which I have quoted, which moves from a commonsense observation to phrases like 'living reality' and 'what *is*', is
obviously in need of closer scrutiny.

§ 42

Let us assume that the following is a verbatim transcript, made for
some formal or legal or scientific purpose, of an actual conversation
you have overheard or taken part in:

—I was thinking, you know . . .
—H'm?
—Well, we *have* talked about it before.
—Yes?
—Sorry, you're still reading the paper.
—What? Oh. *I*'m sorry. No, I'm not. I mean I'm not reading the
paper. I just . . .
—Well, if you're not reading, do just have a look at that chair.
No—that one, by the window.
—Yes? What's wrong with it?
—What's wrong with it? Heavens, I'd have thought anybody
would see that. For one thing it's never really suited this room.
The day your mother gave it to us, eight, no, nine years ago, I said
that neither the shape nor the colour was right for this room. Of
course I said it to you, but you've conveniently forgotten. I didn't
want to hurt her feelings.
—Honour bright, I don't remember.
—The red—well, it's really a ghastly peachy colour, isn't it?
Anyway, it's so garish, it simply kills every colour in the room.

And as for those phony Chippendale legs, they would be just ghastly in any room . . .

—Oh, I don't know.

—Oh, I don't know. How can you say you don't know? Can't you see what is obvious to anybody? It doesn't take much to see what state it's in, those greasy marks at the top. And that old tear across the seat. It's been mended so often, it really can't be mended any more.

—Well, in that case I suppose we'd better have it re-covered.

—Re-covered? Throw good money after bad? That won't alter the shape of the legs, nor those clumsy armrests. And anyway, it's hideously uncomfortable to sit in.

—Really? As a matter of fact I quite like it, you know. It's awful, the way people nowadays try to kill their own past by garbaging its things. I remember when I was quite small my mother used to mend that tear, and she always complained there wasn't enough material to do it properly, yet she always managed to make quite a good job of it. I remember the old man sitting in that chair, the day I . . .

—That's just being sentimental about it, isn't it, darling . . . But what I was about to say: I saw this beautiful Danish teak chair in town this afternoon.

—Look, *darling*. We can't possibly. I mean there's still this enormous gas bill to come in before the end of the month.

§ 43

Here, inside an overheard conversation, is a representation of 'what *is*'. There is no question of the chair being 'imitated' by one partner for the benefit of the other. The chair being given as a part of the room in which they are, what 'she' does is to point to certain of its features, and to certain features of those features, and to omit others: though the wife thinks it necessary to mention that the new chair is Danish and made of teak, she describes but does not think it necessary to name the kind of fabric with which the old chair is covered. In this 'Pickwickian' sense it might be said that she 'distorts' (§ 38) what is before her. Her description—the way she represents what *is*—is shaped ('determined') by what is recognizably true to both of them about the chair as it now stands there; by what they know of its history; by her comparison with that Danish chair which caught her fancy earlier that afternoon; by her taste in colours and shapes; by her expectation of his resistance to the proposed purchase —in sum, by her intention, underlying her choice of every word and argument, to get that new chair. And her description would not be radically different if they weren't at home and she had to preface some of her remarks with 'You remember'. The description might well have to be fuller ('Yes, you *do* know the one I mean . . .'), but there is no reason for thinking that a fuller description would represent more 'living reality', or a briefer description less.

What is true of the chair is also true of the people in the overheard, 'real' conversation. The way they know each other is similar to the way they know the chair: their knowledge of each other is composed of all such occasions (some of them less trivial than this one) in which their intentions—their expectations, hopes and fears, their thoughts and actions—meet upon a common purpose. Perhaps these encounters were inadequate—perhaps they haven't led to a reliable knowledge—yet they are still parts of 'what *is*', part of 'the living reality' of their lives. And since their knowledge of each other is at least partly shaped ('determined') by such conversations as the one we have overheard (and other less trivial ones), that conversation too is an inseparable part of 'what *is*', of the 'living reality' of their lives. We cannot conceive of a description of 'reality' or 'experience' which would not also include conversation. (Not all experience contains conversations, but all conversations occur in experience.) Thinking of it as a part or aspect of experience, we can certainly conceive of a view or philosophy of life which would regard that conversation as in some way inferior to or 'less real' than the rest of experience. The maxim of such a philosophy might be: 'Words don't matter. In the beginning was the Deed.' But similarly we can conceive of an opposite view, under some such maxim as 'Words alone are certain good': and there is no reason why, on *this* view, some other aspects of experience—remembering, thinking, indeed doing any one thing rather than another—might not be regarded in a similar light, as 'less real' than that conversation. To anticipate: to the extent that a literary text will show affinities and resemblances with that conversation, there will be no reason why such a text should claim a special status as once and for all and in every way different from other aspects of experience. This is not to say that literature viewed as 'a self-contained activity' is necessarily a chimera, but that such a

view is always tied to a special purpose in criticism (as each particular evaluation of it—seeing it as either 'more real' or 'less real'
than the rest of experience—was tied to a particular philosophy of
life); a view of literature as 'a self-contained activity' is not something that can be taken as self-evidently given in experience, in the
way in which a conversation can be.

There is no such thing as a literary work of art, however abstract
or esoteric or 'surrealistic', which does not refer to shapes and situations encountered in the experience of its readers, and which does
not in its working transform or modify or illuminate or confuse
that experience. There is no work of literature which does not appeal
to what existed before and will continue to exist after the work has
made its impact on the reader: which does not seek to have an effect,
and which does not rely for its effect on what is outside itself. To say
this is not to say that all responses in the course of which the outside
world is brought to bear on a literary work of art are equally valid.
On the contrary: the purpose of literary criticism is precisely to
distinguish appropriate reactions from inappropriate ones, just as
the purpose of literary history is to debarnacle our texts and rid us
of the false expectations of anachronism.

§ 44

How is that overheard conversation tied to the rest of experience? It
is a conversation about a chair: a something composed of worded
intentions relating to an object already given in the experience of
those two people: it is against this foil of the physical object that
the wife's intention will be realized. And in varying degrees and
ways this will always be the case. If the conversation were about an
Unidentified Flying Object or the pension scheme in Nirvana, it
would still have to be presented in its relation to other objects or
situations already given in the experience of those taking part. And
if it were about love, it would still be a conversation built upon the
rock or the quicksands of shared and available experience.

Moreover, as soon as an object or an activity is given in experience
—is placed in a verbal or visual or whatever relation to it—it is
bound in some way to be foreshortened: yet *for that reason* cannot
be said to be 'less real' or less part of experience. A philosopher may
well call this perspectivism to which all experience is subject 'our
ineradicable habit of lying',[3] but he can only do this meaningfully

within the framework of his metaphysical or moral scheme. Outside it we have a different notion of what it is to lie.

§ 45

Let us now assume that the conversation is part of a short story or novel or a play, a piece of fiction. This is much the same kind of assumption as was the claim that the overheard conversation is part of 'reality' or of 'what *is*'. (What is assumed is not that literature must necessarily contain a conversation of this kind, any more than it was assumed that 'reality' consists of nothing but such conversations—only that it may occur in literature.) The questions we shall try to answer are: What will change if we regard the conversation as a part of literature? and, What is there to justify us in calling it a piece of realistic literature?

Our 'model' (the conversation) is a fragment, its size is determined by the convenience of our argument, and its uses are therefore severely limited. Thus, even if we succeed in establishing the conversation as a realistic passage from the oeuvre of, say, J. P. Snookes (described in the Sundays as '*the* realist of post [Harold? Angus?] Wilsonian England'), an author like Nabokov or Pinter or Beckett might well place a passage such as this in a very different context and thus put it to a very different use (§ 89). No analysis of a fragment will fully answer questions about an achieved whole. To these questions other parts of this study are devoted. Nevertheless, our fragment has of course a verbal texture of sorts, an analysis of which should throw light on the arguments of those who assert, as well as of those who deny, that realistic literature is 'an imitation of real life'.

§ 46

There is a *prima facie* reason for taking this conversation-as-fiction to be a sample of realistic literature: it is, or seems to be, 'the same as' the overheard conversation. If instead of being offered to you in printed form, the conversation had been made available in a tape recording, you could check whether it is 'the same', whether it is 'reproduced verbatim'. Of course, not every verbatim representation of a conversation that occurs 'in real life' is necessarily realistic, nor is realism confined to verbatim representation (otherwise it would all be direct speech). It is certainly possible to think of criteria

F

according to which some other form of writing could be *more* realistic. But if realism in literature has any meaning at all, the case for its sometimes *including* a verbatim representation of, or 'the same words as', a 'real-life' conversation is at least as good as the case for its including any other form of writing. Other things (the wider context) being equal, using 'the same words' *is* a rudimentary form of realism.

§ 47

But in what sense are they 'the same words'? In one obvious sense they are not: the printed words of the conversation-as-fiction are related to the verbatim tape recording in something like the same way as the recording is to the overheard conversation. In each case something is lost or changed in the transition: the visual aspect as well as the physical presence are lost in the recording, both these as well as the audial are lost on the printed page. On the other hand there are certain gains: the conversation-as-fiction (='the text') is made permanently available whereas the overheard conversation is not, it is made visually available whereas the tape recording is not, and these changes have important consequences for the way each enters into our experience and affects it. Yet the words also *are* 'the same', for instance in the sense that the words of the overheard conversation will be found in the same place in the dictionary as the words of 'the text' (they show their 'sameness' when reduced or changed to the dimension of print); or again in the sense that some of the words of the overheard conversation as well as some of the words of 'the text' can be shown to refer to the same physical objects or situations (they show their 'sameness' when translated into non-literary experience).

What 'the same words' means here is the overlapping of certain affinities, not the presence of a single quality or mode or form going all the way through the three conversations, the overheard, the re-corded, and the fictionalized. Above all: even though certain words and phrases ('do just have a look at that chair') refer to the same physical objects and situations and in that sense have the same meaning, we shall see (§ 89) that 'the text' as a whole need not have the same meaning as the overheard conversation as a whole. There are many similarities between them, and many differences, not one.

§ 48

Gains or losses—there are *changes*: the conversation-as-text is a *re*presentation, an offering again of what was there in the first place, though an offering, here and always, in a different form. You cannot have a full-scale model of England in your back garden: 'The ideal limiting case of a reproduction is reduplication, and a duplicate is too true to be useful. Anything that falls short of the ideal limit of reduplication is too useful to be altogether true. And this goes not only for maps, but also descriptions, pictures, portraits and theories'[4]— and conversations, in a room as much as in a book. The foreshortening of 'the text'—its 'falling short of the ideal of reduplication'—is likely to be different from that of the conversation in a room, but in both cases it will be dictated by certain ends in view. (And also by the difference of medium.) While the 'real' conversation may go on in the same vein until its 'practical' end is achieved, Snookes feels that he has done enough (his readers may feel he has done more than enough) to achieve his 'literary' end in view. 'The ideal limit of reduplication' concerns him as little as it does the lady in pursuit of a new chair. Realism is as compatible with selection as is any other mode of experience (of which literature is a part).

§ 49

But is it not plausible to argue that because in the transition from the overheard conversation to the text something is lost, the conversation-as-text is properly described as 'less real'? Granted that we cannot conceive of a description of 'reality' which did not include the printed page any more than we could conceive of a description of 'reality' which did not include the overheard conversation, is it not common usage to refer to books (as Hamlet does to 'Words, words, words!') as 'less real' than social encounters or facts or moments of personal exposure? Is it not 'natural' to feel that 'books are less real than life'? Well, Balzac on his death-bed called for Dr Bianchon (a character he used in a score of his novels) and thus presumably thought of him as 'more real' than the people around him. What is 'real experience'—for a writer, for the good reader—if it is not to include what obsesses them? To deny reality to what happens inside books is no less peculiar—is no less a special plea—than to deny reality to what happens outside them. Of course, in any view of reality, whether literary or not, it is possible to designate some aspect of it as more or less real than another. For instance: 'I think the husband's answers, in that tedious conversation you have cooked up, are so stereotype as to turn him into a cliché—you know, to me he is much less real than she.' Do we feel that this is a literary rather than a 'real-life' judgment? But then, the husband may with equal justice say that his wife's arguments against keeping the old chair are 'not real arguments at all', or are 'a good deal less real than the gas bill that's due before the end of the month', and that surely is in no sense an exclusively 'literary' judgment.

But is there not a body of literature, from *Don Quixote* onwards, which gives expression to the experience of a gulf between books and the world? (Think of the old Tolstoy and the peasants, ill-smelling and venerable.) Have not many modern authors felt themselves to be excluded from 'the real world', and have they not built their finest works from this feeling? May not a special plea on behalf of a single man's experience be true? It *is* true, so long as it remains special: so long as it is offered as a single man's experience. Its characteristic form of expression is lyrical poetry. It becomes available to realism only at the point where the experience is worsted in the disillusioning conflict with the world of other people. A realistic presentation of 'the artist's problem in society' is bound to end in a refutation of the special plea and an encroachment upon the artist's isolation.

Among the countless human sentiments realism can represent is that which makes us call one kind of experience 'more real' than another, but it can only do this on the premise of a single, undivided reality.

§ 50

All these uses of the words 'real' and 'unreal' may be called *qualitative* uses, since they designate a greater or lesser distinctness of perception or feeling, in brief a quality of experience; they are readily replaceable by other words, such as 'substantial', 'strong', 'convincing'; or again 'shadowy', 'defective', 'feeble'. But there are other uses of the word 'real', which may be called *absolute*,[5] and which have words like 'false, inauthentic, an imitation' or 'not the same', 'not real' rather than 'unreal', for their opposite. Take things like 'a

Japanese pearl', 'a Hong Kong-made suit of clothes', 'a counterfeit one-pound note', 'Zeuxis's painting of a basket of grapes' or 'a forged Vermeer': each of these is 'not real' in the absolute sense of being the thing it is (an imitation, a *trompe l'oeil*, a forgery) and not another ('the real thing'). Each of them is related to its 'real' equivalent in a different way: a Japanese (or 'cultivated') pearl is made from different material and by a different process from a natural pearl, the Hong Kong tailor uses the same material and the same cut as the one in Savile Row but charges less, the forged one-pound note may well be made of the same material and even by the same process as the genuine thing but is different by reason of its origin, Zeuxis's painting is different from a basket of grapes in every way save its visual effect, the forged Vermeer is different by reason of its origin and also because it is, or is said to be, artistically inferior to 'a real Vermeer'. But obviously none of *these* relations between the real thing and its imitation are relevant to the difference between the overheard conversation and the literary text save that the things in one group are not the same as, and yet have something in common with, the things in the other group. *This* difference, however, occurs in 'life' as readily as it does in literature, nor is it the only characteristic difference that divides life from literature. It *may* be the difference between them: Schiller's Maria Stuart is not the same as 'the real Mary Queen of Scots'—and 'the real Mary Queen of Scots' is as much the subject of Schiller's play as she is the subject of Antonia Fraser's biography: historical accuracy is not what makes for more or less 'reality'.

A critic who claims that Schiller's Maria must 'fail to represent what *is*' or that she 'is not a living reality' is offering the qualitative use of 'real' where what he has in mind is its absolute use. He is claiming that 'the real Mary Queen of Scots' has more reality than Schiller's Maria Stuart, when all he can properly be saying is that, while they have certain things in common, the one is not the same as the other. (If Schiller's play were in some way fragmentary and radically unintelligible without reference to Mary Queen of Scots, that might make it 'less real', in the qualitative but not in the absolute sense, not because it is a play; and it would, as we shall see [§ 57], make it less realistic.)

What all the things on our list have in common and what makes it appropriate to call them imitations is what makes it inappropriate to call literature by the same word: they are intended to stand for their equivalents, and on occasion they may successfully do so: they approach the ideal limiting case. And since in literature this intended or achieved quality is bound to be irrelevant, to describe it as 'an imitation of real life' can never be more than a defective metaphor: the ideal limiting case (§ 48) is not its concern. Literature of all kinds may be, and realistic literature always is, a representation but not a 'standing for' in the sense of a replacement of that which it represents. Even in naturalism the intention 'to imitate scientifically' falls short of any possible achievement. The country bumpkin who, on visiting a playhouse for the first time, thinks he is present at an ordinary conversation,[6] is a country bumpkin who doesn't know what a drama is, not a witness for the prosecution in Plato's case against poetry. And when Aristotle calls tragedy 'the imitation of an action', he writes in the same metaphorical way in which we speak of 'the music of poetry', not in the way we call a prose fiction a novel or a Japanese pearl an imitation. Aristotle's metaphor underlines what tragedy has in common with life off stage, and ignores those uses of 'imitation' which are inappropriate to tragedy. Whereas when Auerbach uses Aristotle's own word, *mimesis*, he does not have to disclaim what is inappropriate in 'imitation'. Instead, he and others like him are enriching the language of criticism by a term of some technical precision, which however lacks that parallel meaning outside literature which is the distinguishing feature of 'realism'.

§ 51

There is not one set of meanings of the word 'real' reserved for life and another for literature. Literature is not an imitation of life in any of the senses in which the objects on our list were imitations of their real counterparts. The conversation as fiction is not the same as the 'real' conversation, but it is not necessarily and for that reason 'less real'. A literary representation may well be (be felt or thought to be) less real than that of which it is a representation, just as one partner in the overheard conversation may well be (be felt or thought to be) 'less real' than the other partner. However, this is not due to its being a *literary* representation (any more than in the other case it is due to their being partners in a *conversation*), but to its being a literary representation *of a certain quality* or kind.

§ 52

What makes 'imitation' an unsatisfactory designation of literature is above all the absence of any creative element. Aristotle is aware of the objection and forestalls it: the writer of tragedies should not 'try to hang on at all costs to traditional stories . . . [he] should be a maker of his plots. . . . And in fact even if he turns out to be putting actual events into his poetry, he is none the less a poet for that; for there is nothing to prevent some actual events being the kind that might probably happen, i.e., are capable of happening—which is the principle by virtue of which he is their "maker" [*poietés*]'.[7] Now it looks as if, of all possible samples of literature, our conversation is the least suitable for showing what is to be the creative (non-imitative) aspect of a text. However, there may be an advantage in that. If we can show that here too creativeness—a making—is involved, we may *a fortiori* take it for granted that it will be present in other kinds of writing too.

But what is this creative element? In what sense is it involved in the conversation? We can see how it was involved in Zeuxis's legendary painting of a basket of grapes (which we are told were so perfectly depicted that the birds came and pecked at them). With the basket of real grapes before him, Zeuxis mixed and matched his paints and made his brush strokes so as to trace out what was before him, aiming at the one perspective—in the conceiving of which lay his creativeness—from which the finished product would look 'exactly like' the real basket of grapes. Here every detail and every move is calculated to contribute to a known attainable end, which is the successful imitation. To use E. H. Gombrich's felicitous terminology,[8] Zeuxis's *making* is subordinated to his *matching*. In the overheard conversation the wife is not describing the old chair in order to reproduce or imitate it, but on the contrary in order to show it in the worst possible (though still recognizable) light. 'She is playing it by ear': matching her words not to the chair but to her husband's anticipated and actual reactions, and thus to her practical end, which is not imitation but the purchase of a new chair. And something like this, too, is the way Snookes proceeds. He too will be matching his words—choosing some, rejecting others, following with his mind and pen a mixture of memories of overheard conversations culled from a world he half knows, half divines—with a view to *his* end. To paraphrase Aristotle: even if he turns out to be putting an actual conversation into his work, he is a maker of fiction for all that. His creativeness will lie in his choosing this conversation and these words in accordance with the right perspective from which the conversation will appear as part of a world. His end, too, will not be the reproduction of the conversation, but its reproduction as a means of characterizing that couple, the social and economic situation to which they belong, the mores of the English professional classes in 1971—something, at all events, that is represented and illuminated by that conversation but not replaced by it. There is no perspective from which his text will appear the same as, or may be mistaken for, the conversation itself—the goal of naturalistic literature is a chimera.

§ 53

Zeuxis's picture is a whole, the conversation is a fragment of a text. Whether it becomes part of a realistic whole depends on Snookes's choosing a perspective which will place that conversation in *a* world that is continuous with, and at the same time modifies, our expectations of what *the* world is and what happens in it: by which I mean *our* world, in which there are people—creatures, that is, of some appreciable degree of integrity, not fragments of consciousness or psychic tropisms (§ 108), and not trends of history either (§ 120). In building up this world which is his fictional whole, the author will be matching his brushstrokes to his ideas or 'experience' of expectations which he shares with us (expectations of 'events . . . of the kind that are capable of happening'), departing from these expectations but never wholly ignoring them. He will challenge and modify them, refine, enrich, deliberately disappoint but never completely abandon them, and even in the flouting of our expectations he will still be appealing to them by a variety of overt or indirect or hidden Let us now look more closely at some of the features of that conversation about the chair.

§ 54

Let us now look more closely at some of the features of that conversation about the chair.

An indirection: At what point, dear reader, did you decide on the sexes of the two speakers? Probably fairly early on. If you had been present at the conversation, there would of course have been no uncertainty. Does this point to a radical difference between the conversation 'in real life' and in a book? Is this intimation of something not explicitly stated in the text *the* distinguishing mark of literature? Not at all. This intimation is of the same kind as the circumstance that, in the overheard conversation too, the husband guessed at the wife's tactics and purpose early on, well before she mentioned the Danish chair. He guessed because her words were becoming increasingly meaningful, that is, revealing her end in view more and more clearly. And you as a reader guessed for the same sort of reason, because their words (=Snookes's choices) made increasingly more sense as indications of their sexes in a given social framework (that of marriage) in which, in our culture, the wife goes to town to look at furniture, the husband groans and foots the bill, etc. Her reason for resorting to intimation is much the same as Snookes's: they both reckon this is the best way of attaining their respective ends in view. Snookes's is the more complex. Writing in A.D. 1971 and in English, his purpose could be an indirection, a sly way of introducing a homosexual couple into his novel. If you had been present at the conversation, then this particular device would most probably not have been possible. True; but if Snookes were writing in a language less coy about grammatical gender than English, he would have had to resort to much more indirect verbal devices to achieve this particular innuendo. Indirection is as much an option in realistic fiction as in 'real life'.

§ 55

There is such a thing as *the best perspective*, which will get all the relevant details into the picture. To deny this is to deny the possibility of a coherent narrative (which is what Robert Musil does in *The Man Without Qualities*, choosing 'Essayismus' instead).

But which details are relevant? Clearly, all those that contribute, and no more than contribute, to the achieved whole ('the total form') of the realistic fiction: a 'total form' which fulfils and enriches our expectations by way of a continuity. The realistic writer's choices in the building up of that whole are determined by what is available to him *and* by 'what he likes':

The realistic painter
'All nature faithfully'—But by what feint
Can Nature be subdued to art's constraint?
Her smallest fragment is still infinite!
And so he paints but what he likes in it.
What does he like? He likes what he can paint![9]

Is this really 'a mordant comment on the limits of realism'? No doubt, as Professor Gombrich says, this is what Nietzsche intended his verses to be—but are they not rather a comment on the misguided 'scientific' claims often made on realism's behalf? Who would deny that an artist can never do *'all* Nature faithfully' (or the *whole* world, for that matter)? Of course he can only do what he can do. But the operative fact for the realist is that 'what he likes' is *in* Nature ('Er malt zuletzt *davon*, was ihm gefällt'). To say that the operative fact is 'what he likes' is like saying that because an historian or for that matter a scientist shows a personal ('subjective') preference for one topic of research rather than another, therefore his research is determined by personal feelings (is 'subjective'), and discloses not facts about the world but only facts about himself; or that, because in all experience a perspective of some kind is involved, therefore all experience distorts and displays 'our ineradicable habit of lying' (§ 44)—in brief, that there is no difference between knowledge and opinion.

Nietzsche speaks for a whole host of critics who say they miss that accuracy and 'objectivity' to which realistic fictions are said to lay claim; but the claim is usually of the critic's own devising. In any event, the accuracy they miss is absent in all representation that is not reduplication. And when it is agreed that art is not reduplication, they then conclude that there is no such thing as realism:[10]

All realism in art is a delusion. You reproduce what delights and attracts you in an object—but these feelings are most certainly *not* evoked by *realia*! You don't know what is the cause of your feelings! All good art has always deluded itself into thinking it is realistic!

But this is like saying that every representation, because it is a representation, is always of the same quality and kind; or indeed that, outside the realm of art, a realistic way of dealing with a given situation is not significantly different from any other way.

Every matching involves a making, but the two are not one and the same thing. In realism the balance is on the side of the matching.

§ 56

'Here is the rose—here dance!' (Hegel).[11]
What is available to the realistic writer—the means by which he realizes his choices and takes issue with our expectations—is also what dates his work: his means are language, life, and the forms of art at a certain time in the continuum of history. He is the son of his time, his work is his time caught in words, which are also the words of his contemporaries. A good many turns in Snookes's conversation betray their day and age fairly obviously—think of the difference between the two uses of the pronoun, in 'I saw *this* beautiful Danish chair in town *this* afternoon', the first of which is a kind of pro-pitiatory ploy that came in (from American speech) in the 1960s; but think also, less obviously, of turns like 'as a matter of fact', 'it *simply* kills every colour in the room'. There is no such thing as a neutral language and the notion of a 'non-style' is always relative to the purpose of singling out a 'personal style'. No form of writing 'transcends History'[12] because all are part of it, though there *is* an appreciation of the text to which its historicity is irrelevant (§ 120). And since realism is different from pastiche, the extent to which it can return to the past and reproduce its language is limited: 'it is necessary [writes Sir Walter Scott in the 'Dedicatory Epistle' to *Ivanhoe*] that the subject assumed should be, as it were, translated into manners, as well as language, of the age we live in.'[13] Whatever it is that makes for the immortality of a realistic work, it is not the timelessness of its language. Words are born and die within a single span of time, new words and old live side by side in the *parole* of a single speaker. Saussure's notion of linguistic synchrony can never be more than a working hypothesis.[14]

The language of realism needn't of course have the awful flatness of our conversation (though the reader may be grateful that Snookes didn't attempt a 'close transcription' in the naturalistic manner, with all its hums and haws). On the other hand it will have to eschew linguistic creativeness that is the hallmark of symbolist poetry, of the Joycean stream of consciousness, and the like. The verbal innovations it offers ('people . . . kill their own past by *garbaging* its things') will be infrequent and unobtrusive—realism avails itself of what is given in the broad spectrum of natural language as it avails itself of what is given in experience. (And this in the sphere of language too, as in experience at large, doesn't mean that 'it leaves things as they are'.) In the creative acknowledgment of its language lies a rudimentary approval of the world. A writer who condemns his world to the extent of rejecting its *parole* (Karl Kraus and Stefan George offer two different examples of this attitude) by this token cannot be a realistic writer; a world whose language is wholly contemptible cannot have a realistic literature. Just as societies and cultures differ in the demands they make on their writers, so languages differ in the amount of freedom from the bonds of common linguistic usage they allow. The looser the nexus that ties an author to his society, the greater his possibilities for linguistic innovation ('creativeness'), and the less compelling the claims of realistic writing.

§ 57

'I remember *the old man* sitting in that chair. . . .' The obvious dating of this phrase (>1930s) is incompatible with the dating of '*this* beautiful Danish chair' (1960s<): the phrase dates not the conversation but only one of the speakers. Or does it? What is at issue here is not so much a dating as a social (working-class) placing; or again 'the old man' may be used ironically, in a quotational manner, to hide an emotion or by hiding to draw attention to it.

Language, life, and the forms of literature at a certain point in history are available to the realistic writer. Consequently there are three kinds of expectation to which a realistic text addresses itself: verbal, social-existential, and formal. They overlap each other and are not easy to separate, because they have their common ground in the historicity of all literature. As to the first, I have already suggested the kind of linguistic restraints imposed on a realistic writer as well as the kind of lexical and idiomatic resources available to him. To work within these limits and with these resources is to work in an area determined by the verbal expectations of a given public at a definite time and place. (Lyrical poetry works with less common expectations and with fewer linguistic restraints.)

Where our conversation refers to 'those phony Chippendale legs' or to a 'Danish teak chair', however, it appeals not so much to a common verbal convention as rather to a knowledge of what function these things have on the existential and 'cultural horizon'[15] of those two people—a knowledge, again, shared by author, characters, and public alike. Here realism moves among clichés and in the direction of satire: to explore *idées reçues* (the petrified intellectual expectations of a given social class) and then to explode them is a realistic device as old as Petronius's *Satyricon*. The realist's first pitfall is an overburdening of intimation: *we* know that social ambience in which 'Chippendale legs' are always 'phony', to dress lettuce with Heinz's mayonnaise is 'sacrilege' and all that is *'ab*solutely plain', including Danish teak chairs, is always 'beautiful'. . . . Courting ephemerality, the realistic writer must hope that cultural gaps will be bridged by repeated intimations. Literature which does not enable us to bridge such gaps is not necessarily meaningless, but the meanings it yields don't have the continuity of realism. It is for this reason that historical knowledge can never be irrelevant to our appreciation of the realism of a work, and that our ignorance is a vital limiting factor in such an appreciation.

I have called this kind of expectation social *and* existential precisely because what realism appeals to and establishes is that social truth which insists on the interconnectedness of individual and society. (You cannot know the size and shape of a field without knowing its breadth *and* its length.) To claim that the existential-personal portrayal of man is incompatible with the socio-historical[16] is to ignore realism's characteristic achievement.

The descent into banality is the realist's second pitfall. His task is not the mere fulfilment of an expectation ('There he is, up to his usual tricks again—not content with using those wretched catkins as fertility symbols, he has to tell us so, too . . .'), but its fulfilment along unexpected lines which the text coaxes us into accepting as though they had been expected; this is what Aristotle recommends as the 'plausible impossibilities'[17] of the best mimetic actions. When we say that 'at this point the characters come alive', or that 'they determine their own destiny', or again that 'they take the conduct of their lives out of the author's hands', our critical metaphors indicate that the artifice of the fulfilled expectation has been particularly successful.

§ 58

Realism in literature is a fictive dialogue, a writer's singularly direct way of taking issue with the historically and socially formed expectations of his readers. Of course, the mind's readiness to act on predisposive stimuli is not confined to literary experience and involves problems of perception beyond the scope of this study. However, some recent inquiries happily confirm that a little theory of perception goes a long way as far as aesthetic insights are concerned, and that this modicum may well provide something like common ground for an exploration of the different arts. Thus to translate the arguments of E. H. Gombrich's *Art and Illusion* into the language of literary criticism is an exercise as instructive as it is exhilarating:[18]

> We notice only when we look for something, and we look when our attention is aroused by some disequilibrium, a difference between our expectation and the incoming message. We cannot take in all we see in a room, but we notice if something is changed. We cannot register all features of a head, and as long as they conform to our expectations they fall silently into the slot of our perceptive apparatus. Similarly we have come to accept certain forms in pictures as representing heads, and we are not troubled before our attention is roused—though if somebody entered our room with an egg-shaped head . . . we would be sure to notice something wrong.

Here again is the same argument, transposed into musical terms:[19]

> Musical meaning . . . depends for its sheer existence on the clearly implied contrast between that which you hear and that which is contradicted by what you hear. It is this tension varying in intensity according to the structural juncture a composition has reached, between what the composer does and what he makes you feel he was expected to do, that constitutes musical logic.

Within the relationship that springs up between the cliché and the new, music and poetry are conjoined:[20]

> All metre is to some extent contrapuntal. That is what we mean by 'the music of poetry'; the regular expectation is set up and then what we are actually given is 'a spume that plays upon a ghostly paradigm' of form. . . . When, at the age of 15, I first heard Louis Armstrong play a trumpet solo on the basis of a popular tune, I realized that with one part of my brain I was hearing the tune, which by itself would have been intolerably banal, and with another I was hearing his marvellous improvisation, and that the

music came from both of them together. That, more than any
other single experience, made me a writer of verse.

The poet's aphorism has the last word:[21]
Poète pour nous est celui-là qui rompt pour nous l'accoutumance.

§ 59

When I composed verses, I could not fit any foot in any position I
pleased.

(St Augustine)[22]

As for the third, the *formal* expectation raised by a realistic text, it
too conforms to and challenges our sense of continuity—the continuity we expect in experience as reflected in the continuity we
expect in literary forms. When we say (apropos of Snookes's conversation) that the wife chooses her remarks realistically, we mean
that she proceeds 'with an eye for the main chance'. 'From desire,
ariseth the thought of some means we have seen produce the like of
that which we aim at':[23] hoping to attain certain foreseeable results,
the wife conforms in her expectations to a notion of causality
accepted and acted on in a given society and culture. We thus per-
ceive a certain unity in her choice of remarks, and this unity our
author retraces. It is what her situation and his fiction have in
common (Wittgenstein calls it 'the logical form'[24]), even though we
shall see that the ends they aim at are different. And just as in the
real-life situation it would be unrealistic for the wife to believe that
her remarks will have results radically disconnected from the expected ones, so a text which showed her remarks to have quite
untoward results would cease to be a realistic fiction.

Again, the measure of what is radically disconnected is provided
by the cultural framework within which the conversation takes
place. The expectations raised within this framework are the foil
against which both kinds of realism—the literary and the non-
literary—are measured: they *are* that framework in so far as it is
relevant to the writing and reading of the text. Realism, a child of
its age, is as relative as is, *not* indeed the logical form of causality,[25]
but the feeling for what at any one time is an adequate set of causes
in life or an adequate motivation in literature.

What happens when untoward, disconnected effects are introduced into a text? Literary realism (I have argued) is a mode, not just

a style of writing. Thus it may be breached and replaced by another mode even while a single style—that is, a unified verbal texture—is maintained: think of the matter-of-fact 'reports' of Kafka. Or again realism may persist through changes of style: think of the fantasy and *chosisme* in Dickens, the interpolated parables in Dostoevsky, the lyrical passages in *Madame Bovary*. (To account for such composite practices we shall, in chapter 8, have to consider more fully that distinction between ways of assessing situations and ways of describing them which we found (§ 29) to be connected—though rather loosely—with the different connotations of realism in 'life' and realism in literature.)

For the formal expectation to be fulfilled it is necessary that any literary genre once chosen should either be completed or purposefully modified; a stated problem solved or shown to be insoluble within the stated terms; a chosen area of experience charted or shown to be beyond realism's reach. This is the pattern of formal expectations Shakespeare sets up, deliberately repudiates, and takes up again in *The Tempest*. There is nothing inadvertent in the fact that the action of his last play is not confined to a single mode—the introduction of Trinculo and Stephano, or again the dismissal of Ariel, are among the many ways in which the changes of mode are made an issue of and dramatically acknowledged: both realism and the supernatural in turn are, not merely abandoned, but *shown* to be irrelevant. Politics and magic lore, charisma and *eros*, disillusionment and charity, the natural and the Divine are the elements from which, against great odds, the unity of *The Tempest* is achieved. Its dominant mode is neither realistic nor supernatural but a purposeful interplay of both.

Inadvertency is the third of the pitfalls of realism. It is the break in continuity that remains a break, arbitrarily and without acknowledgment; the incoherence of one literary genre or form that does not accrue to the coherence of another. Again, our sense for such coherences is relative to our historical and cultural circumstances, and liable to grotesque misunderstandings—unaided by a critical commentary, what do we make of the *haiku*? All the same, to one side of historical relativity, there is such a thing as defectiveness of forms; and there is a limit to our capacity for reconstructing them.

At the point where realism is abandoned without adequate reason, it turns into *kitsch*, its worst pitfall: sweet *kitsch* where it slips

inadvertently into romance, sour *kitsch* where it lurches adventit-
iously into tragedy. Continuity of meaning within an achieved form,
however, is among realism's finest achievements.

§ 60

'What is the meaning of that conversation between those two
people?' 'I thought it would be fairly obvious by now. She wants him
to buy that Danish chair.' 'Is that its meaning?' 'Well, there is no
other meaning to it.' 'Isn't there? That, surely is the purpose of the
conversation, not its meaning!'

In the translation from overheard conversation to written fiction
the wife's purpose becomes a part of the author's meaning. This is
what he will be doing throughout: converting purposes into meanings, and meanings into an overall meaning which, whatever else it
may be, will be built up from a variety of scenes and sentences such
as these. The whole will be more than its parts but not another thing,
not another reality.

Purpose, then, stands in the same relation to realism in life as
does meaning to realism in literature: they are not the same but they
are closely related (they have the same 'logical form'). We have
already mentioned the way in which the wife's selection of descriptive items was shaped by her end in view (§§ 43, 48). Similarly, the
author's selection of what he makes his characters say is determined
by *his* end in view, which may well be more complex. What is being
established are two distinct but analogous hierarchies of ends. Just
as her immediate purpose (the acquisition of a new chair) is part of a
larger purpose (improving the look of the room), this in turn of one
larger still (keeping up with the Joneses), and so forth, so the author
is pursuing another though similar hierarchy of ends, from the discrete description or scene to the building up of characters and their
interaction in a chapter, and from that to the completion of his
dominant theme all the way to 'the achieved form' of his work.
Whatever the end in view, and whether or not it is clearly conceived
before it is achieved, it is bound to shape the fiction, and therefore
the conversation-in-the-fiction, in something like the same way that
the details of the real-life conversation are shaped by *its* end; though
in each case not the end only but it *and* the available means do the
shaping.

G

§ 61

An objection: 'Isn't there a fundamental difference between the two ends in view—hers, which we may call practical, and the author's, which we may call aesthetic or literary? And, granted that both are, as you keep insisting, aspects or modes or whatever of experience, does *that* diminish the difference between them?'

'Certainly not. We have already enumerated a good many differences between these kinds of experience, and the same applies to the ends they pursue. And we have also seen that, however many and however varied these differences may be, the practical is in no sense "*more* real" than the aesthetic, is in no sense more of "*what is*" (§ 41). Of course, there is also the purpose for which Snookes writes—not the meaning inherent in his work but the purpose it is intended to fulfil in its author's life. It may be anything from *ad majorem Dei gloriam* to keeping the bank manager from the door, it may be the wish to make an object that gives delight or simply the desire for "the clapping of your good hands"—which of these are practical ends and which are aesthetic?'

§ 62

The overall meaning of a realistic fiction is built from scenes and sentences whose importance and generality varies, but only within a single spectrum. Remember the husband's attempt to parry the wife's foray: 'It's awful, the way people nowadays try to kill their own past by garbaging its things!' His generalization may well be a plausible and true observation about what he is sure to call 'the Modern World', but that isn't its function in Snookes's conversation. Its function, which would be achieved even if the observation were plausible and untrue, is to help build up the characters of the two speakers and their ambience. Generalizations are an integral part of a realistic text (as they are of the real-life conversation), they belong to the single spectrum of scenes and sentences and meanings. There are various ways, in life and literature, in which we periodize, and thus bring order into, our experience: 'You always used to . . . but nowadays you . . .' is one of them.

Realism in literature, then, is not some improbable absence of meaning but a close dovetailing of piecemeal meanings. The political implication of this view—realism's sceptical attitude to all utopian and revolutionary ideologies which propose to sacrifice the concrete particular to the abstract general—has already been mentioned (§ 36). But hand in hand with its politics go certain metaphysical and religious implications. For realism at this point emerges as the articulated and fictionalized recognition that 'the Meaning of Life'[26], too, is not something imposed on a sudden and from outside or from above (outside this world realism cannot breathe),[27] but that it too is built up from the meanings of the parts and occasions—the scenes—of life. And where it shows the workings of Divine Grace, realism must show it as that which perfects, not as that which breaks, human nature.

§ 63

There are other ways of establishing a literary meaning. Take this passage from the husband's rearguard defence:

—I remember when I was quite small my mother used to mend that tear . . . I remember my father in that chair the day. . . .
—That's just being sentimental about it, darling. . . .

What the wife calls 'sentimental', the critic of this passage will call 'symbolical'. The familiar chair, in the husband's recollection, becomes more than an object of use, more than a part of his daily life.* Its familiarity is heightened to the point where the object comes to stand for a number of apparently poignant past experiences —it becomes a rudimentary symbol. (To make the name of an object stand for a variety of encounters, recollections etc. [1 : 1, 2, 3 . . .], is not exclusive to literature.) In the real-life conversation the chair is endowed with a symbolical meaning for a perfectly good practical ('realistic') reason. Just so in the fiction the use of a symbol is perfectly compatible with realism (it is not confined to referential, 1 : 1 uses of language, any more than 'life' is), as long as what the symbol stands for is shown to belong to the built-up and achieved unity of the action, is shown to contribute to the single spectrum. At the

---

* In satirizing the 'fetish value' of the commodities produced under capitalism —the table that grows a head and starts dancing—Marx is in fact giving a picturesque description of the way poetic symbols behave in (presumably) all societies. See Das Kapital, I, iv (Ullstein ed., Berlin 1969, pp. 50–1).

point where the object (or situation, or whatever) moves away from its common and shared meaning—the point where what it *is* is swallowed up by what it *stands for*—symbolism takes over.

Realism allows for symbolical meanings, but it limits their range. Symbolist literature moves beyond that range, to the point where a break occurs between '*is*' and '*stands for*', where shared knowledge gives way to intimation; symbolism begins where intimation ceases to be subordinated to a realistic purpose and becomes dominant, an open-ended vision (§ 100). Realism imposes a balance between public and private meanings. It may require historical information. But once that has been provided, it establishes a self-explaining continuity—whereas symbolism insists on the enigmatic break—between the common norm *given* in the language and a contingent, *created* multiplicity of references. Realism's *making* of private meanings is subordinated to its *matching* of meanings against available common norms of usage; and realism ends where a continuity between the private and the public, the symbolical and the referential, can no longer be established. But does not the ability to establish such continuities depend on the reader's subjectivity? Certainly; but then his subjectivity too, like his sense for the continuity in experience and the coherence of forms, is relative to and part of a changing but shared historical situation.

The coherence of symbolical fictions is precarious—some will say they are all the more valuable and poetic for that. Such fictions have aerial roots, they grow 'beyond the world of our common indication'.[28] This is why they occasionally contain prophetic insights which are denied to realism (§ 120). Just so their language displays an originality and a creativeness that leaves the common usage of a given age behind, though it may provide a later age and *its* realism with new linguistic forms.

Symbolism too is concerned with 'the Meaning of life', which it intimates as a thing ineffable; and where it is concerned with the working of Divine Grace, it shows it as disconnected from human nature, as that on which human nature must first be broken.

§ 64

Language can be a part and a form of life in a more specific sense than is usually intended. To quote from Snookes's conversation about that old and worn chair for the last time:

—Yes? What's wrong with it?

—What's wrong with it? Heavens, I'd have thought. . . .

and:

—Oh, I don't know.

—Oh, I don't know. How can you say you don't know. Can't you see. . . .

and again:

—Honour bright, I don't remember.

In the first two passages the wife is pursuing her purpose by quoting the husband's speech habits at him. In the third passage he ventures on a mild joke, quoting from the language of the Girl Guides. These phrases are rhetorical, they don't add much to the description either of the object or of the speakers' reactions to it. They amount to verbatim repetitions of what somebody else has said: bits of language are being *re*considered and made the focus of the speakers' immediate attention. However, these simple language-conscious ploys are being used not for their own sake but in order to push the argument along to its desired goal or to prevent it reaching that goal. We shall see (§ 106) that language-conscious devices are available to literature on a scale stretching from such unsophisticated quotational turns as these to the complex lacework of the *nouveau roman*; and that as soon as this self-conscious mode becomes dominant—for instance, in the form of apparently self-contained language games—it upsets the balance of realistic fictions. My present point is that just as realism was compatible with selection and ellipsis, with intimation, generalization, and symbolical meanings, so it can accommodate language-conscious turns, though again only in their non-dominant, rudimentary forms. A realism composed of nothing but language-conscious fictions is an impossibility, albeit a fashionable one.

§ 65

'Well—so you have made your points. That grey-in-grey conversation of yours is a piece of realism. There are many connections between "life" and "literature", and realism is the mode in which they most nearly meet. Also, there are many differences between them, not just one. Literature is not less "real", no less a part of "what is", than "life". And language *is* a "form of life" . . . Where do we go from here?'

'Where do you want to go?'

'Well, you know, there is a sense in which you haven't said anything relevant at all!'

'No, I didn't know—I hope there isn't'.

'What I mean is this. Literature in general and realism in particular may well be all the things you say they are, but over and above that these are terms that relate to *works of art*. And unless you are saying that this conversation is a work of art . . . *Are* you saying that?'

'No, of course not. I made that clear when I mentioned that it was a fragment, that it *could* be part of a work of art.'

'That's not what you said. You said it could be part of a realistic fiction. And that is something different.'

'Is it? Why?'

'In speaking of a work of art we are conscious of making a value-judgement. Whereas I notice you have carefully avoided using words like "beautiful" or "valuable" '.

'Not quite. I did, after all, say that "realism" itself was a term implying a positive literary achievement. And to call a work "realistic" is to commend it, though in a full evaluation of such a work other factors too will have to be taken into consideration. And a piece of trivial realism. . . .'

'Such as that conversation?'

'. . . clearly represents a smaller value than a serious realistic work, or a serious work of symbolism, or a romance in the grand manner, or any other non-realistic alternative. Moreover, to talk about the pitfalls of realism as I did again implies that positive values are to be found where such pitfalls are avoided. What I say about realism as the fulfilment of a set of expectations is that aiming at a target and hitting it is an achievement, whereas aiming at a target and not hitting it is not.'

'All right. But I remain unconvinced. You admit that your conversation isn't a work of art and you claim that it *may* be part of one, yet you don't define, you don't even describe, what a literary work of art is.'

'Don't I? Surely it's what I have been doing all along. Selection, intimation, the use of symbolical meanings, the dominance of matching over making and all the other topics I mentioned—the fact that they are also to be found "in life", outside a realistic work of art, wasn't meant to suggest that they are not to be found inside it too!'

'Yet you also show that they can all be gathered together in a conversation which, on your own admission, is not a work of art. Surely there is something missing. And surely what is missing in your description is the most important thing of all.'

'And what would that be, do you think?'

'Well—what all old-fashioned aesthetics is about. What gives us that feeling of delight, or insight, or shock, or whatever—the feeling that we are in the presence of a genuine work of art.'

'I agree that something is missing from my description and I certainly want to add something to what I said, though I don't know whether it will satisfy you, because. . . .'

'Let's hear what it is first!'

'Because what I want to add isn't necessarily more important than the various topics I have already mentioned. You see, my difficulty is that I don't think I can produce a list of items, enumerate them all, and then say, "These and these items, taken together and suitably arranged, are a literary work of art". Just as little as I can compile a list of this kind and say, "This is life". Many more items might have to be added, or again omitted, in each individual case.'

'Oh, very well—but what about that one thing you say you have omitted?'

'It's quite simple, really. It must always be present, though this doesn't make it more important than the rest since it is meaningless without the rest. It is the fact that we regard something as a work of art and call it by that name.'

'You must be joking. Calling a thing by that name? This surely is carrying language-consciousness to the point of absurdity. Even Kant says that when it's a question of deciding whether an object is beautiful or not, chatting people up doesn't count.[29] To call a thing by a certain name doesn't mean that the name is correct, that it *is* that thing.'

'True. But it also doesn't mean that it isn't that thing. It means that in doing so we call attention to certain qualities which may or may not be present in it and which, if they are present, we would not otherwise have perceived in it.'

'Them's dark words! And you said it was going to be something quite simple!'

'Well, perhaps it isn't. But simple or not, it is what we do all the time. Look—have a look at this old blotting pad.'

'Yes—what about it?'

'Well, tell me what you see.'

'How ridiculous. Oh, all right. It is an oblong piece of cardboard with a vast number of inkblots on it, mainly black and blue, and some red. There is an area of it that's been smudged and bleached—you probably left it in the garden and it got rained on. There are some rather inane doodles in one corner, and a few monograms, some of them almost illegible. What about it?'

'You can see that it's pretty old. I've had it for years, but I don't think I was ever particularly conscious of what it looked like. If I thought about it at all, I probably vaguely considered that I ought to throw it away and get a new one. But a few days ago a friend of mine came into my study and saw it. Quite out of the blue he said, "Isn't this beautiful?" He also said something about its strange patterns. And suddenly, although all that had happened was that he had called it as he did, I saw it "with different eyes".'

'It's a bit fanciful, but I'll buy it. He was probably a painter.'

'As a matter of fact he wasn't. Just a highly competent critic and ₁over of art. But you're on the right lines. He certainly knew what to look for. And this showed me what I hadn't seen before. A work of art? Of beauty? Something like that. What he did was what a literary artist might do with that conversation. He put a frame round the old blotter, he placed it in a different light, he *ostended* it, if you'll pardon the expression.'

'I won't. But anyhow, it seems like a pretty roundabout way of getting to the old chestnut about beauty being in the eye of the beholder!'

'Perhaps it is. But you yourself implied that this can't be the whole story when you asked whether he is a painter.'

'Did I? Why? I only asked, because to be honest *I* can't see all this beauty. All I can see is just a crummy old blotting-pad with, as you say, odd blotches and shapes. Sorry to disappoint you after you've been trying so hard.'

'Yet you would agree that a painter, or an art critic, or someone of that kind, might truly claim to see the thing as beautiful.'

'Of course. Anybody might.'

'Anybody? With equal justice? But if being a painter means

having a particular understanding for shapes and lines and colours and their arrangements, then clearly it can't be anybody. . . .'

'That's true. But even though some people might be better at discerning this quality than others, it's hard to see what would prevent them from seeing it in anything, in any chance configuration. . . . Especially nowadays, when every tin of baked beans and every cross-examination in a court of law can be "framed" or "ostended" and declared a work of art.'

'Well, the declaration needn't be accepted—either now or in time to come. Every age has its own aesthetic values and anti-values, and its own realism (§ 115). But this doesn't mean that the declaration must be invalid, either now or in the future, or that there can be no overlap of the value-systems of different ages, or that the value-system of an age is static.'

'What you are saying makes the survival of works of art a pretty precarious business!'

'It *is* precarious.'

'And yet you seem to claim that *any* chance configuration. . . .'

'Let's be quite clear, first of all, that we aren't talking about a single quality but the framing or discerning of a number of different ones. But apart from that I agree that this is what my argument implies: anything, any configuration of lines, or colours, or words, *may* be called a work of art. Kant was quite clear about that,[30] and so was Stephen Dedalus in his argument with Lynch. As long as we are concerned with art not as a process but a product,[31] its origin doesn't matter. But though any configuration can be a work of art, it cannot be *any kind* of work of art. Realism, for example, is more limited—only certain kinds of configuration of words can be called realistic. But then again you will recall that, as to the kinds of words it uses—the lexis of realism—we could say no more than that it is co-extensive with *parole*, the common part of the language of an age. After all, there are no diamonds on that blotting pad, no splashes of gold-leaf even. . . .'

'You're telling me. Common language, common knowledge, common experience—it all sounds like a pretty common way of writing.'

'So are bread and salt—pretty common fare. But to come back to what you said about beauty and the eye of the beholder. If some people are better at discerning that beauty than others, and if they are better at it by virtue of a skill they have acquired in contact with other people, then beauty can't be *only* in the eye of the beholder—

I mean quite apart from not being in the eye of just *any* beholder. The work of art isn't a work of art until you have considered it as such, unlike this old bit of cardboard, which is what it is whatever name you give it and whether you look at it or not. However, your considering it as a work of art need not be an act of sheer arbitrariness or untrammelled subjectivity, but may imply—and if you are any good at it does imply—a habit and a practice—learned and shared with other people—of considering objects or configurations in that light, nor is considering it in that light the only thing that makes it into a work of art, but it and all the other perceptions you bring to bear on that old blotter, that old bit of conversation: you as the practitioner of the art of seeing or of the art of reading and you as the person you are, within such and such a socio-historical. . . .'

'I wonder how you are going to finish *that* sentence.'

6

The charm of institutions

Take but degree away, untune that string
And, hark, what discord follows!

(Troilus and Cressida)

§ 66

In describing the life of the solitary man the literary imagination
may proceed as freely as it will; in describing the life of a complex,
closely-knit society it is hampered at every step. In the one case it
portrays a freedom diminished by nothing save the necessities of
nature (and often it transcends even these), in the other it must take
issue with the competing claims of individuals and groups, their
antecedents and consequences, in brief with human history. It is
history that offers the resistance which the realistic writer must
overcome and in the overcoming acknowledge—the resistance of
'That's how things are' to the free-flowing imagination with its
proclivity to fantasy and idealization. In this region of competing
claims, where 'life means entering relationships',[1] realism finds its
richest veins.

Literary realism has no special vocabulary or syntax of ideas, no
'material objects'[2] are exclusively its own. Yet there *is* an area in
which it is most fully at home: it is where human relationships are
formalized and protected against the caprice of solipsism, in the
social institutions of a given age. Even there it may be displaced or
superseded by other modes of writing. Some of the greatest works of
recent literature have either by-passed institutions as inauthentic
'reifications' of individual experience, or turned to the grotesque in
order to show them up as the daemonic opposite of that for which
they came into being. Indeed, so common and pervasive is our

91

experience of the deformation of institutions—their dehumanization and bureaucratization—that we have largely lost sight of their *raison d'être* and their virtues, let alone of the charm they held for other ages. Recent terrors and present perplexities are in our bones. We have no sense of wonder at the sight of that extraordinary and complex living venture that modern Western society amounts to. Nothing is more alien to us and to our peculiar notion of authenticity than the wisdom which proclaims that 'value lies not in particular will'. The characteristic productions of our literature show little appreciation of the fact that Western society offers the only safe-guard we know and can realistically conceive of against the threats of chaos and anarchy, whose full meaning is collective death. So browbeaten are we by egalitarian ideologies that we apologize for rather than rejoice in the variety of men and their conditions, yet we also repudiate the hierarchies which stabilize this variety and render it socially fruitful. We marvel at the progress of science and techno-logy, then again are petrified at the prospect of a further quantifica-tion of our lives, yet we seem unaware that the institution of, say, a liberal university is a more complex and more finely-wrought instru-ment of human ingenuity than any marvel of science, its product. For any of us who are neither hermits nor maniacs the capacity to discriminate between men in their various stations in life is a vital accomplishment (as well as a source of consuming interest), yet we regard this capacity as shameful, and seem unaware that the flexible rule of social distinctions together with the fixed rule of law are the only safeguards we have against the tyranny of natural differences. We profess a belief in social justice, yet would wish to impose it either through the injustice of bloody revolution or by way of some spontaneously generated utopia—in either event without the inter-vention of institutions that must be impersonal and stable if they are to be effective. It is true that we have a profusion of realistic novels and plays of sorts, yet they proceed as if Auschwitz, Hiroshima, and Dresden had never happened. Whereas the most advanced literary trends of our age, which often acknowledge those terrible realities, deny all value and literary interest to the forms of life by virtue of which we actually live. (Here, incidentally, is the missed chance of C. P. Snow's novels: he does indeed do justice to the institutions, but the persons inside them are not quite alive.)

The idea that service for king and country could be presented unblushingly as a value and a worthy object of devotion conflicts

with our vaunted ideas of personal authenticity. The *pietas* garnered
in the album of days and years of a humble clerk's life of service is all
but meaningless to us. Records of stocks and shares and the
ephemeral fluctuations of markets, sheet upon sheet of fine copper-
plate entries, the minutiae of the legal process or of finance ('A fine
man—middle-class boarding house—600 francs income—despoiled
by his daughters who both have 50,000 francs per annum—dying
like a dog . . .'):[3] all these seem to us hardly fit subjects of serious
literature—unless we are able to eke out their actuality by turning
them into symbols, or into evidence for 'the rise of capitalism from
the ethics of Protestantism' or of 'the false consciousness of the
bourgeoisie'; but having turned the rich actuality of the past into
mere evidence, we readily skip it when reading Balzac or Pérez
Galdós 'for their literary achievement'.

§ 67

In our reading of the nineteenth-century realists, the stock exchange
and government offices, municipal administration, the Church, the
army, the law, and parliament figure above all as *the background* to
individual action. And it is true that these institutions and the work
done in them were rarely described in full detail (though surely
George Orwell's remark that Dickens tells us nothing about the daily
work of his characters is as odd as its sequel, that Dickens 'sees them
always in private life, as "characters", not as functional members of
society'). Routine, which is the essence of all institutions, is hostile
to literary presentation, realistic or other, for literature is sustained
by individuation and finds nothing harder to trace or retrace than a
smooth surface unbroken by variety. (Fabrice at Waterloo and Pierre
Bezuchov at Moscow are *tours-de-force* of individuation, and so is
Theodor Fontane's description of the French retreat through the
Prussian countryside and the streets of Berlin. What Evelyn Waugh
evokes in *Men at Arms* is the routine of army life, a portrayal we are
surely wrong to read as a satirical indirection.)

But the word 'background' fails to do justice to the place of institutions in the realistic literature of other ages. Concentration on the
'symbols' and 'image clusters' of Dickens's language has tended to
obscure how much of the foreground of his novels is taken up by
institutions: the school (in *David Copperfield* and *Nicholas Nickleby*);
the Marshalsea (*Little Dorrit*); London business (*Dombey and Son*);

the industrial North (*Hard Times*); the workhouse (*Oliver Twist*); the legal practice (*Great Expectations*); the cathedral and its environs (*Edwin Drood*); and, again and again, the Court of Law. It is true, as George Orwell says, that 'Dickens attacked English institutions with a ferocity that has never since been equalled'. But what also needs saying (because unlike Orwell we can no longer take it for granted) is that Dickens couldn't have 'attacked' these institutions without first recreating them; without first portraying them in their encounters with individual characters, who only become 'functional members of society' through these encounters.

What is at issue in realism is not Dickens's humanitarianism, or Tolstoy's sentimental love of the Russian peasantry; or Balzac's conservatism; or Stendhal's or Flaubert's contempt for the Church, the politics of a petty Italian court, life in the French provinces, or the revolution of 1848. More fundamental than these conative attitudes is the creative acknowledgment on which they rest—the creative acknowledgment of the data of social life at a recognizable moment in history. What is at issue is not 'engagement' but *interest*; an interest which comes before the scorn and contempt and goes beyond them, and which, through the quality of its literary expression, belies those feelings of contempt, and others too:

'So you take love to be the strongest emotion of all?' the artist-hero of Thomas Mann's *Doktor Faustus*,[4] the young Adrian Leverkühn, asks his friend and future biographer.

'Do you know a stronger one?' Serenus Zeitblom returns the question.

'Yes, interest.'

'By that I suppose you mean a love that has been deprived of animal warmth?'

'Let's agree on the definition,' Leverkühn laughed.

§ 68

Adrian Leverkühn is of course a very modern artist indeed, and may be thought an odd witness to call in the present context; besides, his art is music, to which realism by its very nature is irrelevant (§ 31). The alienation and radical solitude from which his work arises are the ultimate destination of the *artistes maudits* of the nineteenth century, and these conditions belong to a social situation uncharted in earlier ages. However, Leverkühn's view, that *interest* is what governs an artist's attitude towards his material, needn't imply those catastrophic-existential conclusions which are recorded in modern art and literature (and of which 'the life and work of Adrian Lever-kühn' is a most poignant memorial). His view is valid beyond his particular predicament. The question we must now turn to is how, in literature, such a creative interest is related to social life and its institutions. It would certainly be absurd to suggest that every literary work of art is defective if it doesn't focus on, or at least include or intimate, the social dimension. Yet the conditions of an artist's exclusions are not arbitrary, his freedom in the face of his chosen theme is not unlimited, he must come to terms with our formal expectations (§ 59).

The work of Goethe provides one of the most interesting examples of an alternative consistently explored. Here is a man who in his several avocations was richly steeped in the social realities of his time and place, whose private and public comments on contemporary political events, on Napoleon and the Germany of his time, are abundant, well-informed, and profound. Yet here, too, is a poet whose greatest works bypass whenever possible what he himself called 'the middle height of life'. Of the three levels of human experience which engage the literary imagination Goethe explores the first, the personal, with an intensity of feeling and language that has rarely been equalled; and the same is true of the third, the metaphysical and religious level. To these, the greater part of his poetry is committed: the self in and out of love, anguished and joyful, falling prey to despair and then again taking courage from life; the self involved in intimate personal bonds of friendship and family; the self in contact with Nature and the Divine, contemplating the sadness of the fleeting moment as well as the consolations of habit and duration, expressing the timeless not in mystical ecstasy but rather in firm contact with the created world: these are the themes that yield his finest poetic achievements. The signs of the social experience which these poems display are all implicit, they all derive from the splendid 'commonness' and centrality of Goethe's language. It lacks all esoteric inventiveness, it explores and appeals to the verbal imagination of the common people no less than of the educated classes. Yet what this language expresses are those rare and privileged moments in which all *other* signs of the social experience are, not avoided or suppressed, but rendered irrelevant by the nature of the chosen occasion itself. And it is a measure of Goethe's achievement that subsequent generations of German writers and readers came to see in the evocation of those privileged, private moments the staple of literature.

But what of the second sphere of experience, the kingdom of the Leviathan, where men are bound not by love but contract, not by worship of Nature or the Divine but by mutual agreement? Where the nature of the occasion does not render the social dimension irrelevant, there Goethe's works show a lack of realistic concern which contrasts strangely with the worldly wisdom and realism which enliven all the reports we have of his activities as a courtier, man of affairs, and critic of contemporary society. No important work of his is seriously and consistently concerned with the French Revolution[5] or any other major political event of his time. Now, it would be foolish for a critic to cavil at his author's choice of themes; need he do more than record the fact that the subject of the Revolution, treated in several minor plays, failed to engage Goethe's finest gifts? But Goethe's lack of social and political concern is more pervasive than that. It is manifest in those of his dramas which, by their very choice of medium and theme alike, raise the expectation of a fully developed political intrigue, and disappoint that expectation by imposing on the dramatic situation a purely private solution, allowing the political issues to remain unresolved. The salvation that Goetz and Egmont attain does justice to their greatness as private individuals. But they are also political leaders, yet the freedom into which they escape in their hour of death has nothing whatever to do with their political function. All the political problems they raised remain unsolved. We are to see them triumphant, yet what they leave behind is chaos.

§ 69

Is a non-realistic concern with social institutions possible? Goethe's *Die Wahlverwandtschaften* (*Elective Affinities*, 1809) is a novel of life among the contemporary aristocracy. Its ostensible theme is the tragically ironic vindication of the institution of marriage, engendered by a conflict of the moral law with the natural. What determines the action are either moral/personal or natural/supernatural causes, acted out in a timeless and island-like setting that is disturbed by hardly a hint of social causality. Within this setting a kind of experiment in natural philosophy is conducted, whose outcome is the destruction of unworldly spirituality and natural piety in its contact with passion and wilfulness. Where a realistic novelist would build up a circumstantial picture of the worldly world as a foil to the heroine's intuitive and 'daemonic' being, Goethe on the contrary devises a setting that has been freed—deliberately, it would seem—from social substance. The conflict is subdued, it takes place in a 'world' of spiritual omens and natural/supernatural affinities. The work thus gains in purity and lyrical poignancy what it loses in liveliness and worldly interest. Yet it is *a novel*: the expectation of something like an 'epic totality of life' *is* raised in the work; and this, certainly, is the way Goethe's contemporaries read it:

> In this novel [writes one of them in 1810[6]], just as in an old epic, is contained everything that is significant and characteristic of the age, and in centuries to come it would be possible to outline from it a perfect picture of our present life.

Everything? The critic, the Berlin classical scholar K. F. W. Solger, offers a strange selection of items to support his claim:

> Just as the details of their [physical] environment evenly sustain and serve as a foil to the entire and real daily life of the characters, so does the inclusion of all that is fashionable today, such as horticulture, love of medieval art, representation of paintings by living people and all other such [fashions], which serve as a foil to the life of the readers and of the entire age.

We need move no heavy Marxist guns to observe that this is not, and cannot possibly have been, 'everything', that from these charming bits and pieces, which make up the extent of the novel's accommodation in the social world, no coherent picture of 'the entire age' emerges. We know, and Goethe knew, that elsewhere richer and more realistic resources of fiction were available. Take Jane Austen's heroines—Emma Woodhouse, Harriet Smith, Jane Fairfax; or again, Fanny Price, Maria and Julia Bertram, Mary Crawford—all exact contemporaries of Ottilie, Goethe's heroine. Plainly, our ability to distinguish quite sharply between these seven girls, all under twenty-one, depends in no small measure upon the state of their bank balance. The size of their private means (or its absence) is neither irrelevant to their characters nor does it wholly determine them. Money is one of the elements that anchor Jane Austen's fiction in a reality we can place and date, and the dating of the reality is one of

H

the charms of the fiction. It is hard to imagine Ottilie in the company of Jane Austen's young ladies, but then it is hard to imagine her in any more robust context than that which Goethe has created for her. Ottilie is certainly no mere idea, but she isn't a full fictional embodiment either. She is an Ophelia, moved into the centre of *L'année dernière à Marienbad*.

Yet what if such exalted spirituality really did constitute the Weimar variant of the *Zeitgeist*?

> To this perfect picture of the age [Solger continues] belong the many reflections scattered throughout the book. There is nowadays almost no other way to affect people and in a higher sense to live sociably in human society than through private discourse and the reflections it contains. For it is principally in this that we must now seek our whole world and the entire activity of our lives. ... Indeed, these reflections are the true life we lead, to the extent that we raise ourselves above the common and the sensuous.

Our quotations are no cockshies. Solger's is the genuine voice of Weimar culture with its insistence on the autonomy of the life of the mind and its relegation of the material and social mainsprings of action to one side of all that is significant. It is this voice, too, expressing the aspirations of the age, not its realities, that speaks to us from Goethe's novel. Is it an anachronism to suggest that what the fiction tells us about the social world, 'the common and the sensuous', is incomplete? The completeness, and hence the coherence, which the realists among Goethe's contemporaries give us is certainly not some list of facts and figures such as a modern social historian may be looking for. (Mail-order catalogues, we shall see [§ 102], aren't necessarily realistic.) The picture the realists present, with its inclusions and omissions, is accessible and meaningful to us to the extent that it fulfils and enriches our informed expectations. They are *our* expectations, but aroused by the themes the realists choose and the situations they depict—by situations and themes which present men not in their privileged moments but in their social roles first and foremost, and in the conflicts of their competing claims on the world they share. Goethe's creative interest, on the other hand, is devoted to the two spheres—the personal and the metaphysical—which are dovetailed round the social and leave it largely though not entirely uncharted. In saying all this I have done little to convey the true dimensions of Goethe's novel: the fine aerial threads of the entanglement, the wisdom of the interpolated 'reflections', the depth and variety of its symbols, and above all the poignant charm of its tragic heroine. All these had to go unheeded. The more an ethereal figure like Ottilie dominates the structure of a novel, the less room is left for a realistic presentation. And conversely: where a similar plot is presented in a wholly realistic manner (as in Ford Madox Ford's *The Good Soldier*, 1915), there a figure like Ottilie is bound to occupy a less central position.

§ 70

It is shifts of balance of this kind that make one ask (§ 117) whether realism has a history (by which I mean a coherent development), or whether we must content ourselves with the kind of picture album that Auerbach presents. Is it likely to be a history tracing the growth of consciousness, or merely a chronicle of its contingent changes? Fielding is much less concerned with individualization of characters than Jane Austen;[7] Thomas Hardy reproduces the speech of poor villagers more convincingly than does Jane Austen, who makes it up from the speech habits of higher social strata;[8] D. H. Lawrence's portrayals of mining communities are more single-mindedly realistic than any comparable working-class portraits in Hardy; where Jane Austen's characters are happily accommodated in the class into which they were born, Hardy's characters challenge their class status, yet not as radically as Lawrence's, etc. Are these changes indicative of a development and progress, or is it merely a case of 'one damn' thing after another'?

It is clear that realism is exceptionally sensitive to the movements of social and political history; and that, more than other modes of writing, it is dependent on its literary antecedents. The literary history of realism would therefore have to be a sequential account of ever new areas of worldly experience becoming available to literature—that is, a sequential account of ever new possibilities of fiction and sentence-making within the *données* of changing historical situations. The narrative resources available to Jane Austen were indeed manifold,[9] yet to us they appear simple enough, not least because today they are wielded competently by almost any run-of-the-mill novelist. Yet the devices that were adequate in her time and for her world are not adequate in ours. Her success, like their failure, shows the unique adequacy of her resources to her task.

The remarkable fact is that these resources were not available to Goethe in his creativeness. What activates the resources of realism is not individual inspiration only, but individual talent in conjunction with a social and literary tradition that is unambiguously committed to the world; a tradition in which observing (=matching) is as much honoured as is creating (=making).* For whatever historical reasons, such a tradition was not alive in the Germany of Goethe's day. His unparalleled originality and creativeness in other modes of writing tend to obscure this fact; yet he was aware of it, and occasionally saw the lack of a realistic tradition in German literature as a direct consequence of her socio-historical development.

Towards the end of his life he remarked that the age of national literatures was over and that the future belonged to *Weltliteratur*: Carlyle, Manzoni, and Sir Walter Scott, he said, were the authors who could help German literature to emerge from its 'narrow circle' and 'pedantic conceit'.[10] He was of course right in his prophecy. The works of nineteenth-century European realism form a common literary enterprise—a concurrence of themes and modes of expression, of descriptions and evaluations which, more than any earlier literary tradition, deserves the name of 'world literature'. The irony is that Goethe's contribution to this tradition is hardly very significant. His finest achievements, and those of the men who wrote in the shadow of his genius, were of a different kind.

§ 71

'I am afraid that my background will eat up my foreground', writes Flaubert, afraid that he may be losing sight of his young man of 'moderate passions' in the turmoil of 1848. There is no such danger.

* See also the following exchange from the *Conversations with T. G. Masaryk*:
    Karel Čapek: 'We [the Czechs] have some fine poetry, but we lack novels and drama. For poetry, personal life is enough; the novel and drama presuppose the accumulated experience of generations. Novels are the work of a whole age.'
    T.G.M.: 'Yes—a poem that springs from a genuine and strong feeling is within the capability of many poets, precisely because it is the expression of certain personal feelings. Novels and drama are quite another matter, and so is the epic. They presuppose the artistic observation of a society, a nation, of classes and estates and so on. I criticize our novels for a certain kind of immaturity, a limited knowledge of our own life and life abroad, a lack of worldliness.' (K[arel]Č[apek], *Hovory s T. G. Masarykem*, Prague 1937, p. 311.) Incidentally, Masaryk entered Czech politics in 1891 as the founder of 'the Realist Party'.

No nineteenth-century novelist was more alive to the interconnections between self and social world; and *L'Education sentimentale* marks one of the highest points in realism's creative awareness that no personal relationship, amorous or any other, can subsist beyond the privileged moment without a network of interpersonal, public bonds. (This is analogous to Wittgenstein's showing that the language of the emotions, including the language of 'private feelings', is always a part of the language and behaviour a man shares with, and has learned from, other people.)

Early sociologists came to insist that the individual self, in any living sense, *even as a self*, is already inextricably involved in a social whole. They were thus re-establishing a unity and a truth which the realistic artists had never ceased to take for granted. (Marx pays tribute to 'the present splendid brotherhood of fiction writers in England, whose graphic and eloquent pages have issued to the world more political and social truths than have been uttered by all the professional politicians, publicists and moralists put together.'[11]) For just as they—the realists—had never questioned the verities of a naïve philosophical realism, whatever doubts idealist philosophers might profess about the existence of the external world, so they never lost their intuitive knowledge that 'Robinson Crusoe is an Englishman and a native of the City of York'.[12] A reader of realistic prose is likely to greet the sociologists' discovery, as he is likely to greet many discoveries of the psychologists, as theoretical reminders of a fictional practice no less familiar than civilized life itself.

The circumstances that prevent this social truth from being available to Goethe in his creative work are also the circumstances that enable him almost to invent or at least decisively to determine an alternative tradition—the fiction of the *Bildungsroman*. Its autobiographical origins in the confessionary tracts of Pietism, which were in due course secularized and aestheticized, to become the apologias of artists, cling to the genre throughout its history and are reinforced by Goethe's own didactic intentions. In its very structure, the 'novel of education and initiation' is designed to let the hero 'eat up the background' and to fill the foreground with those privileged moments—in art, in love—to which the social truth of the interdependence of self and world is only marginally relevant. The genre is solipsistic and unrealistic. It is the only kind of fiction (except for romance) in which the world is presented as yielding before the hero's weaknesses and acts of self-indulgence, and in which the effects of his actions in the social world are invariably cancelled out, usually by his self-consciousness.

§ 72

So strong is the sway of the genre over the German literary tradition that more than a hundred years after *Wilhelm Meisters Lehrjahre* Georg Lukács begins his career as a critic with a study in which he presents the *Bildungsroman* as the 'ideal-type' of the Novel, and includes *L'Education sentimentale* among its representatives.[13] Every aspect of Flaubert's novel proves how untenable this view is. For everywhere we are shown a social world which, far from yielding to Frédéric Moreau's weaknesses, inflicts on him a series of defeats. There is no difference between 'initiation' and 'life', between the close season and the hunt. Events don't merely 'happen' to him, nor are they in any sense neutralized by his self-consciousness (let alone, as in Goethe, Keller, and Stifter, by a higher agency): they modify every aspect of his person, every area of his experience. And the various narrative threads which are united at the climax of this process—the outbreak of the revolution of '48, Frédéric's futile waiting for Mme Arnoux, the illness of her little boy, the consummation of Frédéric's affair with Rosanette—all these form a pattern of experience as unyielding as the ties that bind us to the world of shared experience; as solid, too, as the bars of our prison. Here if anywhere is the fullest and richest harmonization of realistic themes, and thus incidentally the very antithesis of the *Bildungsroman*.

Flaubert's ambivalent opinions about the world as a source of majesty and banality (§ 21) point to one of realism's pitfalls (§ 57). We recall that *The Idiot* was brought to a close on just this feeling of banality, this feeling that 'the world merely goes on' (§ 11). Flaubert in *L'Education sentimentale*, however, makes it his dominant theme. If realism is seen (§ 54) as an ever-renewed and singularly direct appeal to the various kinds of expectation with which we come to a work of literature and which develop—are enriched and refined—in the course of our contact with it, what could be more realistic than a novel in which this aspect of our experience is constantly being acknowledged, a novel written as a series of disillusionments and defeats and brief triumphs ('enjoy'd no sooner but despised straight'), of disappointed ambitions and unfulfilled expectations? But how, with such a theme, does Flaubert avoid writing a banal story? He doesn't take the obvious way out: there are few moments of dramatic tension and very little satire. Instead, there is an unabating interest in and concern for getting each situation into focus and getting it right, where the focus (the making) is dictated by the structure of the whole and the rightness (the matching) by our informed and intelligent anticipations. There is nothing in the least mechanical about the hero's disillusionments or about the fulfilment of our expectations (that would be banality indeed). There *is* a growth in wisdom and tolerance, in sympathy and love, yet this 'development' is cancelled as each of these qualities is challenged and worsted in each new situation: the pattern of experience *is shown and proves* to be unyielding. In this showing and proving lies the poignancy of Flaubert's masterpiece, and its realism.

§ 73

If it is to be available to literature, the social truth about life—no less fundamental for being obvious—needs to be nicely balanced between the two extremes of radical alienation (the domination of the unaccommodated self) and naturalism (the domination of milieu). The realist must somehow bridge the gulf between the exceptional-unique in its chimerical isolation, and the common-repeatable. He isn't concerned to show 'the average' or even 'the typical' (just as he isn't interested in 'the human condition as such'), even though a social historian may find that 'Julien Sorel is a typical product of the post-Napoleonic age'. The average is boring because it conceives men at a flat angle, in respect of what is least distinct and least remarkable about them, presenting their traits according to a premeditated scheme. The typical is boring not when it is first created (which is before it is typical) but when, and because, it is repeated; when and because it is *conceived* as the typical.

A full exploration of the individual and the particular—which is what the realist's undertaking to face all the relevant facts of his chosen situation amounts to—results in a general illumination. To account for this process there is no need to invoke 'the sensitivity of a spiritualistic medium'[14] or any other occult forces. All knowledge, including the social historian's, is grist to the realist's mill. What he seeks while at work is not a state of ignorance but a state of freedom from the distractions of irrelevant knowledge—from such absurd distractions as 'les salons des filles (c'est de ce temps-là que date leur importance) étaient . . .'. He doesn't know that he is speaking the prose of social history; afterwards he may well subtitle a novel, 'Moeurs de province' or entitle a chapter, 'Façon d'agir en 1830'. He furnishes concrete proof of the fact that every generalization must rely for its value and truth on the individual instance only. The figure of Anna Karenina does indeed illustrate 'the woman's predicament' or that of old Golovin 'the evils of the kulak mentality'. Just as our living discourse is punctuated by brief surveys of accumulated experience, so realistic fictions too abound in generalizations, from the homely wisdom of Tolstoy's formal opening,[15]

> All happy families are more or less like one another; every
> unhappy family is unhappy in its own particular way. The
> Oblonsky household was in a complete state of confusion. . . .

to observations with an explicit claim to socio-historical truth:

> A kind of gloom hangs over some families. One notices it in
> particular among the class of small landowners scattered all over
> Russia who, having no work, no connection with public life, and
> no political importance, were at one time sheltered by serfdom,
> but now. . . .

Some are illuminating and true, others merely sententious. But in any event, what is being illuminated is not a truism (§ 62)—about families or the economic status of a class or the spirit of an age—but the fictional life of a single man or woman or family within an age, under certain social and economic circumstances. The truth of such generalizations is suspended, we must match them not against our historical understanding but against our understanding of the fictional whole (the 'totality') in which they occur. And it is from the congruence of this fictional whole that our historical understanding may be enriched.

Each realistic hero is unique, but his uniqueness does not isolate him. Or rather: it may isolate *him*, but not for us who are always seeing his isolation in the perspective of the world he has left, so that we may say of him, with Jocasta, 'Many a man has dreamt as much', or with the soldier in his prayer for the dead, 'There was a bit of a mystery about him. But then, when you come to think of it, there is a bit of a mystery about all of us.'[16]

§ 74

To say that the realistic novelist doesn't conceive his characters with the social historian's eye for 'trends' is very far from saying that he isn't aware of them as part of a manifold social whole:

> Now there emerge before our eyes yet further branches, which seem to have dropped off without really having done so. But who would be able to reveal their secret connections with the intertwining and criss-crossing shoots of the giant liana? Who could track down whether Dámaso Trujillo, owner of the shoemaker's shop 'At the sign of the Lily-Bunch' in the Plaza Mayor belongs to the real line of the above-mentioned Trujillos? Who could ascertain whether the owner of the blanket-stall 'Good Taste' in the Calle de la Encomienda is an undoubted relation of the rich Villuendas? There is a man who claims that Pepe Moreno Vallejo, rope-chandler in the Concepción Jerónima, is a real cousin of Don Manuel Moreno-Isla, one of those Morenos who chain their dogs with sausages; and it is said that one Arnáiz, a badly-paid employee, is related to Barbarita [the rich hero's mother]. There is a Muñoz y Aparisi, dealer in offals in the immediate vicinity of the Flea Market, who is probably second cousin to the Marquis of Casa-Muñoz and his sister, the widow Aparisi. Finally we must mention that a certain Jesuit, Trujillo by name, claims a place in this tangled undergrowth of families, and that such a place also belongs to the right reverend Bishop of Plasencia, Father Luis Moreno-Islas y Bonilla. . . . The cleverest mind is unable to find its way in this extended labyrinth of Madrilene family connections. Single threads cross, are lost and appear again where one least expects them. After a thousand twists and turns upwards and downwards they meet and then again divide. . . .

And again, more explicitly:

> Let us now, dear reader, turn to other matters. The highly respected and wealthy Santa Cruz family had friends and acquaintances in all circles of society, high or low. It is curious to observe how our age [1870–6], unhappy in other respects, presents us with a happy mingling together of all classes, or

rather, the concord, reconciliation of them all. In this, our country has the advantage over others, where the great historic suit of Equality is still not settled in the courts. Here, the problem has been solved simply and peacefully, thanks to the democratic temper of the Spanish people and to the lack of vehement class-prejudice among the aristocracy. A great national vice, job-hunting, also has made its contribution to the attainment of this goal. The government office has been the trunk on to which the cuttings of history have been grafted, and from these grew friendships between the impoverished nobleman and the plebeian raised in his status by an academic title, and from being friends they soon became relations. This intermingling has been beneficial, and thanks to it the contagion of social conflict does not daunt us, since we already have an attenuated and inoffensive socialism in our blood-stream. Imperceptibly, with the help of bureaucracy, poverty and the academic education which every Spaniard receives, there has been a general interpenetration among all social classes, and a dispersal of the members of any one class among all others, with the result that a thick net has been woven binding and solidifying the national mass. With us privileges of birth mean nothing, patents of nobility aren't worth mentioning. We admit only essential differences between people: whether they are well or badly educated, whether they are intelligent or stupid—in short, the differences we admit have to do with people's spiritual variety, a thing as eternal as the spirit itself. Money, the other hallmark of class, has its foundations in economics. It obeys laws as unchanging as the laws of nature. To disregard it would be like trying to drink up the ocean.

These two views of Madrid society in the 1870s are taken from Pérez Galdós's masterpiece, *Fortunata and Jacinta* (1887).[17] They contain evidence of social trends as well as vestiges of the movement of individual lives. The vantage-point from which they are taken is not the social historian's but the realistic novelist's, for whom the lives of his characters—those 'humdrum and random persons'—are 'embedded in the concrete and constantly changing politico-socio-economic total reality of the age.'[18]

These passages (and several others like them) don't amount to a 'profound' or 'scientific' social analysis. To almost any present-day reader, 'the socio-psychological factors with which Galdós deals

[will] seem elementary',[19] and a Marxist critic will no doubt point out that in his remarks about social class and money Galdós shares the 'false consciousness' of the bourgeoisie he is depicting. His mixture of observations, generalizations, and irony is dominated by a metaphor (the 'giant liana', used throughout the novel) which works by way of an indirection, for it is precisely the distinctness and individuality of each branch and shoot and leaf that makes the novel's social dimension so memorable. None of these elements has anything to do with 'science', nor for that matter with 'imitation'; there is no 'liana' or 'tangled undergrowth', the 'criss-cross connections' aren't visible. Without specific knowledge we cannot tell how accurate these observations on 'the Spaniard's democratic disposition', on his passion for job-hunting, etc. really are. And yet, reading these and similar passages, we are sure to exclaim, 'Yes, this is what it must have been like!', and we shall take this ring of truth for a positive thing—a value, though not the only value, in our appreciation of the novel. Why?

Fortunata and Jacinta is a story of the eternal triangle, the patrician Jacinta, her husband Juanito Santa Cruz, and the plebeian Fortunata; of the women's passionate strife for the intelligent, frivolous, and worthless man; of Fortunata's disastrous marriage to Maxí (something of a Dostoevskian 'idiot' figure), her victory and defeat. But *as such*—and not merely by way of 'background'—as such it is also the story of stable wealth versus dismal poverty, high bourgeois society versus the slums, patrician restraint versus the manners of the gutter. (However, every realistic novel reminds us that there is no such thing on land or sea as poverty or wealth, but only poor people and rich.) It is a love story, where love bears all the marks of its time and place, and where even the most heedless erotic passion bears the stigmata of social conflict. To convey the ethos of the Santa Cruz family firm, Galdós involves us in a brief history of the Madrid shawl-trade and its dependence on Paris and London fashions; the ups and downs of equities and government bonds are linked with the violent political upheavals of the time on the one hand and Fortunata's attempts to lead an independent existence on the other; a lengthy discourse on the coffee-house as a national institution serves to show its function in the life of the job-hunting intelligentsia; the daily routine of a convent (part prison, part finishing school, part religious house) is described, and so are the economics of private charities, money-lending, Church appointments, slum-letting. . . . And all these institutional details, firmly linked to the story's characters, provide the ground on which they walk and the horizon of their thinking and loving and suffering —provide the concrete boundaries which their unique and living personalities accept or exploit or attempt to breach. Are all these not surface pictures? In a sense (not the good reader's sense) they are superficial. Perhaps we 'know better' than to accept 'intelligence, education, and money' as adequate indexes of class. *The fiction*—a structured whole—persuades us that they are adequate to Galdós's purpose, that these are indeed all the relevant facts of the situation he has chosen to depict. For as he shows these institutions at work, he is building up that part of the total structure in which the social aspects of his individual characters are accommodated. Again: are we not likely to criticize his reticence in erotic matters as hopelessly outdated? And again we come to see that in the economy of the whole this decorum, this relatively distant vantage-point, is all that is wanted if a balanced whole is to be achieved. Neither close analyses nor deep structures are to his purpose. The whole derives its substance from the parts, the (seemingly superficial) parts draw their sanction from the whole. As the parts are elaborated and rounded off, one by one, they come to establish a world of intertwining interests and cares—a social system, full of iniquities and deprivations and inequalities may be, but also *a system that works*: a system composed of sentences describing social facts, that works in the fiction as the system composed of social facts works in the historical reality. And the ring of truth for which we have praised the novel? Now we understand that it is this coherence which fulfils our relatively uninformed yet never wholly ignorant expectation of what that human possibility called 'Madrid in the 1870s' might be like. It is the implicit affirmation *that* the thing works, emerging from the explicit demonstration of *how* it works, which elicits our positive response and our delight.

§ 75

And the system works all the way to the end: 'We can't change the social order, darling', Juanito tells Fortunata just before he abandons her for the second time. 'It is stronger than we are. For a while we may dance on society's nose, but then comes the hour when we must bow to it. You should always remember that . . .' (II, iii, 1). The reminder is unnecessary—Fortunata knows that in her battle for this charming but perfidious man she has no reliable allies and no real chance of winning. (Juanito, incidentally, is the least successful of the novel's characters, simply because he is uninterestingly predictable; because he fulfils our expectations without enriching them; because, in short, we all too quickly recognize him as typical.) Yet Fortunata has her moment of triumph, and it is Galdós's triumph too, for it is the point where the obvious social truth—the involvement of the self, even as a self, in a coherent social whole—is most finely demonstrated.

Jacinta, Juanito's lawful wife, has almost every advantage over Fortunata. She is a beautiful society lady of great charm and intelligence, in its own way her love for Juanito is hardly less passionate than her rival's, she has qualities which in the end even Fortunata can't help acknowledging and admiring. But Jacinta is childless, and all the pleasures of her exalted station turn to ashes as she thinks of her barrenness; whereas Fortunata bears Juanito two sons, and even in her greatest misery exults in her motherhood and in the advantage this gives her over Jacinta. Of all human feelings, one would have thought, the loving pride of motherhood is the most 'natural', the least socially determined. Not here, not in this situation, says Galdós. Apart from her 'natural' pride and her passionate love, Fortunata has no ethos of her own with which to challenge the Santa Cruz ethos. Over and over again she resolves to leave the gutter and 'become a decent woman', yet the only notions of respectability she has are those of Jacinta's class. When, at the end of the novel, she gives birth to her and Juanito's second son, the vicious pleasure she once experienced in her 'natural' superiority gives way to a generous reconciliation with her rival. On her deathbed she dictates a letter to Jacinta who, Fortunata knows, is desperately eager to have the child, 'the real Pituso', almost on any terms. (The little boy Jacinta had previously adopted had turned out to belong to other parents.)

> ' "I don't want to die without giving you a token of my love [Fortunata dictates to the old family factotum], and so I send you by my friend Don Plácido the gift from Heaven which your husband accidentally bestowed on me. . . ." No, no. Cross out "accidentally". Write instead: "With which God blessed me while keeping it from you. . . ." Oh no, Don Plácido, don't put it like that, it's all wrong . . . because I had it, didn't I, and nothing

was taken away from her. . . . The thing is that I want to give it to
her because I know she'll love it and because she is my friend. . ..
Write: "So that you should find consolation for the bitterness your
dear husband causes you I send you herewith the real 'Pituso'.
This one isn't false but legitimate and *natural*, as you may learn
from his face. I implore you. . . ." '
' "I implore you . . ." '
'You must put it very clearly, Don Plácido. I am giving you the
idea. Now write: "I implore you to look on him as your son and to
recognize him as your own and your husband's natural child. . . ." '

[IV. vi. 13]

This is Fortunata's 'idea', to which she has been clinging throughout the last months of her life, to which she now clings in the hour
of her death: that she has been able to give the Santa Cruz couple
what Jacinta cannot give them—a child, yes, but one who also will
be *'the real and only Son of the House'*. Her last clear thoughts are on
worldly matters: reconciliation with the social order, mother-love,
and pride in having enriched that order by the gift of a 'real Son of
the House' are all united in her 'idea'. Her reconciliation with the
Church is imperfect, enveloped by an air of tragic irony. After such
a life, it could hardly be otherwise. 'I think her suffering is over',
says the priest. 'She wasn't able to make her confession. . . . Her mind
was no longer clear. . . . Poor woman! She said she was an angel. . . .
God will know whether it's true. . . .'

§ 76

The given situation retraced in the chosen form—that is the prescription. Yet just as the given situation is not arbitrary but informed by
what we have called 'the social truth', so the chosen form is not
arbitrary but restricted by the available literary possibilities—that
is, the literary 'tradition' at that point in time, as modified and
enriched by 'the individual talent'. My point so far has been that, in
a novel like *Fortunata and Jacinta*, the chosen form puts the social
milieu on the plane of the main action and not merely behind it.
There *is* a background here, which is taken up by politics. (*Le Rouge
et le Noir* shows a similar structure; in *La Chartreuse de Parme* it is
the other way round; in *L'Education sentimentale* the relationship is
a good deal more complex.) In order to establish as much of this

background as he needs, Galdós resorts to the device of occasional parallels between the main action and the political history of Spain in the 1870s. And again, it is the coherence of the fiction that persuades us that this and no more than this is what he needs.

The political pattern is simple and obvious: Fortunata and her family are plebeian and thus her fortunes are associated with the populist republican cause; the Santa Cruz household and its many offshoots are upholders of the conservative status quo; Fortunata's husband Maxí's two brothers are trimmers who make their way on the principle that for a guzzling priest and a venal official there is a place with perks under any régime: a background of *plus ça change* to the political turmoil of the time. There is a fairly obvious political meaning in the contrast between Fortunata's fecundity and Jacinta's barrenness. And again, the parallels are spelled out in ironical chapter headings, such as 'Victorious Restoration' (III. ii) or 'Defeated Revolution' (III. iii), which of course tell us more about Juanito's return to Jacinta than about Alfonso XII's accession of 1874. Most of these political parallels are associated with Juanito and his infidelities, but they don't add much depth to the novel's least successful character portrayal. At their most explicit the parallels appear in conversational or authorial asides, as when Don Baldero, Juanito's father and head of the Santa Cruz clan, remarks,

> 'I don't know what will happen in the next twenty or, say, fifty years. In Spanish society you can't foretell so far ahead. The only thing we know for certain is that our country is convulsed by fevers which toss it to and fro between revolutions and peaceful conditions. At certain times we all want the firm hand of authority. "Let's have some discipline!" But we soon get tired of it and feel like kicking over the traces. And then come the times when we indulge in quarrels and strife. Finally we start yearning for a strong régime again. That's the way we are and I imagine always will be, till the day the frogs call on the barber.' [III. ii. 1]

which is echoed in the narrator's comment,

> The very thing Don Baldero had said about the country now took place in Juanito: as in a fever he was tossed between his desire for freedom and his need of rest. After two months of the most brazen marital infidelities his wife began to attract him as though she belonged not to him but to another.... [III. ii. 2]

Reconciliations are followed by more broken promises . . . and another authorial indirection, like the 'giant liana' of society, concludes the argument:

> Thus it was that the re-establishment of marital life took place. There are events in the lives of families, as in the history of nations, of which wise men have foreknowledge and which experts predict without being able to say what causes them, and which materialize without anybody knowing how, for even though their approach was felt and divined, yet their driving force remains forever hidden. [III. v. 2]

§ 77

Other balances between self and society, between the social and the political are possible in realistic fiction; other coherences emerge and validate the distribution of action and background—yet always within the charmed circle of the worldly world and its institutions, for outside it realistic fiction cannot breathe. The explicit demonstration of *how* the system works yields the implicit affirmation *that* it works, but no more. Beyond that, for the realistic novelist too, is the mystical, 'the feeling of the world as a limited whole'.[20] Ontology is not his business, he doesn't ask, 'Why is there Being rather than Nothing?' And the mysteries that reality hides are for him what they are for us all: mysteries of *human* experience, whose asymptotic solutions we live and write.

7

The middle distance

§ 78

The system that works—this, and nothing but this is reality for the realist. Galdós knows that when he puts down some such words as 'Maxí—Fortunata's husband—was a qualified pharmacist', he is pulling off the first corner of a coloured transfer, placing before us a situation to which we provide certain more or less fixed antecedents and consequences. (A pharmacist is not an organ-grinder; the Bank is not at Hyde Park Corner; Nantucket is not in the Pacific; and no rose is a rose is a rose.) When he adds, 'Maxí was a peculiar chap, a dreamer, who couldn't be trusted with drugs', he is modifying our expectation and steering it toward his meaning, again in a consequential and firmly determined way. He will then proceed to explain what he means by calling Maxí peculiar and a dreamer, though to our post-Freudian way of thinking his account will not seem very searching. He will give us a few details of Maxí's various illnesses and speculate about their causes; he will tell us the sort of things Maxí does in his peculiar state and how what he does exasperates Fortunata and Doña Lupe, Maxí's aunt, rather than enlarge on a direct description of the mental state itself, though he will say a little about that too. He will mention only those hidden motives which sooner or later will come to the surface of the situation Maxí shares with his family and friends. In a few passages the private thoughts of characters (especially Maxí's and Fortunata's) will be directly reproduced; but they are couched in the same public language as the rest, they too could easily be part of a conversation. When Galdós died in 1920, the practice of extended interior monologue had already been made available in the writings of Arthur Schnitzler, Dorothy Richardson, Proust, Joyce, and Virginia Woolf.

However, these oubliettes of private experience which never see the common light of day belong to a different conception of individual character, and thus to a different age. Replacing the balance between inner and outer characteristic of nineteenth-century fiction, interior monologue comes into being when the social truth ceases to be relevant to the private and individual truth; when 'the system' ceases to be of interest to creative minds. Galdós belongs to an earlier generation. One of the ways of placing his work (one of the ways of forestalling false expectations) is to recognize that the reality of his fiction is not disturbed by any such doubts and requires no such devices.

The realistic novelist needn't confine himself to the 'phenomenal' treatment of thoughts and feelings, yet he may not consistently ignore it. The balance between inner and outer—or, to put it another way, the distance the narrator keeps from his characters—will vary according to the realist's particular purpose and conveyed meaning.

§ 79

Like Galdós, Fontane, Flaubert, and Tolstoy write novels on the subject of adultery, yet each writes from a slightly different perspective, each establishes a different kind of balance. In Fontane's *Effi Briest* (1895) the determination of the heroine's inner life by the social ethos is all but absolute. True, Effi puts up some spirited resistance against the dictates of 'the Code' of the Prussian civil-service aristocracy into which she marries. And yet, almost her entire life (including her relationship to her child) is dominated by the social imperative she so briefly and almost innocently violated, and to which she can conceive no alternative. The words Fontane uses to describe her—'charming, gay, sociable, a delightful companion'—belong to the vocabulary of social decorum and indicate the distance at which the narrator (like the husband, who uses much the same words about her) remains throughout the story. Fontane doesn't side with 'the Code' and doesn't hesitate to show it up as a somewhat inhuman institution. But he also presents it as largely (though not entirely) self-justifying and objectively valid—as the ethical structure of the system that works—and in order to do this he must content himself largely (though again not entirely) with 'appearances'. Paradoxically, there is a lyrical dimension to Fontane's narrative manner, but hardly any intimacy. We are told nothing more private about his main characters than what emerges from their conflicts with and final defeat by the public world.

In Tolstoy's *Anna Karenina* (1877) there is an uneasy balance for most of the way. Anna is able, at least for a time, to lead a full life with Vronsky outside the convention of St Petersburg society, and the convention itself is less strict than that imposed upon Effi. The balance is destroyed and the system breaks down at the point where Anna is forced to judge herself as society judges her. Forced—by what? The grounds of her self-condemnation are moral-spiritual rather than merely 'conventional' and therefore different from the grounds on which society condemns her, yet not wholly different. In her suicide she acknowledges a moral covenant which has, and is shown to have, an objectivity and an existence outside herself. And Tolstoy's only way of showing this objectivity is by adopting, in the bulk of his story, a perspective that will represent Anna in her deteriorating relationship to the society that surrounds her; for though it is foolish and fashionable and occasionally corrupt, this society is not wholly incapable of serving as an embodiment of that covenant. Significantly, Tolstoy comes closest to his heroine in her greatest anguish, which is also the moment when for her the system ceases to work.[1] He comes closest, that is, not in any sentimental sense, but in the sense of abandoning the middle distance that has served him most of the way and entering the stream of her anguished consciousness. (Here, as so often in Shakespeare, conscience and consciousness become one.)

Flaubert's purpose in *Madame Bovary* (1857) is to convey an imbalance between the inner and the outer—romantic passion and desires imprisoned in a humdrum provincial world. He does this in two ways. He creates a social world whose very ineptness and inability to assuage Emma Bovary's desires are a part of its firmness and solidity; her desires and fancies have to face, not Fontane's objective 'Code', not Tolstoy's moral covenant, but calumny and petty material necessity. At the same time Flaubert endows his heroine with desires and aspirations—embodied in her lovers—which are themselves the products of the inept and solid world that encompasses her. (The prison is impenetrable, not least because the prisoner can't conceive of a life outside it.) With such a purpose before him Flaubert must choose a manner that is predominantly psychological: his narrative distance is consistently closer than Fontane's or Tolstoy's—it is in fact as close as is compatible with the creation of a stable world outside; the reality of this world, with its firm social distinctions, economic considerations, and political overtones, is never in doubt. It is indicative of the perspective that dominates the novels we have been considering that none of them quite ends with the heroine's death. (Death *is* an event in the world.) The system is reasserted and the social perspective regained at the point where, for each of these heroines, the world has ceased to have a living meaning.

§ 80

When not deploring its lack of 'objectivity', critics of realism are apt to argue that a concern with subjective states of mind is not the realist's business, that it doesn't belong to the 'kind' of literature he is writing; only that which is available on the surface of shared talk and overt action (we are told), only the phenomenal view is to be regarded as his proper province. Yet the above sketches have shown that writers who on any criteria are called realists (if anybody is) do not, as a matter of fact, work under such restrictions. But even without such august examples it should be clear that any novelist whose stylistic resources are more varied than Ivy Compton Burnett's is bound to transcend this supposedly 'objective' restriction. Almost any quotational phrase—anything beyond the merest 'he said' or 'she replied'—will involve him in an assessment however perfunctory of what is going on in the minds of his characters. True, there are special perplexities to be faced as well as special delights and illuminations to be derived from a strictly delimited point-of-view technique: 'We are shut up wholly to cross-relations all within the action itself', Henry James writes in his preface to *The Awkward Age*, 'no part of which is related to anything but some other part—save of course by the relation of the total to life.' The famous restrictive device of the masterpieces of James's last phase claims its justification from the peculiarly subtle and fragile nature of those 'cross-relations' and from the novelist's very particular ambition to re-enact in the literary form the social relations of 'the action itself'. (The finely-spun style is intended to retrace the finely-spun social network.) However, the high intelligence and single-mindedness of some of James's literary criticism must not blind us to the fact that its prescriptions (rather like those of T. S. Eliot's criticism) are derived from and are meant to apply first and foremost to his own work, and that his attempt to impose them upon writers with a different idea of form lands him in some obvious misjudgements.

As to the question of James's realism (§§ 91, 110), at this stage it is enough to underline the final point of our quotation. James's delight in the artifice of self-containedness should not make us forget that its fullest sanction—for him as for us—derives not from some esoteric hang-up but from 'the relation of the total to life'.

§ 81

Our discussion so far seems to be afflicted by a certain blatant vagueness: what *exactly* is that 'middle distance' from which the realistic writer is said to present his material? Instead of attempting to refute the charge directly it may be convenient to let the philosophers and *philosophes* take over and do our work for us. What they have to say on the subject of 'perspective' and 'distance' and 'accuracy' is relevant not only to the problem of realism but also to the method of considering it adopted in these pages.

The matter is important enough to have engaged the attention of Aristotle, grandfather of philosophers and literary critics alike. Defending the *kind* of enquiry he is conducting in the *Nicomachean Ethics* (and anticipating James's aside that 'everything . . . becomes interesting from the moment it has to consider, for full effect positively to bestride, the law of its kind'[2]), Aristotle writes:[3]

> In studying this subject we must be content if we attain as high a degree of certainty as the matter of it admits. The same accuracy or finish is not to be looked for in all discussions any more than in all productions of the studio and the workshop. . . . Such being the nature of our subject and such our way of arguing in our discussions of it, we must be satisfied with a rough outline of the truth, and for the same reason we must be content with broad conclusions. Indeed we must preserve this attitude when it comes to a more detailed statement of the views that are held. It is the mark of an educated mind to expect that amount of exactness in each kind which the nature of the subject admits.

In my discussion of politics and of the just man (Aristotle is saying), as in the works of artists and poets and literary critics, you will not find *as much* accuracy as you will find in a mathematical proof, but then you shouldn't really expect it. For Aristotle as for the more open-minded of our scientists (the others don't care either way) there is really only one scale of accuracy, stretching from the 'soft options' all the way to the 'hard sciences'. He sounds a salutary warning about the relevance of a mathematical model to 'this kind of enquiry' (and that in itself is an advance on the Snows of today), but he offers no alternative model.

§ 82

In taking up this discussion on a more mundane level, the *philosophes* and *moralistes* proceed with what at first looks like calculated vagueness. Here is Pascal's observation on the reading of books: '*Two extremes, the mean. If you read too quickly or too slowly, you don't understand anything*'[4]; and La Rochefoucauld's observation on those who believe that the best way of pulling on a pair of gloves is to go through the seams: 'The worst fault of penetration [perspicacity?] is not to fail to reach the goal but to go beyond it.'[5] Yes, but *how* to determine that goal, how to find out 'that amount of exactness in each kind of enquiry'—academic or mundane—'which the nature of the subject admits'? La Rochefoucauld doesn't really tell us in so many words, but in his informal way he does take the argument one step further: 'Men and matters have their proper point of perspective. Some, *to be judged fairly*, must be seen close at hand, others need distance.'[6] ('Men and matters, and statues too', says another version of that maxim.) This '*proper* point of perspective', like Aristotle's '*that* amount of exactness', is what it is because it is conducive to a certain end in view (such as the fair judgement of men, or the description of man as a political animal, etc.); and this end is itself part of a given pursuit or art or *technè*. No doubt this is true, Pascal replies,[7] and in some pursuits, such as looking at pictures (and, more doubtfully, painting them), one '*sees*' the 'proper point of perspective' quickly enough. But what about less tangible pursuits? How does one 'see' there?

> If you contemplate your work immediately after finishing it, you are still prepossessed by it, if too long after, you cannot enter it. So with pictures seen from too far off or too near. There is but one single point which is the right place: the rest are too near, too far away, too high or too low. In the art of painting, perspective determines it. But in truth and morality, who shall?

In searching for what looks like a religious answer Pascal is moving to another kind of enquiry. In our context it isn't a question of *who* but what shall determine the position of that 'single point of perspective'. And the answer, which comes from Wittgenstein,[8] is the one implied in La Rochefoucauld's 'to be judged fairly': the answer is, *'the goal'* or 'special purpose' envisaged for the pursuit in hand:

> We don't know the boundaries [of a concept] because none have been drawn. We can ... draw a boundary—for a special purpose. Is it only in this way that we have made the concept usable? Not at all! Except for that special purpose. No more than he who defined '1 pace = 75 cm', made '1 pace' usable as a measure of length. And if you want to say, 'But still, before that it wasn't an exact measure of length', then I reply: very well, it was an inexact one. Though you still owe me a definition of exactness.

And it is also a question of the width and breadth of that 'single point':[9]

> 'But is a blurred concept a concept at all?'—Is an indistinct photograph a picture of a person at all? Is it indeed always an advantage to replace an indistinct picture by a sharp one? Isn't the indistinct one often just what we need?
> [XY] compares a concept to an area and says that an area with vague boundaries cannot be called an area at all. This presumably means that we cannot do anything with it.—But is it senseless to say, 'Stand approximately over here!'? Suppose that I were standing with someone in a city square and said that. While saying it I won't even draw any kind of boundary but perhaps point with my hand—as if I were indicating to him a particular *spot*. . . .

And further:[10]

> The sign-post is in order if, under normal circumstances, it fulfils its purpose.
> If I tell someone 'Stand approximately over here!'—may not this explanation work perfectly? And can't every other fail too?
> 'But still, isn't the explanation inexact?' Certainly. Why shouldn't we call it 'inexact'? Only, let us understand what 'inexact' means. For it doesn't now mean 'unusable'. And let's consider what, in contrast with this explanation, we call an 'exact'

one. Perhaps something like drawing a chalk line round an area? Here it strikes us at once that the line has breadth. So the edge of a coloured area would be more exact. But has *this* exactness still got a function here? Isn't it empty of meaning?

§ 83

If anything can excuse this huddle of overlapping quotations, it is the importance, for any such enquiry as the present, of the question to which they address themselves and which they solve. There is no valid description of 'the middle distance', or indeed of that mixture of meaning and fact and language we call realism (our philosophers and *moralistes* are saying), except one that is related to 'the purpose of the whole' for which the description is intended; and any description that takes its notion of accuracy from some other purpose is bound to be misleading:[11]

> Is it not curious that when reading [xyz's] excellent treatise on the organ called the Soul, the matter seems no more familiar than a treatise on the intentions of the Ring of Saturn. And yet, if in this connection we can talk of space, the former is what lies *closest* to us. But the closeness doesn't help us, for the thing that we *can* bring close to us is not the thing that we *wish* to come close to. If while observing the setting sun I take a step toward it, I come closer to it by however little. With the organ of the Soul it is altogether different. Why, it could well be that by coming too close, as with a microscope, I once again move away from the very thing which I could come close to [if I didn't go beyond a certain point]. For instance, I see in the distance a strange mass on top of a mountain, I come closer and find that it is a castle, closer still I discover windows, etc.; this would be enough. If, unfamiliar with the purpose of the whole, I were to continue investigating, I would soon find myself analysing the stones, which would only lead me further away.

Well, we shall retort, it is all very well for Lichtenberg, writing in the heyday of enlightened rationalism, to take 'the purpose of the whole' for granted, and perhaps even Wittgenstein (who confined his historicism to his prefaces) may argue from 'normal circumstances' without undue embarrassment, but can *we*? Our answer is likely to be uncertain—and so, applying it to our enquiry, is the status of literary realism at the present time (§ 95). And yet, as Lichtenberg remarks on another occasion, 'People don't think about the events of life as differently as they talk about them'. (He isn't talking of high metaphysical matters, and if he were he would still talk of them with the aid of humble analogies.) After all, 'the purpose of the whole', or again 'the proper point of perspective' that determines the middle distance of realism, is the most familiar thing in all literature: it is the fictional creation of *people*, of individual characters and lives informed by what in any one age is agreed to constitute a certain integrity and coherence. ('An age' is no more than a community of agreements in time.) Moreover, the integrity and coherence that realism requires is present in the raw material as well as in the finished product; that is, in the persons and the world to which the realist directs his interest as well as in 'the characters' and 'the world' which he 'recreates' in the pages of his fiction. If literary realism is inseparably related to realism outside literature, then its fictional creations must 'match and make'[12] a world in which the realistic attitude (in its 'real-life' meaning) makes sense. And this attitude in turn only makes sense and works (that is, makes a meaningful difference to things) in a world in which there are *people*, individuals of some degree of integrity and coherence of character. (Literature *can* have other ends in view than the creation of people and of the world they inhabit.) To reverse the emphasis of an earlier argument (§ 71): it is with individuals that the social truth of realism is concerned—not with trends or inchoate masses of humanity, and not with fragments of consciousness either.

§ 84

That middle distance which places individual people and their institutions in one working perspective ('gets them all into the picture' at any one time in history) gives the realist a sharper and finer view than the view of his uncreative contemporaries. Yet what he presents is recognizable to them, is an illumination (why read him if it isn't *that*?) of shapes whose lineaments are reminders, finer and more coherent than they could ever fashion, of that which they know and live. The meaning that emerges from his work may well exceed the situation and understanding of his first readers; there are, for us, intimations of the civil war of 1936 in *Fortunata and Jacinta*. But his only way of intimating such larger and new meanings is by building up his work from details that connect and make for a coherent perspective.

There are occasions, Lichtenberg told us, when a change in perspective results in a change in objective. This is one of the reasons why the realist's room for manoeuvre is limited. If he steps further back (as does Tolstoy in the epilogues to *War and Peace*, or John Dos Passos in *U.S.A.*), to a point where the details of the recreated reality become mere trends or 'waves of history', he will be doing the historian's or philosopher's work. The ground close by, with its microscopic perspective and huge blow-ups, is occupied by the naturalistic writer and the *chosist*, his literary heir. The shape of his fiction and its 'truth to life'—coherence and correspondence: its making and matching—are joined in a nice balance. If a writer is content to abandon an overall meaning in favour of *faits divers*, he will be a mere reporter on the margins of literature (a barrenness not disguised by present talk about our need for 'the bare truth of the documentary'). If, on the other hand, he allows the meaning to exceed the concrete details, underscoring their intimatory function at the expense of their referential function—the making at the expense of the matching—he will be moving toward symbolism (§ 100). If he is forced to create individuals who live in a pre-established harmony with their institutions and whose every significant aspiration is automatically satisfied by a benevolent and paternalistic collective, he will be condemned to the tedious unreality of socialist realism (§ 99). If he portrays institutions that offer no significant resistance to the individual's whim and caprice, he will be writing idylls or the kind of romance that informs the *Bildungsroman*, the novel of initiation. If, on the other hand, he creates institutions from which no meaning can be wrung or whose meanings don't add up to a system that works, he will be writing the kind of fiction whose early example is the demonized Court of Chancery of *Bleak House* and whose greatest practitioner is Franz Kafka.

It is hardly surprising that realism, the product of so many adjustments, should be called 'an unstable compound'.[13] The alternatives I have mentioned contain no elements wholly alien to it. Literature is after all one field, and just as realism is not confined to one literary genre so it may form compounds with other modes of writing within a single coherent work. Only among the realists of the nineteenth century and their heirs do we find a complete commitment to the mode, though even in their writings its instability is obvious. Nor am

I suggesting that unalloyed realism is *in itself* a criterion of literary value. George Gissing, a consequential realist if ever there was one, is not a better writer than Balzac with his notorious excursions into the fantastic and improbable, or *Dubliners* a better book than *Ulysses*. The balance between coherence and correspondence or between middle distance and close-up, or again between symbolism and realism, may be achieved in more ways than can be enumerated. Indeed, it is the hallmark of every great creation that it modifies our critical expectations and achieves a new kind of balance—a balance determined not by a ready-made prescription but by the creative intention, the available means, and the achieved end.

§ 85

'The thing we can bring close to us is not the thing we wish to come close to,' Lichtenberg said (§ 83), but another thing. This, in litera-ture, is the shift from realism to naturalism, which may be illustrated by two passages from German fiction around the turn of the century.

Theodor Fontane's last novel, *Der Stechlin*, was published in 1899, a year after its author's death at the age of 79; Thomas Mann's *Buddenbrooks: the Decline of a Family*, the masterpiece of a young man of 26, appeared two years later, in October 1901. Both are leisurely novels of good society, affectionate tributes to a style of life whose decline they describe, and cast in a form regarded as out-moded by the literary vanguard of their day.

The Stechlins are Prussian landed gentry short of cash, with a ramshackle castle in a village on a lake whose name they bear. At the centre of Fontane's tableau is old Major Dubslav von Stechlin, around him are grouped his servants and family, including his son and heir; glimpses of the rich and cosmopolitan society of Berlin form a counterpoint to the mildly eccentric 'originals' of provincial Stechlin. Throughout most of his career as a novelist Fontane had conformed to the formal precepts of European realism by placing action, plot, and characterization at the centre of his novels and stories; allowing mood and atmosphere to emerge from the action; and displaying no interest in ideas except as means of character depiction. His last work too displays those high skills of the con-versational and socially accommodated novel of which he was the first serious practitioner in German literature. Yet the plot of *Der Stechlin* is something of an excuse. The novel's dominant aspect is its mood, old Dubslav Stechlin's gentle decline toward death. There are a few intimations that this decline is part of a wider historical picture, but they amount to hardly more than casual hints, musings that remain unexplored. The old century is drawing to a close, but the realistic novelist is too deeply interested in the present and its roots in the past to be much of a prophet of the dark things to come.

The young Thomas Mann's scope is a good deal broader and more ambitious, and his narrative means are a good deal more sophisticated. The Buddenbrooks are North German (Lübeck) merchants and corn shippers, fully involved in the public life of their city as senators and honorary consuls. The socio-historical dimension of the plot that covers the years 1835 to 1877 is rendered more explicit than in Fontane. The decline in the fortunes of the family firm is traced out over three-and-a-half generations, and it is given its partial and proximate cause in the Buddenbrooks' inability to adjust to the changes from mercantilism to finance capitalism which are taking place around them. Hand in hand with their economic decline goes a gradual loss of physical stamina and moral fibre, ending with the death of the family firm's last head, Thomas Buddenbrook, in the prime of his life, and the subsequent liquidation of the firm; the decline is completed in the precocious and sad little life of Thomas's son Hanno, who dies of a typhoid infection, aged fifteen. The richness and complexity of the social and psychological substance from which the two-volume work is built, the assurance with which the various threads of the narrative are handled, the dovetailing contrasts of mood, and the interplay of action and ideas—all these have never been surpassed in German fiction.

The world the Buddenbrooks inhabit is substantial enough by any realistic standards. The novel opens with Frau Consul Buddenbrook as she sits 'with her mother-in-law on a straight white enamelled sofa with yellow cushions and a gilded lion's head' examining her grand-daughter in the Catechism. And: 'I believe . . .' Tony begins her recital, looking round the 'landscape room' on the first floor of the Buddenbrooks' rambling old house in the Mengstrasse, with its heavy painted tapestries which were hung so that they stood away from the walls, 'I believe that God created me, together with all living creatures . . . and clothes and shoes, and meat and drink, hearth and home, wife and child, fields and cattle. . . .' All of it, including old Johann Buddenbrook's burst of laughter while poking fun at the Catechism, could be Fontane's prose, we recognize it as 'the very age and body of the time his form and pressure'. And with Fontane this prose of the perfect accommodation takes us all the way, to the very extremity of the human condition as he sees it.

§ 86

Dubslav von Stechlin is dying. The doctors haven't been much use and the strictly illegal herbal cures the village crone has prescribed 'against the congestion' haven't done much good either. But as he sits in his armchair near the french windows that give on to the verandah and the garden beyond, Dubslav is not alone. His regimental batman and faithful servant, old Engelke, is with him, and so is a little girl, Agnes, grand-daughter of the village herbalist and daughter of, well . . . the novelist of decorum mentions Agnes's mother in Berlin, but doesn't ever quite tell us who her father is. Dubslav's is an old-fashioned death, the scene is wholly innocent of that catastrophic view which regards social experience as inauthentic and incapable of accommodating man *in extremis*. It is not only Engelke (*alte Silberputzerseele* Thomas Mann calls him in his tribute to Fontane) and the girl who are with Dubslav in his hour of need. What he feels is fear and apprehension indeed, but it is not that notorious *Angst* beyond all meaning and possible comfort; he is not 'held out', as in a vice, 'into the Abyss of Nothing', that fee-faw-fum of existentialism. Even when Engelke leaves him for a while he is still comforted by the homely wisdom of a traditional tag ('Life is short but the hour is long'), his mind still dwells among those certitudes which his illustrious fellow-countryman, old Immanuel Kant of Königsberg, had formulated ('An eternal law is fulfilling itself')— certitudes which, for the Stechlins at all events, are close enough to the comforts of religion itself. And the novelist too is with Dubslav to the end: gently intimating his own presence when the new day breaks ('It must have been about seven . . .'), commenting approvingly on the child who does as Engelke suggests (untranslatably: 'die Kleine trat *auch* leise durch die Balkontür . . .'), anticipating in his own voice ('the snowdrops were the best . . .') Engelke's last words about the flowers Agnes has brought in from the garden ('Those are the first', said Engelke, 'and will probably be the best'), yet avoiding all sentimentality by cropping his syntax to a bare brevity. A scene of death and anguish, to be sure, but fully encompassed by the incomparable charm of the realistic novelist: focused on that middle distance at which realism portrays and preserves persons and their world in their time-bound, relative integrity:

> Engelke went away and Dubslav was alone again. He felt that the end was near. 'The Self is nothing—one must hold on to that. An eternal law is fulfilling itself, that's all, and we mustn't be frightened of that fulfilment, even if its name is Death. To submit to the law in peace and resignation is what makes man moral and raises him up.'
>
> He thought about this for a while and was glad at having overcome all apprehension. But then the attacks of fear returned and he sighed: 'Life is short but the hour is long.'
>
> It was a bad night. Everyone stayed awake. Engelke rushed to and fro, and Agnes sat in her bed and looked wide-eyed through the half-open door into the sick man's room. It was only at daybreak that the whole house became more peaceful; the invalid was nodding drowsily and Agnes fell asleep too.
>
> It must have been about seven—the trees in the park beyond the front garden were already in bright sunshine—when Engelke came to the child and woke her. 'Get up, Agnes.'
>
> 'Is he dead?'
>
> 'No. He's sleeping a bit. And I don't believe it's so heavy on his chest any longer.'
>
> 'I'm so frightened.'
>
> 'You needn't be. And maybe he'll sleep until he's better. . . . And now, get up and put a scarf round your head. It's still a bit cold outside. And then go into the garden and pick him a few crocuses if you can find any, or whatever there is.'
>
> The girl went quietly out through the balcony door on to the verandah and then towards the round flowerbed, to look for some flowers. She found quite a few; the snowdrops were the best. And then, with the flowers in her hand, she walked up and down for a while, and she saw the sun rising on the horizon. She felt chilly. At the same time she was aware of a feeling of life. Then she came back into the room and went towards the chair on which Dubslav was sitting. Engelke stood with folded hands near his master.
>
> The child came up and laid the flowers on the old man's lap.
>
> 'Those are the first', said Engelke, 'and will probably be the best.'

[chap. xxxiii]

§ 87

Not two or three years but an era and a desolation lie between the
death of Dubslav von Stechlin and the stroke Thomas Buddenbrook
suffers on his way home from his catastrophic visit to the dentist :

> And he went slowly through the streets, mechanically answering
> the greetings that were addressed to him, with a meditative and
> uncertain look in his eyes as though he were pondering how he
> really felt.
> He reached the Fischergrube and began to walk down the
> left-hand pavement. He had gone twenty paces when he was
> overcome by a feeling of nausea. I shall have to go into that bar
> over there and drink a glass of brandy, he thought, and stepped
> into the roadway. When he had about reached the middle of it,
> this is what happened to him. It was exactly as though his brain
> were seized and swung round with irresistible force at an
> increasing, terribly increasing speed in large, then smaller and
> smaller concentric circles, to be finally smashed with tremendous,
> brutal, merciless force against the centre of the circles, that was as
> hard as stone. . . . He made a halfturn and struck the wet cobbles
> face down with outstretched arms.
> As the street was on a steep slope, his body lay much lower than
> his feet. He had fallen on his face, and a pool of blood immediately
> began to form under it. His hat rolled a short distance down the
> roadway. His fur coat was bespattered with mud and slush. His
> hands, in their white kid gloves, lay stretched out in a puddle.
> So he lay, and remained lying there, until some people came up
> and turned him over.
>
> [x. vii]

In its anonymity, desolation, and solitude this is a death in the
naturalistic manner. Its description is as impersonal as the author
can make it. He enters the dying man's mind as though it were the
inside of a clockwork that has broken down. No firm belief sustains
Thomas Buddenbrook in the hour of his need, no distinct self even:
what is being described is not an individual consciousness, not this
one man's fears and anguish, but a pattern of abstract shapes and
mechanical reactions. The narrator's prose registers a case history:
his place of observation and his choice of vocabulary are determined

by a 'scientific' detachment and curiosity. There is a studied break in
the narrative at the words '. . . this is what happened to him. It was
exactly as though . . .'. In much the same way, five chapters later, a
long and fairly detached account of the illness of Thomas Buddenbrook's son Hanno opens and is again resumed with the sentence:
'Now, a typhoid infection proceeds in the following way. . . .' In both
instances (in Hanno's last illness, in Thomas's seizure) the formal,
pedantic break serves to indicate the switch from the close view of
the diagnostician to the distant view of the impersonal reporter. Only
once, almost inadvertently, in the brief repetition of 'So he lay, and
remained lying there . . .' is there a spark of narrative empathy, a
hint of regret. For the rest, the emotion underlying the narrator's
'scientific' attitude is one of distaste. In earlier chapters the Senator's
morbid care for his appearance was established as the desperate
manoeuvre of his decaying will to keep the decline at bay. Now the
physical details of the scene—the hat and fur coat, the sullied white
gloves—are all assembled to mock at that effort and to point to the
utter indignity of Thomas Buddenbrook's death.

§ 88

The stylistic resources of these two passages and the ends they
pursue could hardly be more different. The death of Dubslav von
Stechlin is what it is: the end, as meaningful as such things are, of an
old man's life; symbolical of the end of an age, but only to the extent
that 'the end of an age' is many such deaths. Fontane's perspective is
the middle distance of realism in his time. He could come closer to
his object without losing sight of it, yet not by very much. In his
rendering of Dubslav's thoughts, private and public self are inseparably joined and the social truth is made manifest; beyond this point
he leaves the old man to his God and turns to the new generation.
What Thomas Mann is presenting under the foreshortened naturalistic perspective of the 'scientific' observer is the total dissolution of
both the private self and of the self as the social world (and realism)
knows it. Here too, in the faceless anonymity of the dying Senator, is
a symbol—a symbol of the impersonal force of decadence, reaching
far beyond Thomas and the Buddenbrooks. And the new generation?
'I thought', says the boy Hanno, when scolded for having drawn a
double line under his own name in the family Bible, 'I thought . . .
there would now be . . . nothing.'

8

Description and evaluation

§ 89

Realism combines with other modes to form integrated wholes—this much is obvious; and such combinations are not entirely haphazard. As soon as we look at writings which are partly but not 'completely realistic', we become aware of a curious shot-silk effect: the element of realism assumes a variable function. This complex effect may best be seen in works which are glaringly unrealistic yet at the same time actively challenge a set of realistic expectations.

A picture by Hieronymus Bosch or Salvador Dali, a story by Edgar Allan Poe or Franz Kafka leave us with a strange impression we call 'grotesque'.[1] We are aware of an effect of purposeful incongruity. In Bosch it is the relatively simple case of the hideous and obscene or freakish elements combining with the idyllic, in Dali 'scientifically' exact odds and ends are meticulously assembled into 'surrealist' structures. Poe and Kafka anchor a complexly motivated narrative in several areas of experience, only to undermine it by imposing an arbitrary or untoward motivation in one limited area. In all such works realistic details are used for the purpose of building up a 'fantasy' or a 'nightmare world', the process of *matching* elements of the work of art with ordinary visual or emotional or social experience is subordinated to the *making* of something far removed from such experience. Swift's or Rabelais's satire or Picasso's *Guernica* proceed in the opposite direction. Here it is the details that are fantastic and unrealistic, yet the purpose to which they are subordinated is something as realistic as a critique of our political beliefs or a challenge to our defective moral experience. *Alice in Wonderland* uses a similar structure to different effect: fantastic situations are capped with common-sense, soberly realistic reactions and responses, and it is this incongruity which we find diverting.

Of course, whichever way the elements of fantasy and realism combine, it is our ordinary expectations which are initially invoked and continuously provoked—how else could Bosch or Swift or Kafka achieve their effects save by appealing to and purposefully manipulating our customary feelings for the hideous or the fantastic or the unjust? But the illumination and delight such artists vouchsafe come at the end of a process more complex and more indirect than is the process put in train by the realists, where our expectations are modified and enriched *directly*, by means of fictions that are *continuous* with our ordinary experience.

§ 90

In all such cases, then, we are conscious of a disjunction, or at least a distinction, between means and ends: between *the way* a person or a thing or a situation is presented or described, and *the use* to which such a description is put, that is, the assessment or evaluation or judgment it is subjected to or is made to provide. With this distinction in mind, the purposeful incongruities of a Poe or Kafka appear as structures in which patently non-realistic or fantastic elements combine with one of two kinds of realism: the one that has to do with the detailed *description* of fictional elements, the other that has to do with an *evaluation* of these elements.[2]

The distinction comprehends a work of literature in its entirety, its structure and its texture. However, when considering the realism of description we had best look for it in the texture of a literary work, whereas the realism of assessment emerges most clearly from its structural elements, by which I mean such things as plot, or complex of ideas, or the distribution of foreground and background. (All assessments or judgments are inseparably connected with a sequence of events in time. The various ways of representing time in literature may thus turn out to be best approached *via* the various kinds of assessment—realistic or other—at work in a given fictional whole. But these are problems which are not made explicit in the present study.[3])

The distinction is not concerned with two different vocabularies or static tropes, but with functional and dynamic aspects of a fiction. Nor do the two kinds of realism appear in isolation. They are apt to be organized in leapfrog fashion (§ 96), so that the assessment that flows from a description acts in turn as the description from which a new assessment is built up, and so forth.

The point of the distinction is certainly not to suggest that either kind of realism is more important than the other. Yet when considering realism as a perennial mode of writing we shall see (§§ 112–14) that the structures which display moral and legal assessments translate more readily from one language to another and one era to another than do the textures of descriptive passages. And this is not because actual moral (or whatever) judgments are perennially valid, but because the business of judging (its 'logical form') is a perennial feature of Western literature. The life of the Olympian gods is strange to us; man's attempts to understand his life under the dispensation of some form of justice are not.

Looking back at some of our earlier illustrations, we can now see how the realistic descriptions of the things and people among whom Mr Pickwick moves, including the grim details of life in the Fleet, are put in the service of an overall assessment of the world as a thing harmless and unresistant to his gentle fairmindedness, his generosity and good humour: a realism of description is put in the service of an idyll. Dostoevsky, we recall, acknowledges Mr Pickwick as the Prince's ancestor. Yet whatever may be the affinities of the two heroes, The Idiot derives its characteristic strength from a double realism: the one in terms of which the world of St Petersburg is described, and the other in terms of which the Prince's actions and failures to act in this world are evaluated. It is the latter realism which is here the more effective, for the temptation to abandon it is greater. Are we not, like the Prince's friends, like some of his enemies, expecting a miracle? There is no miracle, the Prince is no saint, it is his humanity that is tested and found wanting. . . . This realistic evaluation gives Dostoevsky's novel an undertone of irony which is lacking in Mr Golding's. The chief virtue of his novel, we have seen, is that its logic is unshakeable. If we ask ourselves why, once we have understood its logic, Lord of the Flies ceases to surprise us and tends to diminish in importance, it is because its dark assessment of the human lot (its realism) remains almost unchallenged, because the terrible temptation to goodness is not intimated strongly enough. The narrative problems which nowadays face realism of both kinds are quite different from the problems it presented to its early practitioners.[4] So commonplace has the realism of assessment become in our literature that it will yield its finest effects only where it is shown to be threatened by its opposite, the irrational, or untoward, or unmotivated. To write realistically today is to write in such a way as to acknowledge something of what is to be said against writing realistically in the old way.

§ 91

Realism is hostile towards ideology and conceptual language generally (§§ 36, 73), yet there appear to be no restrictions on the kind of vocabulary it may press into its service: aren't these two claims incompatible? The paradox is resolved as soon as we recall (§§ 62, 73) literature's freedom to evaluate and treat conceptual terms as integral parts of a fiction, to treat them as though they were 'objects' or data of the same order as other 'objects' or data: as contents of a fictional consciousness, or as the play of authorial irony. Henry James's portrait of Merton Densher (the man who will betray Milly Theale, heroine of *The Wings of the Dove*) bristles with the 'abstract' vocabulary of generalization:[5]

> He was ... not unamenable, on certain sides, to classification—as for instance ... one of the generally sound and generally civil; yet to that degree neither extraordinary nor abnormal. ... You would have got fairly near him by making out in his eyes the potential recognition of ideas. ... He represented what her life had never given her and certainly, without some such aid as his, never would give her; all the high and dim things she lumped together as of the mind ... he had rendered her in especial the sovereign service of making that element real.

The irony of this kind of 'abstract' diction is that it both hides and points to a wholly realistic assessment of the character of one man and one man only. I will dip this character into all the social and intellectual generalizations you care to think of (the author is saying), and in this way will show the various personae behind which he hides: and as you peel off the layers of generalization, one by one, this single man in his world will emerge. A generalization is indeed being made—Merton Densher will in the end stay in the reader's mind as the *measure* of a certain *type* of ambitious young man. But the general truth emerges as the third stage in the process, not the first (§ 73). It is when this kind of conceptual diction moves in the opposite direction, when it *uses* the particular in the service of a general, non-realistic assessment not encompassed in the fiction,[6] that the fabric of realistic fiction is breached.

§ 92

La haine, le dégoût d'exister, ce sont
autant de manières de me faire exister, de
m'enfoncer dans l'existence. (J.-P. Sartre)

The assessment of characters and situations in Henry James's last novels, like the interplay of ideas and character in the work of Gide or Thomas Mann, belong among the ruses of realism—they are acknowledgments and conquests of what is to be said against writing 'in the old way'. A novel like Sartre's *La Nausée*, on the other hand, proceeds by way of a separation. Here realism is confined quite strictly to one area, which in the novel and in Sartre's philosophy is called 'existence', and it is sharply divided from another, non-realistic area, which is called 'Being'. In abandoning an overall realism, has Sartre abandoned the unity of fictional form altogether?

Obviously *La Nausée* isn't a novel of which it could be said that it is epistemologically naïve or philosophically incurious (§ 37). The question of what is reality, what is 'really real', is central to Sartre's literary and philosophical undertaking. (The two are closely connected, but they are not one.) Sartre presents a solitary man for whom 'the system' has all but broken down, who finds the social world in which he has 'gratuitously' placed himself bereft of a positive meaning and value, and who does nothing for that world in order to create a meaning and a value in it. The 'research' Roquentin has come to pursue in Bouville (=Le Havre) is as trivial and meaningless, and as arbitrary, as his weekly *petit cinq-à-six*, as the daily tasks of the respectable citizens of that provincial backwater among whom he moves. The world of *Madame Bovary*? Yes, but sixty squalid years on. The realistic evaluation is an unambiguous condemnation of that world, but it doesn't take us all the way. 'Existence', the actuality of things and people in this world, clings like an unclean 'film', like a blur, to all that surrounds Roquentin: if nevertheless, there is to be 'any value that does have value, then it must lie outside all that happens and all that is as it is.'⁷ This 'existence' without value is contrasted with pure 'Being', a metaphysical haven behind and beyond sordid 'existence'.

Why is he there rather than somewhere else? Why is he collecting data for an historical monograph rather than doing something else? Why (shades of Heidegger) is there this—e.g. Roquentin's—existence rather than non-existence, nothing? Trying to find reasons, trying to find (in a very literal sense) a *raison d'être*, Roquentin must penetrate beyond and behind the film that clings to the world that surrounds and engulfs him. Does he find the answer, the real reality of Being? He *is said* to find it: in the song of the Negro singer on the record that he listens to over and over again in the café—over and over again that record of poor old 'Some of These Days' becomes the unique, timeless thing. He *will* find it, he hopes, in the story he resolves to write as he is leaving Bouville—'a story . . . of something that could never happen, an adventure. It would have to be beautiful, and hard as steel, and make people ashamed of their existence. . . .'⁸ But *La Nausée* is not that story.

He is said to find the answer . . .: the search on which Roquentin sets out will take him into a region uncharted by realism: a world of Being unrelated to and rendered meaningless by all that Bouville very firmly is and stands for. Does the song intimate that world of Being? Is *it* that 'value that does have a value'? The song cannot carry the weight of that assessment, the weight of the meaning put on it, and Sartre knows it. And so, in order nevertheless to say something about that search for the real reality behind Bouville and Roquentin, he resorts to a vocabulary that is explicitly and unashamedly conceptual, and disconnected from the diction which describes the sordid and violent and arbitrary bits and pieces of experience called Bouville.

La Nausée is thus composed in two styles: the one dictated by Bouville, the other by Roquentin's search for a way out of Bouville and a goal beyond; the one is dictated by realistic fiction, the other by philosophy. They are not and cannot be one, but they belong together. There is no play of irony that would unite them, the philosophy points at Being, not at *this* man but away from him, into a region not encompassed by the fiction.

The strength of the writing as a novel (as distinct from its interest as philosophy) lies in a combination of realistic description with ontological assessment, a combination however determined by the realistic element. It is this element which traces out the hither border of the *terra incognita* of pure Being. A description of *that* would require 'une autre espèce de livre. Je ne sais pas très bien laquelle— mais il faudrait qu'on devine, derrière les mots imprimés, derrière les pages, quelque chose qui n'existerait pas. . . .'

As for the meaning—our meaning—of the novel, that too is not the 'Meaning' which Roquentin hopes to reach, but the meaning Sartre achieves in the realistic anchoring of Roquentin's search. Here 'everything is as it is and happens as it happens. (In [this world] there is no value, and if there were, it would be of no value.)'[9] Ballast, rubble, detritus weigh down this world. Outside it the novel cannot breathe. 'Existence' will have to be changed, we are told, transformed into a weightless, eternal moment of art, a harbinger of pure Being. ('Du sollst dein Leben ändern' is the cry of Rilke's sonnet.) But before that happens we have only Roquentin's experiences to go by, among which is his longing to be delivered of his experiences.

§ 93

True, the logic is unshakeable, but it won't stand up to a man who wants to live.

And:

'But I am not guilty', said K., 'it is a mistake. How can a man be guilty, anyway. We are all simply men here, one as much as another.' 'That's true', said the priest, 'but that's the way all guilty men speak.'

And again:

'It may be that you don't know what sort of a court of law you are serving.' He got no answer. 'But these are only my experiences!' said K.

Sentences such as these point to that endless cat-and-mouse game with realism which is conducted in Kafka's writings. And it is here that the break between realistic description and transcendental evaluation becomes programmatic and the fragments are joined into consistent narrative patterns. Psychology (the never-ending more-or-less, to-and-fro, on-the-one-hand-and-on-the-other of the weak) and institutions (the law court, the castle, the penal colony, the academy, all strongholds of power) are the chief sources of Kafka's realistic descriptions. But of course these cool and realistic explorations of mind and world, of the subtle lacework of psychology and bureaucracy, are all subsumed under assessments of a wholly different kind. The more meticulous and convincing the build-up of Kafka's stories, the more destructive and inhuman their implications. Critics who have claimed that 'Kafka's work gives very little recognition, if any at all, to the world in its ordinary actuality' or who speak of 'the self-contained Kafka world', fail to account for the better part of what is distinctive and unique in his writings. Were his stories really so hermetically sealed off from our world, they would be a great deal more sensational and a great deal less interesting (and, given his Prague literary background, a good deal less original). *The Trial* is a meticulous and as it were horizontal elaboration of its first sentence, 'Someone must have laid false information against Josef K., for without having done anything wrong, he was arrested one morning'. *The Castle* is a protracted elaboration of the situation of a man who arrives in an alien community and seeks recognition from the powers that govern that community. *The Metamorphosis* is an ostentatiously factual account of the very ordinary reactions of a very ordinary family to the extraordinary degradation of one of its members. The wholly negative transcendental judgments that are imposed upon the 'heroes' in these situations seem indeed to be disconnected from 'the world in its ordinary actuality'. But it is precisely because this destructive evaluation is superimposed on or (more often) insinuated into such utterly banal realistic situations, their humdrum nature reflected in their drab, lack-lustre diction, that Kafka's novels and stories and fragments achieve their *changeant* effects of the familiar and the strange; and it is from these effects that he builds up his picture of a timeless world bereft of positive meaning and grace, the dark side of the moon. So perfectly in control is he of this purposeful combination of descriptive realism and transcendental judgment that he can create his effects from a minimum of narrative paraphernalia and rely on the barest few strokes of the pen:

It was early in the morning, the streets were clear and empty. I was walking to the railway station. When I compared the time on the clock-tower with the time on my watch I saw that it was much later than I thought, and that I had to hurry; the shock of this discovery made me uncertain of the way, I was not very well

acquainted with the town as yet. Fortunately there was a
policeman not far off. I ran to him and breathlessly asked the way.
He smiled and said, 'You want *me* to tell you the way?' 'Yes', I
said, 'as I can't find it for myself.' 'Give it up, give it up', he said
and turned away with a wide sweeping movement, as people do
who want to be alone with their laughter.

Unreflectingly following the convention of our time, we shall place
this story within three frameworks, each narrower than the last,
labelled 'literature', 'a very short story', and 'Kafka'. Its shortness,
together with the realization that it isn't a joke (which is what very
short stories usually are) will make us read it with special attention.
And since we may be assumed to have some notion of 'Kafka' or 'the
Kafkaesque' even though we mayn't actually have read anything
by Kafka (it is hardly a very daring hypothesis), we shall read with
some degree of wariness, suspecting a trap of some kind. Now, as the
story proceeds, our mind will be divided between two sets of expectations. The one is very ordinary indeed, and will be more and more
fully and flatly satisfied as the description proceeds. Empty street;
planned journey; discrepancy between clock time (=public? =true?)
and watch time (=private? =false?); the strange town; shock or
fright (*Schrecken*); the policeman; the exchange of questions: all
these ordinary words designate ordinary bits and pieces of experience
whose place in our scheme of things is quite familiar to us. They are
part of a system that works smoothly and unproblematically: 'X
goes to catch a train, he doesn't know the way, his watch has gone
wrong, etc.': flatly, the failure vindicates the system. At this point
the whole thing looks almost like a shaggy-dog story. What then of
the third—the 'Kafkaesque'—expectation? It will have been raised
at every sentence, at every bit of information conveyed, but in vain,
for the story gives every impression of leaving it disappointed. But
since the story is very short, this second expectation hasn't time to
dissipate; on the contrary, the tension continues to mount as nothing
out of the ordinary happens. But now, at the point where the policeman first reinforces the questioner's question and then gives the
answer, the realistic description is broken off, the ordinary expectation is falsified, and the momentous verdict is pronounced.
Momentous? What is there momentous about 'Give it up!'? What is
'*it*'? The journey? Life in the strange town? Existence out of step, in
isolation, appealing to power but bereft of it? Is '*it*' 'existence itself'?

We don't know. We slither through the three frameworks, unable to make complete sense of the transcendental assessment, equally unable to reject or to accept it. The bits and pieces of ordinary experience have disappeared.

For Kafka, certainly, realism is not enough, the 'ordinary' system no longer works—but then (he makes us ask) does it work for us, at any tolerable level of awareness? The stories are neither ambiguous nor devoid of meaning. They create a mood of uncertainty and weakness (in the hero; but also in the reader), on which they then impose or insinuate an absolute verdict. The verdict is unacceptable, its connection with the initial situation unconvincing—to the hero, to us who live the ordinary lives of our age. But (Kafka asks) aren't such 'ordinary' lives the most extraordinary examples of weakness and uncertainty and sin? And if so, is the connection really unconvincing? What do *you* (Kafka insinuates the question) regard as convincing, and why? What does Josef K.—what do *you*—oppose to the priest's suggestion (in *The Trial*) that 'the court proceedings gradually merge into the verdict'? This is the cat-and-mouse game of Kafka's stories, in which the transcendental verdict devours all realistic description and the world.

§ 94

If there is such a close kinship between realism in literature and realism in life as I have claimed in various parts of this study (e.g. § 29), then clearly the present distinction inside literary realism should also throw light on statements like 'She is clever enough to be relied on to make a realistic decision' or 'He just hasn't the realism it takes to be a successful politician'. And it is obvious that all such non-literary, commonplace uses of our terms imply or invite a sifting of the relevant from the irrelevant, the arraying of the relevant facts for the purpose of an assessment, of a decision leading to an action, etc. In life outside literature, too, we distinguish between our *understanding* of a situation, which is dependent on our description of it, and the *judgment* we base on that understanding. Yet we notice a difference. In literature, the realism of description seems to occur as frequently as the realism of assessment; at least, there may be historical reasons for the preponderance of one kind of realism over the other (e.g., were novelists like Defoe able to describe realistically before they knew how to motivate realistically?); and I shall suggest

(§ 113) that what is spontaneously and immediately available to us from the literary monuments of the past are not so much descriptive passages as rather those scenes and situations that are informed by assessments which we—spontaneously and immediately—identify as realistic. Nevertheless, there are in literature no logical reasons for a preponderance of one kind of realism over the other. The 'real life' uses of our terms, on the other hand, are heavily slanted towards the realism of assessment. We recall that the synonyms of the common, non-literary use of 'realistic' that sprang to mind (§ 29) were 'accurate'; 'facing the facts'; 'cutting one's losses'; 'an eye for the main chance'; 'clever'; 'not very generous'; 'sharp'; 'cynical'; 'ruthless'. . . . They all point in the direction of judgments, and not very cheerful ones at that. (The synonyms that sprang to mind in literary contexts were 'accurate'; 'life-like'; 'rich'; 'colourful'; photographic'). In literary talk, we conclude, 'realism' may refer either to assessment or description or both, whereas in real-life talk 'realism' seems to be largely confined to assessment. Why this lack of symmetry?

The commonplace, real-life uses of 'realism' and 'realistic' have no possible meaning outside that fragile sphere we call civilized life, outside the framework of more or less compatible and attainable ends which we have called 'the system that works'. The terms have no meaning at the catastrophic margins of existence or in the realm of Grace, where 'the system' breaks down and 'a man's time is no more'. (And here, we have seen, literary realism too breaks down.)

To speak of realism in 'real life', therefore, is to speak of it always within this infinitely vulnerable sphere of attainable ends. Here the realism of assessment predominates because the sphere of attainable ends is time-bound through and through: because here all hurries on, ineluctably, in one direction. Everything that lives and has its being in this sphere presses for decision, refuses to tarry over description, seeing description and understanding as means to an end—means to decision and action and the attainment of new ends. 'Realistic' here is the watchword that distinguishes the possible from the impossible, the tried from the untried, the effective from the ineffective, the true from the false, the purposeful from the capricious and illusory. 'Realistic' is the word that expresses the likelihood of a successful translation of talk and thought into another mode of experience, into the mode of action (which of course does not have to be bereft of talk to be another mode of experience). And it is this translatability, this duality of modes within 'life' that distinguishes it from 'literature'. (Literature is only possible in that part of the fragile sphere where words are not simply equated with deeds and action is not imagination—a point too obvious to need making but for the perverse claims of the votaries of *littérature engagée* and the evil practices of totalitarian politicians that go hand in hand with those claims. The classic statement is Andrey Sinyavsky's: 'The most elementary thing about literature—and this is where the study of literature begins—is that words are not things, and that words and literary similes are conventions.'[10])

Literature, on the other hand, is all one field. It is all in one medium and knows no translation into another. It may tarry over description to its heart's content, it may play with description and with assessment too. At the level of verbal texture it builds up holes in leap-frog fashion or (to recall the peculiar plasticity of the language of Kafka's *The Trial*), here 'the proceedings merge gradually into the verdict'. But whereas in 'life' the verdict is final, in literature it may be the beginning of a new round of events.

Yet there is a bridge. If the realism of assessment predominates in 'life', the realism of description is by no means excluded from it. And if that relative predominance enabled us to show up one of the differences between 'life' and literature, the presence of the descriptive meaning of realism in 'life' brings the two together again where they may properly be joined. For of course we can say 'He gave me a very realistic picture or description of that meeting' without suggesting that the speaker had done something other than *describe* the occasion, and no decision or action of any kind need be implied. The point to insist on here is not that in a rudimentary way such usage is connected with a literary meaning, though undoubtedly that is true. The point is that such 'literary' usages and effects are part and parcel of everyday talk and everyday experience. They unite the sphere of life and literature. They show that even within the ineluctable flow of time, pressing for evaluation and judgment, there are occasions for description whose end is illumination and delight, bridges to the pleasures of literature.

The distinction between description and evaluation seemed to account quite satisfactorily for various combinations of realism with its various opposites. (Satisfactorily, that is, at that middle distance at which most of this enquiry is conducted.) The examples chosen are not meant to suggest that such combinations are peculiar to modern literature. The distinction is bound to be present whenever transcendental or supernatural phenomena are to be integrated into a humanly convincing story. Yes, but what is and what is not regarded as 'supernatural', or again as 'humanly convincing', at any one time? Is it not this, above all, that a history of realism ought to tell us?

9

Distensions, alternatives, concentrations

§ 95

Realism in life and literature alike (I have argued) depends upon a balance between mind and world, inner and outer, at a certain point in time. It is this balance of inward making and outward matching which creates the fiction of a shared reality. In literary realism such a balance is achieved by the co-operation, on more or less equal terms, of four factors: world, self, meaning, and language.

How relevant is such a balance to the function of literature at the present time? The alienation of men from their social, natural, and technological environment has now become so radical that those writing at the highest level of creative consciousness (those who in a more confident age contributed to 'the best that is known and thought in the world') write on the assumption that a realistic account of this state is impossible. Western society works (they agree), it has certainly never worked better. But its working reveals it as a self-contained system, without meaning and value: 'More than ever before / things fall away: the things we can live. For / those that oust and replace them are imageless acts.'[1] Finding nothing significant to *retrace*, literature is now faced with the novel task of having to *create* meanings, as it were *ex nihilo*. It turns away from realism to writings determined by other kinds of balance. The documentary, the literatures of solipsism, of symbolism, and of language-consciousness are alternatives in which the elements of world, self, meaning, and language respectively assume dominant, value-creating roles. And this development is reflected in contemporary criticism and theory, which imply or assert that one or another of these modes embodies a deeper and greater truth about contemporary life than does realistic literature; or again (§ 40), that realism 'is really' some-

142

thing quite different from what it is commonly said to be, or has ever been before, etc. However, it is possible to take the contemporary alternatives to realism[2] seriously without disparaging its capacity to describe the world that is not 'beyond the reach of common indication'.

Jakob Boehme had a vision of eternal reality in a brightly gleaming tin bucket, Goethe saw man's destiny in the flickering light of a candle, T. S. Eliot in a rose-garden, Samuel Beckett in the eternal recurrence of deadly patter to the point of garbage. The question that concerns us here is not whether such symbolical modes of apprehension and creation vouchsafe a greater or deeper truth, but in what ways they are different from the realistic mode. They are different by virtue of assigning a central, dominant function to certain compositional elements which are present in realism at a lower level of intensity, as non-dominant elements in a complex structure.

About documentary literature no more need here be said than that, being assembled from the world's *faits divers* on the peculiar principle of 'less art=more truth', it expresses not so much the life of the contemporary world as the death-wish of contemporary literature; not so much an alternative to as a distension of realism. It is where one of the other three elements—self, meaning, language —assumes a dominant role that genuine alternatives to realism arise.

§ 96

'Do you mean, Dr Howe, that there aren't two opinions possible?'
    It was superbly done in its air of putting all of Howe's
intellectual life into the balance. Howe remained patient. 'Yes,
many opinions are possible, but not this one. Whatever one
believes of *The Ancient Mariner*, no one can in reason believe that
it represents a—a "honey-sweet world in which we can relax" '.
    'But that is what I *feel*, sir.'

(Lionel Trilling)[3]

The solipsist's claim that one man's reality is another man's fantasy, or that I am the creator and sole occupant of my reality, or that life is a dream I dream and share with no one, is easily made but a good deal harder to sustain. And if, as in Schopenhauer, reality is said to be a total dream, a set of brackets in which all life is included and nothing is left outside,[4] then everything realism is concerned with (and everything that has here been said on its behalf) remains unaltered anyway.

The claim is readily made in respect of each individual adventure Don Quixote undertakes. In each instance the author seems to be encouraging us to say that the way his hero set out to deal with this or that 'adversary', or the way he set out to interpret this or that fact or situation, was to Don Quixote an integral part of his reality and his world, than which he knew no other—and why shouldn't it be Sancho Panza who is deluded? Why should it not be true to say that 'the barber's basin is a barber's basin to Sancho, to Quixote it is Mambrino's helmet and to another man it may well be something else'?[5] The author's stratagem is to encourage the solipsistic claim, and in following it up to falsify it. For the barber's basin as Cervantes presents it isn't an isolated bit of reality for very long, and as soon as it makes its appearance as the property of people who live, and are shown to live, outside Don Quixote's noble vision, it becomes again the barber's basin it has always been. The claim on behalf of solipsism *is* made—it couldn't otherwise be falsified; the life of Don Quixote *is* a challenge (among the most poignant in all literature) to our customary notions of reality, but the challenge is rebutted at every point. Don Quixote leads his sorties against a multiplicity of facts, of which the fact that the barber's basin is a barber's basin is one. As the objective totality of the world is established, so its subjective totality (the false, unstable totality of solipsism) breaks up into a series of misunderstandings, misinterpretations, and mistakes, for these alone are the forms under which solipsism becomes available to the realistic mode: the delusion which realism portrays is never total. The fact that Don Quixote comes to grief in each of his adventures is thus not an authorial caprice. The disasters follow from Cervantes' initial decision for realism—once he has decided to cap each realistic description by a solipsistic (=fantastic) assessment, and to cap *that* once more by a realistic assessment, and to stop at that point. Each catastrophe is the necessary practical proof— and realism requires and is susceptible to no other—that the 'reality' Don Quixote has constructed in his mind from the debris of old books doesn't work. Or rather, that it works only so long as it doesn't come into sustained contact with the 'constructs' of other minds, 'constructs' which have the advantage of being shared by many people, a whole age (at which point it ceases to be relevant to call them 'constructs').

§ 97

What has here been said about Don Quixote applies, *mutatis mutandis*, to a whole host of fictions in the nineteenth century, when solipsism ceases to be an oddity, and becomes a common temptation and a lure. (This is why Kafka, turning the story round, presents Sancho Panza as 'a free man' and 'Don Quixote' as the name he, Sancho, gives to his devil.)[6] From Pushkin's *Eugene Onegin* (1833) and Lermontov's *Hero of Our Own Time* (1840) onwards this lure becomes one of the major themes of Russian literary (and political) realism. *Oblomovshchina* is the name given to it by I. A. Goncharov, to exorcise its spell men like Lenin, Trotsky, Gorky, and Stalin assumed their hortatory pseudonyms. When Zahar, Oblomov's servant, tries to shame his master into some kind of purposeful activity and some kind of decision, he does it by pointing out that '*other people* are no worse than us, and if *other people* can move house, surely we can . . .', or again, 'There's nothing extraordinary about a wedding. You are not the only one, *everybody* gets married!' The immense, endless, heedless outbursts occasioned by Zahar's mild reproaches are the highlights of Goncharov's masterpiece,[7] for it is here that all the defences of solipsism are brought into play against the importuning claims of a shared reality. Poor Zahar has no arguments with which to refute his master's outbursts. It is 'life itself'— the pathetic consequences of Oblomov's lethargy and sloth, his inability to emerge from the despondency of selfhood—that provide the refutation.

Reality may well be nothing nobler, or more stable, or less contingent, than 'the *fable convenue* of the philistines'; indeed, not much fastidiousness is needed to look askance at those who would greatly extol its virtues. But, whatever else may be said for or against them, the realists don't worship at its shrine, or at any other. They merely take reality for granted. The relentless praise of *Dasein* and of the Earth[8] is not for them, for they suspect (meanly and realistically) that, the more intense the song of praise, the more Being and Earth recede behind the song, and the more the song becomes an end in itself and an apologia for the praising self. The realists are certainly committed to 'the very world, which is the world/ of all of us', even though they are by no means sure that it is also 'the place in which, in the end,/ We find our happiness, or not at all'.[9] It isn't the realists who would gild the gates of their and our own prison.

§ 98

'Now you know that there are other people besides yourself.'

(Kafka)[10]

Literary critics are forever being inveigled into philosophical fashions. A few years ago they were full of the dark talk of Death, which they seemed to think was a discovery of the Existentialists. Nowadays they are apt to regard the fact that men live in groups, depend on them for their survival, and feel estranged in solitude as a discovery of the young Marx. This is not so. No ideology, only the realization that 'no man is an island, entire of itself' is needed to refute the claims of solipsism, and it is one of the tasks of realism to show up the peculiar and incongruous consequences of such claims. Perhaps solitude really is the 'existential' or 'authentic' condition of man. Perhaps it *is* the never-never land in which men are said to live by no other values save those they themselves have created.* A realistic portrayal of solitude may well show it as the touchstone of courage, or stoic endurance, or some other virtue—but first and foremost it must show it as the collapse of the social bonds. To the extent that the solitary is conscious of his condition—and it is by virtue of this consciousness that he becomes 'authentic' and the hero of existentialist literature—he acknowledges himself as one who lives in the exception, outside common humanity. He may regard his condition as more genuine, more valuable, or 'more real' than the condition of the common herd. But once he attempts to communicate this evaluation to other men, he is bound to do so in the social terms they understand—by means of 'their' language which is his too, and by deeds that have an impact on their lives, and hence on his too. He must share their reality, if only in order to persuade them to quit it.

The peculiar failure of Nietzsche's *Thus Spake Zarathustra* is a case in point. While the book's best thoughts may be found again in

---

* The one man who, though ignorant of the finer points of this doctrine, came closest to practising it, was Hitler.

his later writings, its parables and dialogues represent Nietzsche's attempt to dramatize his habitual soliloquy. So much for its intention: the expectation raised is of a genuine dialogue. In the event the book turns out to be an uncontrolled flow of revolutionary moral insights decked out with lurid images and embarrassing dithyrambics. Zarathustra speaks of disciples and has none, speaks of companions and has none—and this for no better reason than that Nietzsche's mimetic gift is poor and limited. It is limited to the portrayal of that one prophet, that stentorian Self, surrounded by nothing but puppets and emblematic beasts. Since Zarathustra's 'victories' over common humanity are predetermined by Nietzsche's uncompromising individualism (as Don Quixote's defeats were by Cervantes' ironic realism), it follows that such humanity as there is in the book is mere decoy, and Zarathustra's 'victories' are without substance. Intended as a work of art which should challenge our customary too-tidy distinctions between art and philosophy, the book is an artistic disaster. Intended as a refutation of the New Testament, full of hollow echoes of Luther's Bible, *Zarathustra* yields none of the drama and poignancy of the Gospels, because its invocations of common humanity are no more than invocations. The story of Christ, which the story of Zarathustra parodies and seeks to supersede, is not a story of 'existential solitude' at all but of companionship. The companionship is imperfect—'And he cometh and findeth them sleeping, and saith unto Peter, Simon, sleepest thou? couldest thou not watch one hour?'—but the moral insights—hardly less revolutionary than Nietzsche's—are continuous with the portrayal of that imperfection in its full humanity: 'Watch ye and pray, lest ye enter into temptation. The spirit truly is ready, but the flesh is weak. And again he went away, and prayed, and spake the same words. And when he returned, he found them asleep again (for their eyes were heavy), neither wist they what to answer him. And he cometh the third time, and saith unto them, Sleep on now, and take your rest: it is enough, the hour has come.'[11] Realism, we recall, is a condition not a content. The Bible read as literature? It isn't for that phrase, 'for their eyes were heavy' that we read the Gospels. Yet it is through it that their absolute assessment gains a foothold in our minds. Without it the Gospels would be what *Zarathustra* is—a hollow invocation.

§ 99

'Listen, darling', she said after a while, 'Shall we agree not to be jealous of each other at Party meetings?'[12]

'Listen, Comrade Lopatkin', Tepikin said suddenly, 'Today you are the victor. And we are all amazed at the way you went through hell and high water. But your nature, comrade, is selfish. You are a lone wolf. Before I met you I should have said that in our country it was impossible to fight alone. I still say it's difficult. The collective helps you, defends you, takes care of you and gives material support to you at the right time. But you kept out of the collective. Yet we were always ready to extend to you. . . .'[13]

Among the solipsistic distensions to which realism is subject at the present time is the theory and practice of 'socialist realism'. By this I mean the doctrine which prescribes that every plush-covered sofa complete with *pralinés*-nibbling mistress is a relic of bourgeois days; that every family quarrel is due to a politicized generation conflict, in which Dad is always sound at heart but ideologically out of date; every gathering is an officials' or workers' meeting, convened (often 'spontaneously') to improve production; every forest, river, and lake is a recreation ground, and every cloud as a silver lining; every private betrayal is the prelude to a political defection; every unhappiness is a-social and contagious, likely to lower the working morale; every sanctioned loyalty is ultimately to the 'Collective' ('I could not love thee, dear, so much, loved I not the Workers' Executive Council more'); and every human conflict is sooner or later solved by a return to whatever happens to be the established orthodox interpretation of the Party line at the time. It is a literature of muddled tenses, in which every utopian 'shall be' becomes an 'is', and every drab 'is' becomes a vanquished and dead 'was'. Its pictures of 'reality' follow directly from the ukase that 'the record achievements of our literature should, in the handling of dialectics, be measured by the record achievements of the revolutionary practice of the [German branch of the] Communist Party and of the Comintern'. (A few months after this was written, the Berlin branch of the German Communist Party achieved its 'revolutionary practice' by joining the National Socialists in a strike.)[14]

It is a part of this doctrine—a part of its confusion of words and deeds—that every *literary* challenge to such clichés as I have mentioned is bound to be evaluated as a *political* challenge to 'the Collective' and thus to the Party. And yet the fact that this 'Boy Meets Tractor' literature has been imposed on whole societies and that it 'works', albeit at this level of creative interest, is not wholly due to the political coercion behind it. Undoubtedly it is an attempt to gain and make meaningful for literature the area of workaday life which realism in the West has neglected.[15] But this gain has been paid for by an enforced restriction of themes and evaluations, so that, like the system it defectively portrays, this literature is least effective where it is meant to be strongest: in the realistic portrayal of that change which the system can neither accommodate nor wholly suppress. 'Socialist realism' is not merely a condition (§ 31) but a form and a content as well. And as such it is the reduction of a reduction. While the Marxist two-class theory is itself a simplification of an older, pyramidal view of society[16] (a simplification, incidentally, which has surprisingly few echoes in literature), 'socialist realism' 'simplifies' the social truth (§§ 70–1) even further by, in effect, reducing the two classes to one. All that happens outside the interests of that single class is identified as 'deviations' from the established norm; no radical challenge to the system that works is ever seriously considered—there simply are no narrative means to record it. Its collective solipsism and its inability to portray change are one: both derive from a predetermined devaluation of what is to be said on the other side, and any challenge actually recorded must be falsified before it has got under way. In all this, of course, literary theory and practice faithfully reflect political doctrine and practice. The three novels[17] to which I have referred in the previous paragraph belong to the period of 'the Thaw': the Russian and Czech stories contain elements of political protest, the East German is a love-story that attempts to salvage an area of private emotion. But the literary style in which these protests are registered—cliché descriptions, predictable evaluations—has little to do with life, it is the defective life-style of the ideology. (If realism is a prison, then this is the prison within the prison.)

But how do we know that these pictures of life are false? Partly in the same way as we know that Solger's list of 'all that is significant in our age' (§ 69) is incomplete and thus false, because it contradicts our ordinary expectation of completeness without showing that expectation to be irrelevant. But we also know because we have a witness to the truth which this literature falsifies. The work of Alexander Solzhenitsyn, with its roots in Tolstoy and Thomas Mann,[18] and its scheme of crypto-Christian values, owes nothing to the doctrine. On the contrary, it is the greatest single creative indictment of the ideology and its literary doctrine alike, as it is among the few white hopes of realism at the present time. It shows up 'socialist realism' as incapable of portraying a system that works (as to that, Solzhenitsyn leaves the reader in no doubt). More important, it proves that realism is adequate to the portrayal even of that system, even at this time. Can realistic writing of distinction be achieved at a lesser cost in personal suffering, under less exacting conditions? One man's work cannot assure the survival of a literary tradition. But it can refute the claim that the tradition is dead.

§ 100

If once the eye of art and poetry was fixed upon the externally real, seeking there the friends and playmates, the enemies and tragic occasions of the inward soul, then now, on the contrary, it must be the artist's goal to build for the outward things, seen and used and abused by all, a sanctuary in the heart within.

(Erich Heller)[19]

Goethe's *Werther*, Benjamin Constant's *Adolphe*, Rilke's *Notebooks of Malte Laurids Brigge*, Hofmannsthal's *Andreas*, Proust's *A la Recherche du temps perdu*: each of these seems like the refracted image cast by some masterpiece of realism in the literature of inwardness. These are works in which the fiction of an objective narrator is dispensed with—not occasionally or at the behest of an omniscience required by a narrator in straits, but consistently and to the point of dominance of the sentient self. Of course, the bits and pieces of experience that go into a realistic fiction, too, are chosen and assembled by a sentient self, and occasionally both the self and the act of choosing are visible in the work; but in realism the emphasis is on the things chosen, not on the chooser or the choice. In the literature of inwardness, on the other hand, the resistance of the world of shared reality is replaced by the resistance encountered by a self whose dominant characteristics are feeling, introspection, and recollection. The width and breadth and riches of realism are replaced by depth, by an exploration of a world whose landscapes and persons and configurations remind us of the everyday world we know, but only vaguely, or with the especial clarity of a dream. For they—the landscapes, persons, configurations in that world—are but the names of states of mind and soul. The ruler of this world is Orpheus, whose song[20] had such power

> ... that from a single lyre
> more mourning rose than from all keening women;
> that a whole world of mourning rose, wherein
> all things were once more: forest and vale,
> and road and hamlet, field and river and beast;
> and that round this world of mourning turned,
> even as round the other earth, a sun
> and a whole silent heaven full of stars,
> a mourning-heaven full of dis-figured stars ...

The world of shared reality is here too. (And in each of the works I have named, and in the many that might be added to that brief list, the dominance of inwardness over the outer world is achieved by different means, to a different degree and with a different intensity.) But whereas in realistic literature the worldly world was dominant to the point of determining all that went on in the fiction, in such a way that each private aspiration conceived in that world had to break on it, like waves on a rock, and that each recollection had to serve as a help or hindrance to the commerce of the world, here the world is but the point of departure for the voyage into recollection and inwardness.

§ 101

How carefully we read the map of that inward world, how anxiously we compare it with our real map: 'Sainte-Agathe' is really Epineuil-le-Fleury (we say), 'les Sablonnières' is really the Château de Loroy and it isn't in ruins at all, nor is it on the road from Epineuil to Vierzon, and how could Augustin Meaulnes hope to find it in that direction. . . . How anxiously: because we want to know where the story starts from on its journey into the lost region of childhood and youth, because we want to be sure of the point of departure before we abandon ourselves to the voyage. It is this need for assurance which the critic supplies as he earnestly enumerates all the data of geography and biography and history he can lay his hands on, interrupting his scholarly labours only to tell us that 'the facts don't *really* matter'; it is that very need for assurance which the story is designed at once to evoke and render irrelevant.

For this, this re-ordering and re-creating of the past in all its exuberant hopes and shy, half-conscious longings, its palpable fears and sustaining illusions and disappointing fulfilments, which goes by the name of *Le Grand Meaulnes*—

> Je n'ai pas gardé d'autre souvenir que celui, à demi effacé déja, d'un beau visage amaigri, de deux yeux dont les paupières s'abaissent lentement tandis qu'il me regardent, comme pour déjà ne plus voir qu'un monde intérieur. [III. x]

> Ce ne sont plus des coquilles abandonnées par les eaux que je cherche. . . . Je cherche quelque chose de plus mystérieux encore. C'est le passage dont il est question dans les livres, l'ancien chemin obstrué, celui dont le prince harassé de fatigue n'a pu trouver l'entrée. Cela se découvre à l'heure la plus perdue de la matinée, quand on a depuis longtemps oublié qu'il va être onze heures, midi. . . . Et soudain, en écartant, dans le feuillage profond, les branches, avec ce geste hésitant des mains à hauteur du visage inégalement écartées, on l'aperçoit comme une longue avenue sombre dont la sortie est un rond de lumière tout petit.
> [II. ix]

> Ils parlèrent. Mais invariablement, avec un entêtement dont il ne se rendait certainement pas compte, Meaulnes en revenait à toutes les merveilles de jadis. Et chaque fois la jeune fille au supplice devait lui répéter que tout était disparu : la vieille demeure si étrange et si compliquée, abattue; le grand étang, asséché, comblé; et dispersés, les enfants aux charmants costumes. . . . Il s'enquérait de tout cela, avec une passion insolite, comme s'il eût voulu se persuader que rien ne subsistait de sa belle aventure, que la jeune fille ne lui rapporterait pas une épave, capable de prouver qu'ils n'avaient pas rêvé tous les deux, comme le plongeur rapporte du fond de l'eau un caillou et des algues.
> [III. vi]

—this, and the strange landscape of which these scenes are a part, is what realism cannot give us. It gives us all of our common reality. It may even (think of Andrew Bolkonsky's agony on the battlefield[21]) give us the intimations and distant echoes of infinity that stir behind, beyond it—as intimations and echoes. What realism cannot do is to allow these glimpses and intimations to dominate a fictional structure. What it cannot do is to relate everything to them until they and not 'the reach of common indication' become the true theme of the fiction.

Le Grand Meaulnes has a story, the story of many betrayals. It is worked out in fine detail, no ends are left untied. Each detail of the hero's journey and of that night at the feast in the nameless castle will eventually be accounted for, will be corroborated and filled in, by Great-aunt Moinel, by Valentine Blondeau, by Augustin's diary, by Yvonne de Galais herself. How could it be otherwise? The days and months that pass are counted off as carefully as the litany of names of the villages. The *things*, too, are all there: school smocks, gaiters, straw hats, the fine embroidered waistcoat; the schoolroom and its stove with the washing on it; M. Seurel dictating problems; the cold and empty attics through which Meaulnes takes his nocturnal walks; frosty days of winter and the unexpected and not wholly pleasant warm sunshine of a November day; the bank of the Cher where the fateful picnic takes place, 'its ground sloping gently to the river divided up into little garden meadows, into willow plantations fenced off like so many tiny gardens . . .' (III. v): all these are what they are, and they are also the 'dis-figured stars'—shapes on the map of the country of the soul. It is the topography of the castle, the lost domain, that matters, not its reality. And in attempting to establish its map (retracing what is before his inner mind), is not the author in the same predicament as that well-meaning critic who plied us with all those bio- and topographical facts while telling us they didn't 'really' matter? (Except that the author was there first, and knows better how to move in that dreamlike domain.) How else can the author ever make sure of the substantial form he needs, the vessel in which to carry his libation to the past beyond recall which is here recalled, except by giving it 'a local habitation, and a name'?

'Whereof we cannot speak . . .'? But Alain-Fournier does speak—to a purpose no less purposeful and with a precision no less precise than those of realism, but different. The story that matters is the story of the sentient self. Whose self? Not that of Grand Meaulnes, nor that of François Seurel, the narrator, either, but of the spirit of lost and mysterious youth, choosing these two for its vessel and uniting them, their brief joy and long suffering, into a single complex experience.

§ 102

Somewhere in the vast, unfathomable depths of one of literature's strangest creations the persevering reader will come across this unexpected apologia:[22]

> So ignorant are most landsmen of some of the plainest and most palpable wonders of the world, that without some hints touching the plain facts, historical and otherwise, of the fishery, they might scout at Moby Dick as a monstrous fable, or still worse and more detestable, *a hideous and intolerable allegory*.

In order to allay our suspicion that he is allegorizing, need Herman Melville really ply us with this apparently endless array of facts and circumstances? Passage after expatiatory passage in this catalogue of the whaling trade is held together by nothing better than enumeration: 'Either because . . . or because . . . or . . . how it was exactly there is no telling now, but . . .', or: 'Consider . . . consider also . . . consider once more . . . consider all this; and then. . . .' But no sooner have we got the soporific idea (that warehouses and chandlers' shops full of things are needed to tie down the flights of his metaphysical fancy) than we are startled out of it:

> Consider all this; and then turn to this green, gentle, and most docile earth; consider them both, the sea and the land; and do you not find a strange analogy to something in yourself? For as this appalling ocean surrounds the verdant land, so in the soul of man there lies one insular Tahiti, full of peace and joy, but encompassed by all the horrors of the half-known life. God keep thee! Push not off from that isle, thou canst never return!
> friends. . . .'   [xxi]

And:

> 'Well, well, my dear comrade and twin-brother,' thought I, as I drew in and then slacked off the rope to every swell of the sea— 'what matters it, after all? Are you not the previous image of each and all of us men in this whaling world? That unsounded ocean you gasp in, is Life; those sharks, your foes; those spades, your friends. . . .'   [lxxi]

And again, on the third and last day of the chase:

'Oh! Ahab', cried Starbuck, 'not too late is it, even now, the third day, to desist. See! Moby Dick seeks thee not. It is thou, thou, that madly seekest him!' [cxxxiv]

Clearly there is no way of keeping 'the hideous, intolerable allegory' out. The story of the chase matters, of course, and keeps the reader going, but it is not enough—at least, not in view of the metaphysical purpose that informs Melville's undertaking. What unity there is in the book is carried by the symbolical meaning;[23] which is neither a thing of inwardness only (as in *Le Grand Meaulnes*), nor a meaning built up from the realistic details (§ 60). It is what the story and the facts point to and in themselves aren't—a surplus value at some remove from the realistic description. But what is Melville's grand purpose, that it requires him to push beyond the boundaries of realism?

§ 103

Faust II was published shortly after Goethe's death in 1832, *La Chartreuse de Parme* in 1839, Eugène Sue's *The Wandering Jew* in 1845, *Dombey and Son* in 1848, and *Moby Dick* in 1851. The figures of the old Faust, Vautrin, Count Mosca, Ahasuerus, Mr Dombey, and Captain Ahab (and, incidentally, the Balzacian figure of Karl Marx) are variations on the theme of the demonic human will. These men are 'the creators' of the worlds they command—at the moment when Mr Dombey's domineering will fails him, 'Mr Dombey's World' dissolves also; and on this metaphor of the creative will Schopenhauer's entire philosophy is based. But while Dickens, and to a large extent Balzac too, are content to portray these embattled personalities[24] in terms of the *données* of their world, for Melville the seven seas and all that lives in them are but examples, imperfect manifestations of his theme, and his theme is the demonic will engulfed in cosmic solitude: 'The intense concentration of self in the middle of such heartless immensity, by God! who can tell it?' (xcii). To this grand theme, all things particular and discrete and self-contained are by definition inadequate, and the reader is left in no doubt as to their inadequacy. However absorbed in the 'straight' narrative he becomes (and there is a mail-order-catalogue fascination even in the lists of the names of whales, and the book contains a loving description of clam chowder), the pursuit of the white whale is forever turning into the pursuit of the great cosmic meaning, and fiction into metaphor-encrusted philosophy.

§ 104

Symbolism—whether we think of it as the dominance of meaning or in some other way[25]—raises as many problems as does realism, and to consider them at all fully would require a whole set of alternatives to the arguments of this book. Its characteristic forms are not extravagant structures like *Moby Dick* at all but poetry; which is another way of saying that poetry is the most intensive use of language we know, yielding most meaning from fewest words. And it is this concentration of meaning and richness of reference, rather than the presence of poetic attributes like rhythm or rhyme, which makes large areas of poetry unavailable to realism. The judgment that Dante passes on Francesca and Paolo in love, or (on a more mundane level) Byron's on the infatuated Don Juan, to say nothing of Chaucer's on his clerk, lose nothing in realism for being couched in verse. Yet it is significant that we identify this realism in the structural, paraphraseable aspect of a poem.

Examples of realism in poetry, it is true, will be found most frequently in epic and narrative poetry, but they are not confined to those genres. Literature (I have claimed more than once) is all one field. The spectrum of literary kinds, stretching from symbolist and vatic poetry at one end to naturalist and documentary prose at the other, depends upon a variety of adjustments within a constant set of elements—world, self, meaning, language—none wholly isolated from the rest and each capable of exercising dominance over the others. Realism is, among other thing, a *meaningful* mode of writing (and not the mindless 'objective' dummy of anti-realistic polemics). It is constituted from the same elements as all poetry, including the symbolical. What is incompatible with realism is not poetry as such but the dominance of intimatory meaning and self-conscious language (§ 107) from which poetic symbols are created.

But doesn't our definition of the symbol as a high concentration of meaning imply that all literature aspires to its condition, so that all literature comes to figure as a sort of *symbolisme manqué?* Several *fin-de-siècle* purists have held such a view, yet it is no more convincing than its opposite, the view that realism is the sole carrier of truth in literature. The concentration of meaning we call a symbol involves a loss as well as a gain, obviously it is not attained at that middle distance from which realism portrays the world; indeed, symbolism isn't confined to any one stable perspective at all. It is a making rather than a matching; a 'dis-figuring' of the things the world contains rather than a retracing of them: 'Garlic and sapphires in the mud', or 'Le transparent glacier des vols qui n'ont pas fui', or 'Rose, o reiner Widerspruch, Lust . . .'

§ 105

The dominance of meaning constitutive of symbolism is not a Platonic notion impervious to the changes of history. On the contrary: if we accept that the meaning of words is made manifest in their ordinary use, then it must be use at a certain period in time; and if symbolism is abnormal or extravagant use (a rose as the pure contradiction of petals closing in like lids on no man's sleep; of petals closing in like poems on no man's experience . . .), then again it is 'extravagant' relative to a norm in time. While the realistic convention depends on a perspective (=a set of meanings) both stable at any one time and also changing from age to age, the configurations of symbolism arise from no single stable perspective, and it is this instability which modern literature exploits.

Just as the sea-changes of time turn yesterday's common and stable norms into the quaint eccentricities of today, so yesterday's realism provides the vocabulary for the symbolism of today. (Balzacian and Dickensian criticism is full of such mutations.) Yet while it is true that some of today's eccentricities will provide the norms of life tomorrow, there is no assurance that today's symbolism will provide the vocabulary for tomorrow's realism, for there is no assurance that there will be a realism tomorrow. Seeing that realism hasn't been the dominant mode of writing during most periods in the history of literature, this is hardly surprising. Yet a comparison of the contemporary literary scene with earlier ones is apt to be misleading. For whereas earlier periods of non-realistic literature were dominated by a variety of religious and therefore shared symbolisms, our symbolisms are largely of a private and 'creative', that is self-determining kind; and coming in the wake of a realistic tradition, they are not as dominant as the symbolisms of other ages. They arise in a world experienced by some of its best minds as a self-contained system without purpose and value. In this world all or almost all common occasions and meanings are experienced as equally unpoetic and prosy, and thus they all offer equal and endless possibilities for symbolism—possibilities, that is, for grafting intense, extravagant meanings at almost any point and from almost any perspective. What governs this symbolism in a world without purpose and value is 'the terrible compulsion to relate everything with everything else'[26]— Faust with Don Juan, Don Juan with Mephistopheles, Mephistopheles with Christ, Christ with Nietzsche, Nietzsche with Hitler—until no image and no experience remains meaningful in and by itself, each becoming an 'archetype' and symbol of something other than itself. Yesterday's symbolist devices for the poetic apprehension of *les moments fugitifs et ephemères*[27]—'more and bigger and better correspondences, all quivering with vitally appealing sense and senses'[28] —become the mainstay of literature in the wake of realism.

These are tentative remarks, for the present scene is certainly difficult to make out—it is a good deal easier to speak of a recession of realistic writing than it is of a dominance of symbolism. Yet they have implications for the history of realism which are no less important for seeming paradoxical. Most literary discussions, including the present, tacitly assume that there is such a thing as 'an age'—a system of agreed meanings in time; that it 'speaks' in a certain 'voice'; and that literature is the voice, or at least is among the voices, of that age. The truth of these assumptions will be confirmed by anyone who has accurately dated a passage and thus experienced the thrill of reconstituting the temper of an age from the way a few odd words were put together on a page. But there is another tacit assumption, which (we can now see) is clearly not tenable: that this voice of a given age is always its most realistic literature. Realism is a perennial mode of writing, but its dominance at any one time is a literary and cultural option. Just as there are cultures and political régimes whose representative ritual is disconnected from the shared realities of daily life, so there are ages whose representative voice is not the voice of realistic literature, and ours, it appears, is one of them. It is not an age without common norms of meaning (there is no such thing: 'an age' *is* a system of agreed meanings in time), nor is it an age without images, but the two don't meet at the level of its highest literary achievements. Realism—the meeting-ground of images and common meanings—has shifted from the peaks to the deadly plains of contemporary literature. Or has it changed, out of all recognition, breaking all continuity?

§ 106

Last among the contemporary alternatives to realism I shall mention is the literature of language-consciousness. As documentary literature was dominated by the world's *faits divers*, symbolical structures by meanings in excess of the common norm, and the literature of inwardness by the sentient self, so here fictions are dominated by language, or rather by an articulated consciousness of the creative process, its psychology, technicalities, and institutionalization. In its least sophisticated form this is the fiction of *Künstlerromane* and *Künstlerdramen* and of the 'artist and society' theme from Goethe's *Torquato Tasso* onwards, an extension of the literature of the sentient self (§ 100). Where the fictional self betrays itself as identical with the creator's self, its story readily becomes the self-conscious story of artistic creation, the novel in search of a novel, the characters in search of a play. James Joyce's artistic development, from *Stephen Hero* and the *Portrait* to the complex language games of *Finnegans Wake*, illustrates both the consummation of this kind of literature in its relatively naïve form and the progressive loss of realism entailed where it becomes dominant. In the *Portrait*, where it is embedded in and contained by a rich social configuration, articulated language-consciousness functions as the five-finger exercises of the budding artist and remains an integral part of the novel's realism. Only where this self-conscious 'wording' of the creative process becomes a major theme, drawing all others into itself, does an altogether different mode arise.

Like Wordsworth's Cambridge dons, a good deal of realistic fiction from Don Quixote onwards is 'of texture between life and books',[29] if only because it is built on the ruins of old books. Parody, quotational devices and puns (§ 64) are among the many language-conscious elements which are inseparable from realism as they are from the life of any natural language it employs. And there is, so far as I can see, no way of separating these self-conscious elements categorically, as a class, from language in its unselfconscious aspects. Yet this is no reason for inferring that all language 'is about' language, or that ours is peculiarly an age in which 'the practice of writing',[30] without which admittedly no fiction occurs, is most 'responsibly' pursued as the practice of writing about writing. (The sense in which *any* sentence is said to be about the making of sentences is made up of the ruins of that sentence.) Wittgenstein was by no means the first to recognize that 'language is a form of life'[31]—the view, once perhaps general,[32] was handed on to him by a long-established Viennese tradition. Yet if this recognition has meant a liberation from a narrowly instrumental and merely descriptive view of language, language for all that is not the only aesthetically or fictionally viable form of life. And again: the present *may* be defined as the 'age of suspicion of the novel', but outside publishers' cocktail parties it hardly amounts to a very central definition. (It seems to go hand in hand with those Jourdainian statements which enliven undergraduate essays, to the effect that 'Hippolyte searches in vain for a way out of the repressive form of the alexandrine' or 'Phèdre has been blinded to the relentless logic of the play's structure', or 'Iphigenie, as she wandered among the ruins of Tauris . . .'.)

§ 107

Non, décidément non, ça ne va pas. . . . J'arrache la page. . . . Je jette. Je prends une autre feuille. Je tape. A la machine. Toujours. Je n'écris jamais à la main. Je relis. . . . Non et non, encore une fois. J'arrache. Je jette.

(Nathalie Sarraute)[33]

M. Jourdain's case is indeed an instructive one, for at a mercifully crude level it may serve as an example of the kind of redoubling of language from which *nouveaux romans* derive their characteristic themes, while pointing to the strictly limited use Molière makes of such devices. The information[34] that he has been speaking *prose* for upwards of forty years amazes M. Jourdain and fills him with great expectations, which however are promptly disappointed: thus enriched, his consciousness has not made a different man of him. On the contrary, the discovery and the unfulfilled expectation alike are thematic only by being particularly brilliant examples of Molière's realism of assessment—his 'perfectly realistic' ridiculing of intellectual pretentiousness. The sentence (nowadays known as 'the message') on which M. Jourdain tries out his discovery—'Nicole, apportez-moi mes pantoufles, et me donnez mon bonnet de nuit'— *may* be 'decoded' as a piece of prose ('quand je dis: "Nicole . . .", c'est de la prose?'), or indeed as the object of any number of diverse informal linguistic analyses, but the decoding is not a significant part of the overt dramatic action.

Like contemporary linguistics, language-conscious fictions are sustained by the irrefutable fact that *any* number of analyses are possible and may lay *some* claim to significance: the play on pronouns in Mme Sarraute's *Martereau*; the play on *les mots* in *Entre la vie et la mort*; the circular discussions of *Les fruits d'or* in *Les fruits d'or*, all work with the same deliberate inanities as M. Jourdain's 'message', but here the 'decoding' is given the pathos of an existential activity. It is offered as moves in a strategy of self-defence and as signs of complex inner processes intended to reveal 'the automatic flow of impersonal, anonymous tropistic movement, common to all men'[35] (or at least to all *nouveaux romanciers?*).

Whatever may be the interest and function of these 'tropisms', it is clear that, where they are elevated to a dominant narrative device, they are bound to undermine that integrity of persons[36] and foreshorten that middle distance to which realism is committed: not just Balzac's or Tolstoy's or Dickens's realism, but every conceivable kind. At some point or other, beyond the silent interplay of *sous-conversations* and subconscious stratagems and anonymous moves, realism is bound to insist that that sentence—*Nicole, apportez-moi* . . .—should *also* emerge and become available within 'the temporal reality of the surface world', in its simple, referential meaning, as a message not a code.

A code is an instruction for using a set of words. The preponderance of message over code is one of the basic conditions of any realistic fiction, as it is of life in the world at large.

§ 108

'Gosh! Quails in aspic again!'

(Pont)

Fascinating like Dr Coppelius's clockwork mechanisms, occasionally exhilarating like M. C. Esher's 'World in a Puddle', literature in the language-conscious mode vaunts its own limitations. Dispensing with 'names, occupations, houses, sets of personal possessions, a full complement of external signs', this fiction is not calling into question some ideological aberration peculiar to the nineteenth century, some mere 'arabesque'[37] of the age of heedless individualism: it is offering

M

an alternative to a whole literary and historical tradition. Western literature may have its *origins* in anonymity (though whether that anonymity has the slightest resemblance to these 'anonymous tropisms' may be doubted), but it becomes available to us—in the Old Testament, in Homer and in Greek tragedy—precisely at the points at which archaic ritual ceases to be inchoate and anonymous, and is refracted in the medium of individual 'names, occupations, houses'. What prevents the literature of language-consciousness from being *un réalisme d'aujourdhui* is that it is trapped inside a self-reflective circle which, in the last resort, turns out to be yet another form of inwardness. The fact that literature in this mode may yield important criticisms and illuminations of the creative process does little to widen the circle. There is no self-evident analogy between the literary and other kinds of creativeness, yet to spell out the analogy inside the 'writing' goes against its grain. The better this language-conscious prose functions—the more it achieves its ideal of internal coherence and self-containedness—the fewer pointers does it provide to activities outside the process of 'writing'. (The value and validity of a symbol like Rilke's rose [§ 118] lies precisely in its indeterminacy and openness.)

The situation 'where every act of creation is inseparable from the critique of its medium, and every work, intensely reflecting upon itself, looks like the embodied doubt of its own possibility'[38] is both fascinating and tedious; and fictionalized doubts concerning literary forms (as we know from some of Thomas Mann's and André Gide's *novelle*) are apt to become less than riveting. (Samuel Beckett observes that literature is the only occupation where the avowal of failure is rewarded.) True, the claim that literature in this mode represents 'a recognition of the reality of language and of the writer's responsibility with respect to that reality',[39] does offer a justification and an escape of sorts: to the extent, at all events, that language is 'a form of life'. But there are other 'forms of life', which language may describe, represent, define, reflect, intimate—but which it '*is*' not, in the sense that when you take language away from one of these other 'forms' (not, of course, from its description) something is left: and these other 'forms of life', with which a substantial part of realistic literature is concerned, are not available to literature in the language-conscious mode. To put it another way: there *may* be occasions, though hardly for the common reader, when 'l'écriture (l'expérience radicale du langage) est une question de vie ou de

mort';[40] life and death, on the other hand, may be described, represented, etc. in language, but the one thing they are not is 'l'expérience
radicale du langage'.

§ 109

A number of curious moves with curious political overtones are
combined in this 'Practice of Writing': all experience is placed under
the hegemony of language; literary creativeness is identified with
creativeness as such; the distinctions between making and interpret-
ing, fiction and criticism, between writer, critic, and reader, tend to
be obliterated; the writer is said to provide merely 'the notation' for
a text which the reader is expected to re-create for himself; a supposedly 'élitist', 'authoritarian' notion of literature (literature as a
vatic and esoteric pursuit) is replaced by the 'democratic' notion of
literature as a mixture of a do-it-yourself and a read-in. All this is
based on a misunderstanding as old as Plato's *Menos*. It is true that the
slave-boy could *follow* the Pythagorean proof, but this doesn't mean
that he could have devised it. The fact that the borderlines between
fiction and criticism are not fixed once and for all and have to be
redrawn every time anew is itself a part of criticism, and doesn't
imply that there are no borderlines. And when a printed page
becomes a meaningful text this is because it is read by a person with
a mind, but that again doesn't imply that the mind that reads it is in
the same relation to the text as the mind that created it. Realistic
literature has never been particularly 'élitist' in its appeal, nor is it
mere 'notation' for the extemporizing of 'creative' readers.
Criticism remains in the main what it has always been: the
debarnacling of texts from the accretions of arbitrariness, an
account of the most faithful understanding possible of what is given
in books.

§ 110

The balance in which the elements of language-conscious fictions are
suspended is easily dominated by them. To take Henry James's
famous 'late style': it is this attention to his own linguistic devices
—the *façons de parler* of his chosen milieu, the inverted commas,
the vocabularies of logic and rhetoric, the intricate images—which
sets a limit to the realism of the masterpieces of his last phase; leaving

us with the open question whether the language is in the service of a complex vision of the predicament of men and women in a complex society, or whether this vision is in the service of an ever more grandiose and remote exploration of the language of fiction.

Realism (to recall an earlier argument, § 95) attempts to preserve the balance: neither the heightened meaning of symbols nor the sentient self nor language-consciousness in its several forms is a stranger to it. To exclude them would be to produce not another form of literature, but no coherent fiction of any kind. A writer will enter his novel and withdraw again, he will modulate his narrative line from the particular occasion[a] to the generalization[b] arising from it, to the self-conscious mode,[c] to the fiction-conscious,[d] and back again through the generalization[b] to the particular[a]:

> ...[a] de même que Rosanette n'avouait pas tous ses amants pour qu'il l'estimât davantage:—car,[b] au milieu des confidences les plus intimes, il y a toujours des restrictions, par fausse honte, délicatesse, pitié. [c]On découvre chez l'autre ou dans soi même des précipices ou des fanges qui empêchent de poursuivre; [d]on sent, d'ailleurs, que l'on ne serait pas compris; il est difficile d'exprimer exactement quoi que ce soit; [b]aussi les unions complètes sont rares.
> [a]La pauvre Maréchale n'en avait jamais connu de meilleur ...
> [*L'Education sentimentale*, III. i]

Or, even more subtly, he will close his work by bringing together his own sentient self, his hero and heroine, *his* fiction and fiction itself, in one final act of homage to the work and the values that have informed it:

> Elle s'étonnait de sa mémoire. Cependant, elle lui dit:
> —Quelquefois, vos paroles me reviennent comme un écho lointain, comme le son d'une cloche apporté par le vent; et il me semble ques vous êtes là, quand je lis les passages d'amour dans les livres.
> —Tout ce qu'on y blâme d'exagéré, vous me l'avez fait ressentir, dit Frédéric.
> [III. vi]

And he will do all this without infringing any proprieties of the realistic canon, without (for example) abandoning that overall pattern of disappointed expectations which is his thematic line.

§ III

What, finally, is at issue here is not the value and interest of the language-conscious mode, but the claim that this mode fulfils the function of realism at the present time. What makes the balance I spoke of precarious is, among other things, its being subject to historical change. If in order to write a Victorian novel, a novelist conscious of living 'in the age of Alain Robbe-Grillet and Roland Barthes' displays something of the artifice involved in such an act of re-creation;[41] if, in order to anchor 'his' characters in 'their' time and place and yet enrich the narrative with the perspective of 'his' time, he shows them to be aware of Sam Weller, adding that they were not aware of Karl Marx; if, in order to trace their potential for freedom against the limits of his manipulative fiction, he writes more than one ending to their story, then all these moves are compatible with realistic fiction provided they are in the service of that fiction: provided, for instance, the articulation of the limits of the fictional world serves to exhibit the characters' potential for freedom and not the other way round; or again, provided the anachronisms help to round out the characters' historicity, not to air the problems of fiction-making.

From Laurence Sterne's and Jean Paul's times to ours novelists have delighted in making their preoccupation with the technical problems of wording and narrative explicit in their fictions; the contemporary claim on behalf of this preoccupation, however, is a good deal more serious in its intention:[42]

> Le réalisme, ici, ce ne peut donc être la copie des choses, mais la connaissance du langage; l'oeuvre la plus 'réaliste' ne sera pas celle qui 'peint' la réalité, mais qui, se servant du monde comme contenu (ce contenu lui-même est d'ailleurs étranger à sa structure, c'est à dire à son être), explorera le plus profondément possible la réalité irréelle du langage.

Barthes arrives at his polemical definition by turning one defective notion—language as a mere means of 'painting' or 'copying' the world—into its equally defective opposite: the world as a mere occasion for setting the exploration of language in train. But if 'the world as content' is seen as 'foreign to the structure, that is the being, of the work [of art]', then that work itself can surely be no more than the chimera of a self-contained, non-referential language system. Moreover, if the world and its values are seen as alien to the work of art and to language that is said to constitute it, by what criteria can we judge one kind of exploration to be 'deeper' than another?

What Barthes calls 'realism', it goes without saying, is no longer a way of facing all the relevant facts of a chosen situation (§ 37), and it is wholly disconnected from the real-life meaning of the term. Well—why not (it may be said), is this more than a quarrel over critical terms? I have already suggested (§ 40) that not all such disputes are without substance. By virtue of its radical denial of a connection between world and 'the practice of writing', Barthes's definition of 'realism' ceases to be exclusively literary (ceases to be what he tells us all literature is), and becomes a value judgment about the world. For it implies that there are, in what he calls our 'reality', no non-linguistic facts and situations worth the artist's interest, and that the precariously defined 'unreal reality of language' is the only *valuable* reality there is—for the artist, and presumably for ourselves too. In this way our common world, indeed anything less hesitant, less esoteric, and less solipsistic too, than language games in a void, is devalued. But (to return to the argument with which this chapter began) what if our common world *is* without value, so that what Barthes is defining is a realism which takes issue with just this situation? It is at this point that his definition ends up by contradicting itself. Claiming for its justification the way things are today, the state of life and the possibilities of literature at the present time, Barthes's view of 'realism' is founded on an interpretation of historical facts and personal experience: facts and experience, once again, which are expressed in language, and in some ways involved in language, but which no conceivable 'knowledge of language' will disclose.

And, finally: can this Manichaean view of the world be sustained? For the symbolist, the solipsist, and the language-conscious writer alike, the proposition 'The system works, but its working reveals it as a self-contained system without meaning and value' (§ 95) is a viable proposition only because it remains untested, because these writers are not directly concerned with the working system at all. Instead, they by-pass it, creating meanings and values that remain on the margins of the world in which we all live. For the realist on the other hand the proposition is not meaningful. The working of the system is, for him, certainly not identical with meaning and value, and yet the meanings and values he is concerned to build up in his fiction cannot be wholly disconnected from the working system; or rather from his creative acknowledgment (§ 67), which is one of the sources of his fiction, that the system works.

This is not a sign of some harmless sociability, some indestructible euphoria[43] at the heart of realism. On the contrary: the working of the system as the condition of a full and unsparing rendering of the tragedy, or the waste, or the desolation inherent in human relations is one of realism's ways of exploring, no less 'deeply' than other modes, the condition of man.

The realist cannot present—as we cannot live in—a wholly meaningless world. The attempt to make a fiction from, and match it against, such a world leads beyond the limits of realism. But equally it may be doubted whether, if this is a man's experience of the world, he will choose to eke out its lack of meaning with fictions built from 'the knowledge of language'.

10

A perennial mode

The Eumenides, the last play of Aeschylus's *Oresteian Trilogy*, ends with the trial of Orestes before twelve Athenian Elders, convened at Athene's bidding to found the Areopagus: 'Citizens of Athens! As you now try this first case / Of bloodshed, hear the constitution of your court'.[1] Pursued by the Furies, Orestes is seeking sanctuary in the temple of Athene in Athens. The facts of his crime are not in question. He has confessed to the murder of Clytemnestra his mother —last in a line of terrible acts of violence originating before the beginning of time in Prometheus's act of impiety—and now asks his protector, the god Apollo, to plead on his behalf. Was the matricide justified by Zeus's superior command in revenge for Clytemnestra's murder of Agamemnon, 'father, husband and king'? Or are the accusing Furies right when they insist that one who has shed his mother's blood cannot be cleansed of his guilt and must forever remain a fugitive, bringing their curses on any city that dares offer him refuge? The detailed pleas for defence and prosecution alike are bound to strike a modern reader as a strangely mixed lot. The arguments over the precise extent of Apollo's (and Zeus's) authority in bidding Orestes revenge the death of Agamemnon, the quibbles concerning the primacy of one kinship relation over another as reflected in the relative gravity of the two murders, all suggest a court whose jurisdiction extends equally over the legal, moral, and religious aspects of the crime. Moreover, politics too is involved, in the Furies' threatening Athens with their curse should Orestes go unpunished, as well as in Apollo's promises of his and Zeus's blessings on the city if its Elders acquit Orestes and give him refuge within its walls. (This political aspect of the action Aeschylus is likely to have had much at heart at a time, in 462 B.C.,[2] when the ancient authority of the Areopagus was being challenged by an anti-traditionalist reformist movement.)

It is far from easy for us to see this grand trial in realistic terms. The gap between myth and history—between the gods with their rivalries, the ghastly Furies spurred by Clytemnestra's ghost, Orestes, and the twelve good men and true—is hard to bridge. The ancient family curse and the petty quibbles, the universal myth and the liturgical technicalities don't seem to add up to 'a system that works'. We are apt to impose a false aesthetic unity—false because created for the purpose in hand—on a situation which Aeschylus's audience will have felt as a single continuum of life more readily than ever we can, and yet not wholly so: classical scholarship confirms our sense that here 'the deity speaks from a greater distance'[3] than it does in Homer.

Our greatest and least adventitious difficulty of interpretation has to do with the active presence of the divine in the characters of Athene and Apollo. It lies in accepting this presence as *a part* of the institution of the court. There is of course the danger of too readily imputing our doubts and velleities to another age. And yet, can this difficulty of the transition from the human to the divine, from the visible to the invisible, have been wholly unfamiliar to Aeschylus's audience? Can it ever—except in their moments of ecstasy—be wholly alien to men whose thinking is in so many other ways familiar to us? Take their idea of justice:

Chorus He chose to become his mother's murderer.
Athene Was there not some compulsive power whose wrath he
feared?
Chorus And who has power to goad a man to matricide?
Athene One plea [the Furies'] is now presented. Two are to be
heard.

Again:

Apollo This man
Has my protection by the law of suppliants.
I cleansed him from this murder. I am here to be
His advocate, since I am answerable for
The stroke that killed his mother.

And again:

Athene And from your polity do not wholly banish fear.
For what man living, freed from fear, will still be just?

The audience before whom this is enacted may well have ideas as to what constitutes admissible evidence, what is the purpose of justice, or what is just, which are radically different from ours; they may above all have a very different—a more abundant—idea of moral responsibility. Yet they have a conception of justice. They understand justice as a thing connected with the human lot and available at least to a class of men, different from revenge and the rule of might—they understand justice as *an institution* and thus as a thing relatively stable rather than subjective and arbitrary. To that extent at all events Aeschylus's audience is our kith and kin. The content of their conception of justice is different from ours, for it is not an exclusively human institution—

Athene This is too grave a cause for any man to judge;
Nor, in a case of murder, is it right that I
Should by my judgment let the wrath of Justice loose

—yet its 'logical form' is the same; we recognize the equation, even though we aren't always familiar with the values of the symbols on each side.

§ 113

The founding of the court is the *mise en scène*, and through it Aeschylus is building a bridge from the visible to the invisible. This is how, in this scene, he is acknowledging the difficulty of which I have spoken, and at the same time solving it. And in that acknowledgment as well as in the solution lies his realism, the perennial mode as it is accessible to us. Perhaps not only there. Classical scholarship may well be able to show that Aeschylus's realism is not confined to his assessment of how to join the human and the divine. Other elements of the play too may have been experienced by his audience as realistic and may be so experienced by us. (In the study of realism as in every other study there is always room for better knowledge.) What the Greekless reader is concerned with in the first instance is an irreducible minimum of realism, a realism that is close to the surface. There is a sense in which its words don't matter, for it is (§ 90) in the structure of the situation depicted (in its 'logical form') rather than in its verbal texture.

This is how Aeschylus builds the bridge. By constituting the Court of Twelve, Pallas Athene is taking the fate of Orestes out of the hands of the partial gods and hostile Furies, and not Orestes' fate only but that of his ancestors and family too. The curse that is upon them, their dreadful deeds and suffering, are to be justified and consummated, or left unjustified and unassuaged, in accordance with a human decision. Yet Athene also resolves (and incorporates her decree in the constitution of the Areopagus) to reserve for herself the right to vote in favour of the accused, which will make her vote decisive in the event of the jury's failing to reach a majority verdict; and this is what happens. The final outcome of the trial is an act of supreme reconciliation and a work of assuagement, because in it all three parties—the gods, human kind, and the Furies who, their wrath spent, will turn Eumenides—are equally involved, equally vindicated. (An *act*, not, as in Goethe's *Iphigenie auf Tauris*, an inwardly motivated change of heart, solves[4] the tragic issue.) True, it is Athene's—the divine—vote that is decisive. But hers is in no sense an arbitrary interference or a superseding of human justice. On the contrary: the condition on which her presence becomes decisive— the circumstance without which her vote would either not become a casting-vote or would amount to an arbitrary act of *force majeure* —is a *human* decision: it is the rational verdict of six mortal men for and six against Orestes' acquittal. In Athene's verdict the judgments of all three parties to the trial are *aufgehoben*,[5] that is, suspended *and* preserved *and* raised to a higher level. The will to justice of all three parties is preserved, because both procedure and verdict are to be the pattern of justice 'in this court / Which I ordain today in perpetuity, / That now and always justice may be well discerned'; and also because the verdict of the supernatural coincides with the principle of *in dubio pro reo*, which almost any society acknowledges as the verdict of 'natural justice'.

Realism designates a creative attention to the visible rather than the invisible, an unabating interest in the shapes and relations of the real world, the system that works. It is the view from below (§ 35). At a time when the invisible too is a part of the world, the system, realism is bound to be concerned with building such bridges as Aeschylus builds here. That perennial, all-too-human doubt about the world's connectedness with the divine is its source and inspiration. The motivation of Orestes' acquittal and full cleansing, followed by the great Panathenian procession and festival, reveals itself as the most realistic assessment of the circumstances necessary for the working of that world. As such it is not just a neutral representation of a man and the institution under whose authority he has placed himself, but a representation *and* an advocacy, not however of a party or faction in that world but of the whole of it, its weal and woe.

§ 114

Auerbach's chapter on Homer takes for its text the recognition scene from the *Odyssey* (canto 19). A concentration on what has here been called the realism of description is characteristic of his procedure even where he bases his interpretation on dramatic texts (in the Shakespeare and Schiller chapters). This kind of realism is found more readily in epic poetry than in classical tragedy, if only because that tragedy is 'the imitation of an action' through and through, so that even the recitals of the Chorus are largely commentaries on past and prophecies of future actions. Auerbach's emphasis, however, tends towards a kind of perennial *chosisme*[6] (which presumably is the reason why he has nothing to say on Greek drama) and needs correcting by an alternative emphasis, on scenes and situations which we recognize as realistic because they display ways of judging with which, once we have had the circumstances described, we are reasonably familiar.

Think of Oedipus's utterly human and familiar insistence on finding out the truth about himself (ignored in Freud's disastrous reading of the play); think of Antigone's despairing-defiant cry:

What help or hope have I,
In whom devotion is deemed sacrilege?
If this is God's will, I shall learn my lesson
In death; but if my enemies are wrong,
I wish them no worse punishment than mine. . . .

or of old Cadmus's lament to Agave (in the *Bacchae*) at the sight of the mutilated corpse of Pentheus, her son and his grandson, 'Your suffering is worst but mine is next. Dionysus, god of joy, has been just. But he has been too cruel.' The scene of the great haggle in Brecht's *Mother Courage*, in which the *vivandière* forfeits the life of her son, Schweizerkas, has no less majesty than this, the harsh material necessity that presses upon her is her *moira* still.

Literature knows no more realistic assessments of the human lot than such scenes as these. What makes them so familiar is what I have called their logical form, which is also the condition of their realism. But (and this is the other side of the dialectic of all authentic interpretation) these familiar assessments are imposed on scenes and situations which have no equivalent in our world, and which we would falsely appropriate if we did not preserve a sense of what is unfamiliar and alien about them.

In thus emphasizing the continuity of our ways of judging—the continuity of the moral experience preserved in literature—we are brought back to the problem posed by human recalcitrance and scepticism in the presence of the divine. Morality has no meaning outside an area of relative freedom, which in turn depends on a less than absolute dominance of the divine. Ages in which this problem is not at issue, either because the presence of the divine is taken for granted (as in the Middle Ages) or because its absence is (as in our own time), are not favourable to literary realism. A world governed by a divinely pre-established harmony would be as little amenable to realistic considerations as a world of absolute freedom, composed of *actes gratuits* and governed by total self-determination; such a world, we say, 'just isn't realistic'.

Once again realism turns out to be a middle mode which has its being between two extremes. Its judgments are ways of rationalizing, mediating, and if possible integrating into the human scheme decrees which in their pure form must remain unfathomable. The function of Apolline art (as Nietzsche describes it) is just this: to make possible a realism which would draw boundaries to our world ('the gods are just') and at the same time intimate its precarious, vulnerable, infinitely exposed situation ('but they are too cruel in their justice').

This is not the speculative precariousness of idealist philosophy with its 'doubts about the reality of the external world'. On the contrary, only when man's 'epistemological situation' is firmly and unproblematically given does realism vouchsafe such poignant glimpses of his cosmic weal and woe.

§ 115

... our empirical confidence in our spontaneous faculty for
understanding others on the basis of our own experience.

(Auerbach)[7]

All *historical* knowledge goes against the grain, for it must come
from our sense for the differentiae, the alien nature of other ages; all
historical *knowledge* must emerge from our sense for their similarities and affinities with our age. If realism has a history, it too must
emerge from a dialectic in which both the familiar and the strange
are *aufgehoben*—suspended *and* preserved. In this way the task of
literary history turns out to be very nearly the opposite of what some
fashionable Marxist theoreticians[8] take it to be. It is not the deliberate amalgamation of 'the text' with 'the life of the text' (which is
apt to mean its posthumous history as a series of answers to successive political needs), but the debarnacling of the text. To acknowledge what difficulties this freeing of worded experience from the
accretions of time offers to the literary historian, what pitfalls of
anachronism and misunderstanding, is one thing; to make a virtue of
anachronisms and deliberately bury the text under them for the sake
of some ephemeral and spurious notion of 'relevance', is quite
another.

Every age—at all events since 'the Greek revolution'[9]—has its own
realism. It is the representative mode of that age in the sense that it
re-presents—makes and matches in words—the reality, the system
that works in that age (§ 105), but not in the sense that it is necessarily the dominant or 'typical' or the most common mode of writing
in that age. (Goethe, we have seen, § 69, is a representative writer of
his age, though rarely a realistic one.) In every case the question of
what was and what was not experienced as realistic literature is
inseparable from a knowledge of how 'the system worked' at a given
time; a question of history, not of philosophy. Now to the extent
that realistic literature is one of the sources of that knowledge, our
argument appears to be circular. Yet this is not a vicious circle, for
realistic literature is of course not our only source of historical
knowledge. Just as our reading of it is illuminated by other, non-
literary sources, so these sources are to some extent verified and the
information they contain is given its appropriate place in 'the system'

by what, in the course of this dialectical process, emerges as the historical testimony of realistic literature.

It may again seem paradoxical to claim that while an age cannot exist without a consensus and common norm of meaning (§ 111), it may well exist without a translation of this consensus into literature at any considerable level of literary achievement and interest. Yet this is no more paradoxical than the complementary claim (§ 73), that while realistic writing represents a positive value (aiming at a target and hitting it) this is, even in a wholly realistic work, by no means the only value to consider. In both cases the paradox is resolved as soon as we recognize that other modes of writing are not necessarily less concerned with the human condition. Less direct, less *re*presentational modes—the different balances between making and matching we find in lyrical poetry and symbolism, in allegory, romance, etc.—are not for that reason less telling, less illuminating of man's lot on earth and under the starry sky. If the history of literature is seen in terms of a Hegelian history of mankind, as the intellectual conquest of ever new and previously uncharted areas of human knowledge-and-experience, may realism and literature itself not find themselves ousted to areas in which they have nothing very interesting left to conquer?

§ 116

What speaks for the Hegelian view is the curious fact of the gradually narrowing focus of literature. Looking back over the most recent phase of literary history, we see that among the themes and devices of literature in the twentieth century, the one that is wholly novel and unprecedented is the atomic view of things and of human experience. With that in mind, we observe a singular progression: from the emblematic characters of Greek drama with their psyche left relatively unexplored, in which social status and divinely ordained role are inseparable from the acting person, through the medieval characterology of humours, through the interaction and conflict of individual passion and political role as we find it in the characters of French classical drama and Shakespeare, through the formal, descriptive, and psychologically unsearching realism of eighteenth-century novels, to realism's peak in the synthesis of description and assessment among the great realists of the nineteenth century (from whose works most of the material of this study derives), and then beyond it, to the social trends and blow-up technique of naturalism, to Proust's celebration of the sentient self ensconced in a world of its own creative recollection, to the interior monologue and *chosisme* with their obliteration of social status and common world, to the dissolving of all persons other than the individual self, ending up in our own time with the fragmentation of that self, too, into a series of drives, 'tropisms', microscopic episodes, and linguistic ploys.

European realism thus appears as the dominant and representative mode of an optimal period—the moment between the way up and the way down—before the culture of the West is superseded by the Atlantic civilization. It is born of a spiritual effort in a setting of material dearth and social inequality, in a moment of history before that effort is channelled into technological solutions in a setting of material abundance and social engineering.

It has its place in a literary history which is 'progressive' in as much as it shows literature as producing ever subtler and more precise images—ever more conscious accounts—of the individual psyche and of its entanglement in the net of social organizations. And at the point where these organizations and their destruction assume global size, ever smaller psychic and physical facts receive ever more minute attenion. (Halfway between the Somme and Auschwitz, Virginia Woolf, the first of the *nouveaux romanciers*, describes the death of a pale-brown fieldmoth.) A history of this kind is conceived on the analogy with the history of science, yielding ever more detailed knowledge of physical nature. Such observations as 'Yesterday's realism is today's convention',[10] or again, 'like the scientific attitude or the democratic ideology, with both of which its destinies are linked, [realism] is a characteristic expression of modernity',[11] spring from a view of literature conceived as a *development*, on the analogy with the progress of the natural sciences or technology or many another praxis. Yet this is only one side of the coin.

§ 117

As against this, it is a sobering thought that 'Anyway, the thing about progress is that it looks greater than it really is'.[12] As we have seen in our discussion of 'the middle distance' (chapter 7), changes of focus involve losses as well as gains: 'the witches in *Macbeth* would be "real" to a Jacobean audience in a way we cannot re-capture',[13] 'disease has a metaphysical function in Balzac's scheme which has no parallel in ours', or again, more questionably, 'a hand-shake in *Madame Bovary* has more sexual impact than the most strenuous bedroom encounter a novelist of our own day can devise for us'.[14] Our own conclusion must once again be that 'the thing that we *can* bring close to us is not the thing we *wish* to come close to' (§ 83). New areas of experience are charted because they are re-garded as important where before they were thought of as trivial. More complex psyches are analysed because, in conditions of highly structured societies and greater material comfort, more complex psyches become available for analysis, their complexity augmented by the analysis. (There is a sense in which to draw a walnut requires greater subtlety than to draw an apple, but the craftsmanship in-volved is not the only hallmark of excellence in painting.) The objects on which literature focuses are not the unchanging objects of the physical sciences, and the systematic elimination of 'observational feed-back', central as it is to the natural sciences, is merely the peculiar tenet of naturalism. The analogy with the history of science breaks down at the point where we acknowledge literature as an activity of the mind whose objects are again minds, 'objects' which are determined by and part of a living process of change.

The history of science is not only a history of supersessions and peremptory burials, nor is the history of literature only the history of achievements and living victories. Both build on what has gone before: partly on dead wood, partly on what proves amenable to modification and development. But while the progress of science obliterates past discoveries and invalidates them in every way except where they can serve as stepping-stones to new discoveries and insights, the history of literature proceeds in a more complex fashion.

§ 118

Rainer Maria Rilke—admittedly an odd witness to call at the end of a study of realism—in his famous epitaph spoke of the poem (sym-bolized by the rose) as 'pure contradiction'. A vision of poetry is hinted at in this phrase, in which poetry is seen as both a rehearsal and an image.

Within this 'contradiction', poetic process and product are held

N

together. The literary work is one man's project of being (*ein Daseins-entwurf*), his sketchy and tentative and never quite accomplished rehearsal of man's varied and seemingly infinite possibilities of being and living. Yet it is also and at the same time his absolute achievement, the unique and unalterable mark he makes and leaves behind, the final and definitive creation that cancels out the contingent circumstances of its generation and hermetically preserves them (the fly in the polished piece of amber) against the ruins of time. Similarly, each passage in a novel, each scene in a play, each poem and image calls for such a double apprehending—as a part which communicates with the whole and helps to build up its total meaning, *and* as a moment, self-contained and self-sufficient, of beauty and arrest. 'Pure contradiction' is the name Rilke gives to the paradox of the work of art as a thing in and out of time. (The full implications of this view lead beyond the theme of this study, for Rilke's poetic vision is not confined to aesthetic problems but indicates their analogical kinship with other modes of experience. The episodes in our lives, too, are parts of a progression and a continuous questioning which ends only with death—'but is *that* an answer?' the dying Heine asked indignantly—an uncertain growing in and groping for a knowledge of the ways of God and a tentative maturing, at best. Yet there are some among these episodes that are also 'perfect in themselves', moments of beauty or poignancy or insight, to which all effortful trying as well as all considerations of maturing, progress, and historical determination are irrelevant and distracting.)

The double view I wish to advance is intended to do justice to the dual nature of our experience of literary works, as both stepping-stones and monuments. They are the creations of individual talents and responses to given existential and socio-historical situations which they in turn modify, parts of a diachronic continuity in which new styles and themes develop from old ones to be in turn superseded, and of a synchronic continuity of affinities and influences within and across national boundaries. It is as such that literary works belong to (general) history and constitute the history of literature; a history of literary realism as a perennial mode is located in the area of the richest and closest contact between the two. But at the same time the works of literature are finished and complete creations of the mind, 'responses' to nothing but their makers' creative urge, achieved forms whose excellence and beauty is not superseded. They are objects of historical interest (like the past achievements of science) but also of perennial delight, images of the human condition available to any generation that cares for them. (They are not necessarily or automatically available; literature is more vulnerable and prone to corruption than any other art, the threat of barbarism is present in ever new forms.)

In this 'monumental' view of literature, the historicity of the reader or spectator is not in question. It is the freedom he needs for that experience of beauty and arrest which is precarious and unnecessary, a mere option; but then, so is literature itself.

§ 119

Different modes and genres of literature fulfil this double function in different ways. The works of realism bear witness more directly to life in the world than any others we know. They accompany man's history and offer a running commentary on it, courting as though deliberately the oblivion of passing circumstance, in need of 'historical context' and explanatory information; at the same time they are like the stars that form the night sky, all equidistant from us, timeless, transfixed images of the possibility of human existence.

Just as there is no single factor that makes them into works of art (save that this is what they are, § 65), so there is no single factor that makes them live (save that this is what they do). Kindred and familiar ways of judging may be one; but then again it may be the portrayal of a virtue which we must acknowledge as alien; it may be the charm of a description familiar by analogy, or again the circumstantial elaboration of the life of a will that is strange to us in its intensity as well as in its circumstances—all these are among the scenes and themes and works that survive. The familiarity realism presupposes need only be of the most rudimentary kind (such as we have in mind when we speak of a work as belonging to 'the culture of the West'); the recognition a work evokes need do no more than initiate the process of literary appreciation. Interpretation is always an appropriation of some kind, but the appropriating self is a living self, neither a shapeless amoeba nor an embattled fortress.

What makes for literary survival? Marx asked the question when, in a note (1857)[15] that remained unpublished in his lifetime, he attempted to reconcile and explain 'the unequal development of material and artistic production':

> The difficulty does not lie in [our] understanding that the Greek epic and art are tied to certain forms of social development. The difficulty is that they still offer us artistic pleasure [*Kunstgenuß*], and in a certain sense represent for us a norm and an unattainable standard.

Two years later, in the version intended for publication, Marx has solved the 'difficulty' by ignoring it: 'The manner of production of material life determines the entire social, political and intellectual process of life.' But how in that case (he does not ask) can 'the products' that 'correspond to a particular stage of development of [the] material means of production'—'the products' of an age other than our own—be accessible to us, unless we are capable of some degree of freedom from this economic determination? A freedom, that is, from the implications of the 'production' metaphor run wild?

§ 120

Karel Kosík, one of the Prague philosophers of 'socialism with a human face', takes up Marx's puzzle and offers to solve it by arguing[16] that since

> social reality as the natural condition of man is inseparable from its products and the forms of its existence;

since also

> reality consists not only in the production of the new but also in the (critical and dialectical) reproduction of the past;

since furthermore

> the work of art is an integral part of social reality, an element in the building of this reality, and a manifestation of the social-spiritual production of man ... it is a work and lives as a work because it *calls for* an interpretation and *is effective* through many meanings,[17]

it follows that

the literary and artistic work [is] a structure of meanings whose concreteness consists in its existence as a moment of social reality. . . . The work lives [and survives] not by virtue of the inertness of its institutional character and tradition. . . . Its life issues not from the autonomous character of the work but from the mutual interaction of work and humanity. Its life is founded in . . . the 'life' of mankind as a productive and receptive subject.

On the basis of Kosík's 'dialectics of concreteness' a new kind of 'Rezeptionsästhetik' has been projected, providing the methodological foundation of a literary history seen as 'a process in which the passive reception of reader and critic is converted into the active reception and new production of the author, or (to put it another way) into a process in which the next work can solve formal and moral problems left unsolved by the last work, and set new problems in its turn'[18]—problems arising from the social world in which and for which an author writes and whose 'horizon of expectation'[19] he shares.

Does Kosík's theory solve Marx's puzzle? It certainly disposes of two conceptions of literature which, though mutually contradictory, have both helped to bring histories of literature to their present impasse: the Platonizing, anti-historical conception of literature as a shrine of timeless and immutable human values, and the crude Marxist 'reflection theory' (e.g. Lukács's equally inert conception of art, and especially realism, as the mere reproduction—a matching without a making—of socio-economic conditions through 'typical' characters and situations, and the proscribing or devaluing of all literature that cannot be readily seen as 'reproductive' or 'reflecting' or 'realistic' in that sense).

The merit of Kosík's theory lies in its dynamic nature. By insisting on the 'productive' aspect of the literary work and on its 'effective life', Kosík convincingly challenges the compartmentalizing of literary studies, whereby 'social background' is seen as something that has to be briefly mentioned and disposed of before we can approach the work of art in its disembodied purity. His theory accounts for the changes in the socio-historical reality of each successive generation of artists and readers, where that reality itself is seen as 'a product of the mutual interaction of work and humanity'. But here too lies its pitfall. Where the survival of the work is explained exclusively in terms of its 'life'—that is, in terms of its ever renewed

effectiveness in and relevance to ever new historical situations—
there the question of how to distinguish between a true and a false
interpretation[20] receives no convincing answer. It is true (as Kosík
observes) that 'the effective function of the work'—its capacity to
emanate illuminations which are themselves factors in the changing
reality of the world—is not 'a quality of the work analogous to the
way that radiation is a quality of radium, for that would mean that
the work would live, that is, be effective, even if no human subject
were to "take it in" '. But to infer from this that 'the life of the work
cannot be understood from the work itself' because 'whatever
happens to the work is a manifestation of what the work is', is to
place not only the *possibility* of interpretation but also *the limits of
an authentic interpretation* in the social reality outside the work.
(What happened to the poetry of the 1920s at the hands of the Soviet
critics is not a manifestation of the works of Yesenin, Pasternak,
Mandelshtam; nor is what happened to the literature of classical
Weimar at the hands of National Socialist critics a manifestation of
the works of Goethe, Schiller, Kleist, and Hölderlin.)

If there is such a thing as an authentic text, there must also be an
authentic reading of it. And though such a reading may be hard to
achieve, to place an exclusive emphasis on 'the life of the text' is to
discredit the attempt before it has got under way. To place the limits
of interpretation outside the work is to expose it to the arbitrariness
of the prevailing notion of 'relevance' or 'historical necessity'[21] or
whatever fashionable interpretation happens to be at hand. (An
example of this arbitrariness is the claim, made frequently by
Marxist critics, that great realistic literature contains, and bad literature ignores or obscures, forecasts of future socio-historical develop-
ments. But since the same ideological interpretation—the same conception of development—is forced on the facts of the past and on
the works of literature alike, it is hardly surprising that only those
'forecasts' turn out to have been truly prophetic which are identical
with the partisan hindsights of the ideology.)[22]

Realistic literature faces the problem of authentic interpretation in
its most critical form, precisely because realism is more closely and
more directly connected with life outside literature than any other
mode (and for that reason, too, it is not particularly 'prophetic').
Kosík's exclusive emphasis on the work as a configuration of words
that answers the questions our situations compel us to ask it, is
misleading. It must be corrected by an equal emphasis on the work

as a configuration of words that answers the question *it* asks, the text whose wording alone provides the limits of its interpretation. The text is not like the wind that isn't when it doesn't blow. The wording is not the palimpsest to which Walter Benjamin compared it.[23] It is more like the dust-covered, almost invisible mosaic on the floor, revived and restored to its old radiance and splendour by the custodian's pailful of water.

§ 121

A brief vacation from the kind of consciousness. . . . (T. S. Eliot)

The works of realism live, often without any manifest relevance to our own situation. They draw on our 'spontaneous capacity for understanding others', which is a factor of our relative freedom from the trammels of our historical situation. Kosík's argument underestimates that capacity and that freedom, just as—for reasons which are wholly honourable and understandable in the situation from which and for which he writes—he is apt to exaggerate the reality-changing capacity of literature.

To say that the work of art requires for its 'life' a human subject that will 'take it in' is one thing, and to say that the question of what constitutes an authentic interpretation of the work is answered by that subject in its socio-historical situation is quite another thing. It is, at best, to regard the work as a stepping-stone and to ignore its existence as a monument.

The work lives and is a monument, not because it preserves certain values which 'in one form or another' are said to belong to the perennial stock of human values, or because the situation it depicts is familiar, or because it happens to answer questions which bother us, but because, while it is fulfilling one or more or several other such conditions, we come to recognize and accept it, usually in agreement with an already established and in that sense 'authoritarian' tradition, as a thing of beauty and a monument. This is 'the frame' (§ 65) we place round it, and this framing of the work is the only invariable condition, within a configuration of variable conditions, which makes for its 'immortality'. The 'frame' is both related to and distinct from 'the life of the text'—the sum total of previous interpretations—just as the work itself is both related to and distinct from the sum total of the 'causes' that have gone into its generation.

Do we, at the point of recognition and acceptance, cease to be historical persons? We certainly don't cease to apply such skills and use such knowledge as we have acquired in the interpretation and experiencing of literature, nor do we collapse in an aesthetic swoon. On the contrary, we become what we are rarely willing to become: readers, spectators, able to attend to situations and concerns quite unlike our own, given over to literature, the most necessary of the unnecessary pursuits of mankind.

§ 122

When M. Jourdain ceased to be astounded by his discovery, the rules of prose didn't cease to be valid, they only became irrelevant. Language is history and growth through and through, yet we use it most of the time without any reference whatever to its historicity, nor do we for that reason use it badly. We don't cease to belong to our world when we decide (the world having enabled us to make our decision) to ignore it and to devote ourselves to some specialized study or pursuit patently disconnected from it. Nor do we cease to be historical persons when, having explored the manifold historicity of a work of art, we give ourselves over to a relatively disinterested contemplation of it. What we do is to exercise a freedom. The two attitudes—the historical and the aesthetic, in the traditional, Kantian sense of the term—are neither incompatible nor necessarily connected. But they are in need of each other, nowhere more so than in the reading of realistic literature. And it is only through the exercise of our freedom, especially in situations which discourage or proscribe it, that we are able to bring the two views of literature together.

'If quality of consciousness matters . . .' (§ 39): literary realism as it has here been considered illuminates our necessities and occasionally helps to remove them. It does something to bring about that situation of freedom—that escape from collective solipsism—in which alone its achievements are discernible, but it does this only incidentally and in an indirect manner. (To rely on literature to do what is the purpose of political institutions is to be of disservice to both.) Refusing all invitations to journeys into the ineffable, realism displays very abundant connections with the non-literary, social and historical aspects of the world it depicts. It therefore also offers very special difficulties of disentanglement from non-literary considerations, requiring the temporality and worldliness of things and situations to be preserved in one form and obliterated in another. But it repays this special effort by confirming for us, more directly and with greater clarity than other kinds of literature, the reality of other ages, other people.

Notes

1 *Three samples*

1 R. P. Blackmur, 'The Loose and Baggy Monsters of Henry James' in his *The Lion and the Honeycomb*, London 1956, p. 268.
2 See *The Notebook for The Idiot*, ed. E. Wasiolek, Chicago 1967, p. 239.
3 Op. cit., pp. 191, 14.
4 See J. P. Stern, 'War and the Comic Muse: *The Good Soldier Schweik* and *Catch 22*', in *Comparative Literature*, XX, 1968, pp. 193–216.
5 'Мы требуем, а не просим!'
6 *Thus Spake Zarathustra*, end of part ii.
7 The note is reprinted at the end of the New York (1962) edition of the novel.
8 *Poetics* chap. iv, 48 b 4, quoted from L. J. Potts's translation, Cambridge 1959, p. 21.

2 *Aims, methods, metaphors*

1 Ludwig Wittgenstein, *The Blue and Brown Books*, Oxford 1964, p. 17.
2 I shall refer to *Mimesis: dargestellte Wirklichkeit in der abendländischen Literatur*,[2] Bern 1949, and also to W. Trask's translation, New York, 1957.
3 *Literary Language and its Public in Late Latin Antiquity and in the Middle Ages*, trans. Ralph Mannheim, London 1965, p. 20.
4 *Mimesis*, ed. cit., pp. 159 ff.
5 This is the title of Erich Heller's essay in his *The Artist's Journey into the Interior*, New York 1965, pp. 89 ff.
6 This is René Wellek's conclusion in 'The Concept of Realism in Literary Scholarship', in *Neophilologus*, xlv, 1961, p. 20.
7 Wittgenstein, *Philosophical Investigations*, Oxford 1953, § 79, end; my own translation.
8 Wittgenstein, *Tractatus Logico-Philosophicus*, London 1922, 6.54.
9 *Correspondance* (Paris 1926–33), v, p. 260 and iv, p. 357.
10 But see below, §§ 41 ff.

11 See I. A. Richards, *The Philosophy of Rhetoric*, London 1936, pp. 96 *et passim*.
12 Ibid., p. 93.
13 See Aristotle's *Ethics*, I. vii, and also § 81 below.
14 See Harry Levin in 'What is Realism?', *Comparative Literature*, iii.3, Oregon 1951; though this argument, like all attempts to ground meaning in etymology, is misleading if it is made to support the view that 'realism' is especially concerned with 'things'.
15 See J. P. Stern, *G. C. Lichtenberg, a Doctrine of Scattered Occasions*, London 1963, pp. 257–9.
16 See Wittgenstein, *Philosophical Investigations*, ed. cit., e.g. i, § 38.
17 See Wellek, op. cit., p. 6.
18 Quoted from Wellek, loc. cit.
19 It is fully represented in G. J. Becker's anthology, *Documents of Modern Realism*, Princeton 1947; recent contributions to the discussion in *Realism* by D. Grant (The Critical Idiom series) London 1970, and *Begriffsbestimmung des Realismus*, ed. R. Brinkmann, Darmstadt 1969, both with full bibliographies.
20 Ernst Fischer's chapter, 'Der Realismus' (in *Von der Notwendigkeit der Kunst*, Hamburg 1967, pp. 113 ff.) contains a sketch of such a history from a moderate Marxist point of view.
21 I am here, and in several other parts of this essay, in happy agreement with E. B. Greenwood's 'Reflections on Professor Wellek's Concept of Realism', in *Neophilologus*, xlvi, 1962, pp. 89–96.

3   *Transcendent matters . . .*

1 Friedrich Schiller, 'Über die tragische Kunst', 1790, my italics.
2 *G. C. Lichtenbergs Aphorismen*, ed. A. Leitzmann, Berlin 1902–8, L 557.
3 G. C. Lichtenberg, op. cit., B 238.
4 At several points in this comparison I am indebted to an unpublished essay by D. H. Green, parts of which are now to be found in his *The Millstätter Exodus: a Crusading Epic*, Cambridge 1966, esp. pp. 230–1, 236, 299; cf. also my *Re-Interpretations*, London 1964, chap. 1.
5 D. H. Green, op. cit., p. 169.
6 Wittgenstein, *Tractatus*, 6.4311.

4   *. . . and ideologies*

1   Johan Huizinga in his essay on 'Renaissance and Realism' in his *Men and Ideas*, New York 1959, p. 290.
2 Bertolt Brecht, *Versuche 13: Der kaukasische Kreidekreis*, Berlin 1954, p. 106.
3 Quoted from W. K. Wimsatt and C. Brooks, *Literary Criticism: a Short History*, New York 1957, p. 469.

4 Georg Lukács, *Geschichte und Klassenbewußtsein*, Berlin [1923] 1968, pp. 222 ff.

5 One thinks of the novels of André Malraux, George Orwell, Arthur Koestler; but also of Andrey Belyi's *Petersburg*, and Conrad's *Under Western Eyes*.

6 Karel Kosík, *Dialektika konkrétního*, Prague 1965, p. 11.

7 'Anna Karenina lives . . . a life just like the life of other women in her sphere. The only difference is that she follows this road consistently to the end . . .' (Georg Lukács, *Studies in European Realism*, London 1950, p. 188).

8 G. C. Lichtenberg, *Physikalische und mathematische Schriften*, Göttingen 1803–6, ix, pp. 145–6.

9 V. Nabokov, *Speak, Memory* (Penguin) 1964, pp. 130–1.

10 Iris Murdoch, *The Sovereignty of Good over Other Concepts*, Cambridge 1967, p. 10; see also 'The Sublime and the Beautiful Revisited' (*Yale Review*, xlix, 1959, pp. 247–71), which deals illuminatingly with many of the topics of this study.

11 Murdoch, *Sovereignty*, p. 14.

12 Hugo von Hofmannsthal, *Buch der Freunde* [1922], Frankfurt-am-Main 1967, p. 23.

13 Michael Oakeshott, *Experience and its Modes*, Cambridge 1935, p. 59.

5 *A conversation*

1 See Egon Schwarz's contribution to 'Realism: a Symposium', in *Monatshefte*, lix, 1967, p. 103; my italics.

2 Ibid.

3 Nietzsche, *Jenseits von Gut und Böse (Beyond Good and Evil)*, § 192.

4 Renford Bambrough, 'Principia Metaphysica', in *Philosophy*, xxxix, 1964, p. 98.

5 Not, however, in the sense in which J. L. Austin uses 'absolutely' in his discussion of 'real' in *Sense and Sensibilia*, Oxford 1962, p. 70. There is at least one other group of uses of 'real' which has no opposite and may be called *affirmative*, as in 'a real stroke of luck'.

6 Matthias Claudius, 'Korrespondenz . . .' (1769), in *Werke* iii, Wien 1927, pp. 24 ff.

7 *Poetics* 51 b 15; G. F. Else, whose translation I quote, adds: 'In translating such a statement it is hard to repress the terms "creator" and "creation" ', seeing that in English 'we are condemned to render "poietés" ("maker") by "poet", in which the etymological meaning does not shine through sufficiently.' (G. F. Else, *Aristotle's Poetics: the Argument*, Cambridge, Mass., 1957, p. 320.)

8 In *Art and Illusion*,[3] London 1968, passim.

9 Nietzsche, *Die fröhliche Wissenschaft (The Gay Science)*, 'Scherz, List und Rache' no. 55 (see Schlechta ed., *Werke*, München 1966, ii. 30); I quote E. H. Gombrich's charming translation, op. cit., p. 75.

10 'Nachlass zur *Morgenröthe*', Hyperion ed., München 1924, xi, pp. 80–1.

11 G. W. F. Hegel, *Grundlinien der Philosophie des Rechts*, end of Preface.
12 Roland Barthes, *Writing Degree Zero*, London 1967, especially the last chapter.
13 Quoted from Georg Lukács, *The Historical Novel*,[2] London 1949, p. 69.
14 Ferdinand de Saussure, *Course in General Linguistics*, London 1960, pp. 90 ff.
15 The phrase is Nietzsche's in the second *Unzeitgemäße Betrachtungen*.
16 See René Wellek's criticism of Auerbach, loc. cit. in n. 6 to chapter II above.
17 *Poetics*, chap. xxiv, 60 a 26, in Else's version.
18 Op. cit., p. 148.
19 Hans Keller, 'Towards a Theory of Music', *Listener*, 11.vi.1970.
20 John Wain in *Observer*, 18.vii.1971.
21 St-Jean Perse, *Poésie* (Nobel Prize speech), Paris 1960.
22 *Confessions*, iii.vii.
23 Hobbes, *Leviathan*, i.3.
24 *Tractatus*, 2.18.
25 Which is what, heedless of the consequences for the reading of his own book, H. Marcuse claims at the end of *One-Dimensional Man* (London 1967).
26 See *Tractatus*, 6.521.
27 See Wittgenstein, *Philosophical Investigations*, § 103.
28 Wordsworth, *The Prelude*, 'Residence in London', line 636.
29 See *Kritik der Urtheilskraft* (*Critique of Judgement*), i. § 34: 'Ich muß unmittelbar an der Vorstellung [eines schönen Gegenstandes] Lust empfinden, und sie kann mir durch keine Beweisgründe angeschwatzt werden.'
30 See his distinction between *Kunstschönes* and *Naturschönes*, op. cit., esp. § 48.
31 See Northrop Fry, *Anatomy of Criticism*, Princeton 1957, p. 66.

6 The charm of institutions

1 Peréz Galdós, *Fortunata y Jacinta*, 1887, vol. I, chap. i. This novel, said to be Galdós's finest and unquestionably a European masterpiece, is not available in English. I had to make do with a somewhat modish German translation (Zürich 1961), but received generous help with my quotations from Dr A. J. Close.
2 R. Brinkmann, *Wirklichkeit und Illusion*,[2] Tübingen 1966, chap. i.
3 Balzac's note for *Le Père Goriot*; quoted from Harry Levin's *The Gates of Horn*, Oxford 1966, p. 192.
4 End of chap. viii.
5 Not even (though Lucien Goldmann in a lecture attempted the interpretation) the dyke-building scenes in *Faust II*, act V. I have considered the political implications of *Die natürliche Tochter* in chap. i of *Re-Interpretations*.

6 K. W. F. Solger, quoted from *Goethe über seine Dichtungen*, ed. H. G. Gräf, I, i, Frankfurt-am-Main 1901, pp. 478–9.

7 I. Watt, *The Rise of the Novel*, Penguin 1966, p. 283.

8 R. Williams, 'The Knowable Community in George Eliot's Novels', in *Novel*, spring 1969, pp. 255–68.

9 G. G. Hough, 'Narrative and Dialogue in Jane Austen', *Critical Quarterly*, autumn 1970, pp. 202–29.

10 *Conversations with J. P. Eckermann*, 25.i and 15.vii. 1827; other examples of this awareness are his observations on the state of German literature in book vii of *Dichtung und Wahrheit*, and his essay 'Literarischer Sansculottismus' of 1795.

11 Quoted from *Marx und Engels über Kunst und Literatur*, ed. M. Lifschitz, Berlin 1950, p. 231; cf. also Peter Demetz, *Marx, Engels, and the Poets*, Chicago 1967, p. 45; for the connection between literature and sociology, see George Watson, *The Study of Literature*, London 1970, chap. ix; and also below, §§ 117–18.

12 E. H. Carr, *What is History?* London 1964, p. 31.

13 *Theorie des Romans*, Berlin 1922.

14 Thomas Mann, *Die Entstehung des Doktor Faustus*, Amsterdam 1949, p. 126; see also Georg Lukács, *Essays on Thomas Mann*, London 1964, p. 115.

15 The quotations come from the opening of *Anna Karenina* and from M. E. Saltykov-Shchedrin's *The Golovlyov Family* (1876) part vii.

16 Herbert Manning, *Her Privates We*, London 1932, last chapter.

17 Vol. I, chap. vi, sections 1 and 2 (cf n. 1 above).

18 Auerbach, op. cit., pp. 459, 431.

19 S. H. Eoff, *The Novels of Pérez Galdós*. St. Louis 1954, p. 3.

20 Wittgenstein, *Tractatus*, 6.45.

7   *The middle distance*

1 Part vii, chap. 29–31.

2 I quote again from the 1908 Preface to *The Awkward Age*.

3 *Nicomachean Ethics* (109 4b) I, iii, 3–4; I have conflated H. Rackham's translation (Loeb 1956, pp. 7–9) with J. A. K. Thomson's (Penguin 1956), pp. 28–9.

4 Pascal's *Pensées*, ed. Brunschvicq, no. 69.

5 La Rochefoucauld, *Maximes*, ed. Régnier, no. 377.

6 Op. cit., no. 104, my italics.

7 *Pensées*, ed. cit., no. 381; cf. no. 114.

8 *Philosophical Investigations* i, from § 69. I follow and occasionally depart from Miss G. E. M. Anscombe's translation (Oxford 1953).

9 Ibid. § 71.

10 Ibid. § 88.

11 G. C. Lichtenberg, ed. cit., L 10, written in 1796; his italics. The 'intentions' (*Absichten*) of the Ring of Saturn are presumably a spoof on astrology.

12 I return here to E. H. Gombrich's leitmotif in *Art and Illusion*,[3] London 1968.

13 G. G. Hough, *A Preface to The Faerie Queene*, London 1962, p. 108, contains a schematic outline of literary concepts between the two poles of 'image' and 'theme'; these correspond in several ways to the 'details of reality' and 'overall meaning' of my argument.

8 Description and evaluation

1 See W. Kayser, *Das Groteske in Malerei und Dichtung*, Hamburg 1960.

2 The distinction is briefly suggested in the last chapters of Ian Watt's *The Rise of the Novel*, Penguin 1966, pp. 300–1; see also his 'Second Thoughts . . .' in *Novel*, vol. I. 3, 1968, esp. pp. 213–14. A somewhat similar distinction, between 'Conscious Realism' and 'Conscientious Realism', is worked out in D. Grant's *Realism*, London 1970, chaps ii, iii. Similarly Ernst Fischer speaks of a 'realism of attitude ('Realismus der Haltung') and 'realism of style or method' (see *Von der Notwendigkeit der Kunst*, Hamburg 1967, pp. 116–17).

3 I must take refuge in St Augustine's statement (which admittedly did not prevent him from speculating on the matter), 'What, then is time? When nobody asks me, I know; when I wish to explain to one who asks me, I do not know.' (*Confessions* XI, xiv.) Without attempting to take issue with Käte Hamburger's *Die Logik der Dichtung* (²Stuttgart 1968), I find myself in agreement with Roy Pascal's criticism of its treatment of 'fictional' and 'lived' time ('Tense and the Novel', in *Modern Language Review*, lvii, 1962, pp. 1–11). Professor Hamburger's entire argument is founded on the premise, itself unexamined, of a categorical difference between 'fictional' and 'literary' narration ('Erzählen') on the one hand and 'fictitious' and 'real' narration on the other. (See also H. Weinrich, *Tempus: Besprochene und erzählte Welt*, Stuttgart 1964, pp. 20 ff.) The present study, on the other hand, sets out to examine what *Die Logik der Dichtung* takes for granted: the otherness of 'literature' and its alienation from 'life'.

4 E.g. to Fielding, whom Ian Watt (*The Rise of the Novel*, ed. cit., pp. 300 f. *et passim*) sees as the first serious practitioner of this kind of realism in the novel.

5 *The Wings of the Dove*, I, ii, quoted from Dorothea Krook, *The Ordeal of Consciousness in Henry James*, Cambridge 1967, pp. 221–2; cf. also p. 199.

6 E.g. in Ernst Jünger's work; see J. P. Stern, *Ernst Jünger: a Writer of our Time*, Cambridge 1952, pp. 29 ff.

7 Wittgenstein, *Tractatus*, 6.41; the translation is mine.

8 Jean-Paul Sartre, *La Nausée*, Paris 1938, p. 222.

9 Wittgenstein, loc. cit.

10 *On Trial: the Case of Sinyavsky and Daniel*, London 1967, p. 261.

9   *Distentions, alternatives, concentrations*

1   Rilke's Ninth Duino Elegy:
> . . . Mehr als je
> fallen die Dinge dahin, die erlebbaren, denn
> was sie verdrängend ersetzt, ist ein Tun ohne Bild.

2   For a historical parallel see, e.g., the quotation from J. Huizinga, § 36 above.

3   From 'Of This Time, of That Place', 1943.

4   See J. P. Stern, *Re-Interpretations*, chap. iv.

5   Dorothy van Ghent, *The English Novel*, New York 1967, p. 29.

6   In 'The Truth about Sancho Panza', 1917.

7   For the quotations from I. A. Goncharov's *Oblomov* (1858), see I, viii, and again III, iv; my italics.

8   See again R. M. Rilke's Ninth Elegy.

9   Wordsworth, *The Prelude*, book xi, 'France', lines 727-8.

10 Franz Kafka, 'Das Urteil' ('The Verdict'), 1912.

11 Mark, xiv. 32 ff.; see also Matthew, xxvi. 36 ff.

12 Christa Wolf, *Der geteilte Himmel*, Leipzig, n.d., chap. xii.

13 V. Dudintsev, *Not by Bread Alone* [1956], London 1957, IV, chap. vii.

14 Georg Lukács, in 1931 (see *Schriften zur Literatursoziologie*, ed. P. Ludz, Neuwied 1961, p. 316).

15 I have already spoken (see § 66) of C. P. Snow's somewhat similar undertaking in respect of our social institutions; however, this is restricted by a defective individual imagination unable to see the men beyond the smoothly working system, not by an embattled ideology.

16 See George Watson, *The Study of Literature*, London 1969, chapter 10.

17 V. Dudintsev's and C. Wolf's novels are mentioned above; the third is Jarmila Kolárová's *Of Family Affairs Only*, Ostrava 1965.

18 See Georg Lukács's two remarkable essays, *Solschenizyn*, Neuwied 1970.

19 *The Artist's Journey into the Interior*, London 1966, pp. 152-3.

20   . . . daß aus seiner Leier
> mehr Klage kam als je aus Klagefrauen;
> daß eine Welt aus Klage ward, in der
> alles noch einmal da war: Wald und Tal
> und Weg und Ortschaft, Feld und Fluß und Tier;
> und daß um diese Klage-Welt ganz so
> wie um die andre Erde eine Sonne
> und ein gestirnter stiller Himmel ging,
> ein Klage-Himmel mit entstellten Sternen . . .

from R. M. Rilke's 'Orpheus. Eurydike. Hermes', in *Neue Gedichte I* (1907); my translation adapts J. B. Leishman's in *R. M. R.: Requiem and Other Poems*,[2] London 1949, p. 102.

21 *War and Peace*, book XI, chapters xix ff.

22 Herman Melville, *Moby Dick; or The White Whale* (Everyman ed.), chapter xliv, my italics.

23 Obviously, what Melville calls 'allegory' includes what we commonly call a literary 'symbol'.

24 The contemporary (1825) German term is *geschlossene Persönlichkeit*; see J. P. Stern, *Idylls and Realities: Studies in 19th century German Literature*, London 1971, chap. ix.

25 E.g. the various definitions given in a recent account of *Russian Symbolism: A Study of V. Ivanov and the Russian Symbolist Aesthetic* by J. D. West (London 1970), pp. 108 ff.

26 Erich Heller, *The Ironic German: a Study of Thomas Mann*, London 1958, p. 192.

27 Baudelaire in *Le peintre de la vie moderne*.

28 Heller, op. cit., p. 193.

29 *The Prelude*, book iii, lines 575 f.

30 Stephen Heath, 'Nathalie Sarraute and the Practice of Writing', in *Novel* iii, 2, 1970, pp. 101–18.

31 *Philosophical Investigations*, § 241. The Viennese tradition includes Johann Nestroy, whom he quotes, Fritz Mauthner, whom he repudiates (*Tractatus*, 4.0031), and Karl Kraus, whom he briefly admired.

32 Michel Foucault (*The Order of Things*, London 1970, chap. iii), attributes it to the French Classical Age; it was certainly central to Herder's cultural history, and to poets like Hölderlin, Blake, Mallarmé.

33 From the first paragraph of *Entre la vie et la mort*, 1968.

34 *Le Bourgeois Gentilhomme*, ii, iv.

35 Heath, op. cit., p. 105.

36 'Le lecteur qui se laisserait aller à son habitude de chercher partout des personnages, qui perdrait son temps à vouloir caser à toute force les mouvements, les tropismes qui constituent la substance de ce livre, s'apercevrait que ses efforts pour les loger convenablement l'ont amené à construire un héros, fait de pièces disparates, qui peut difficilement tenir debout.' (From Nathalie Sarraute's introductory note to *Entre la vie et la mort*.)

37 Heath, op. cit., pp. 104–5 (quoting Hofmannsthal).

38 Heller, *The Artist's Journey*, ed. cit., p. 226.

39 Heath, op. cit., p. 117.

40 Philippe Sollers, quoted from Heath, op. cit., p. 113.

41 John Fowles, *The French Lieutenant's Woman*, London 1969. The self-consciousness works on the lines of D. H. Lawrence's notorious 'Surely enough books have been written about heroines in similar circumstances. There is no need to go into the details of Alvina's six months in Islington' (*The Lost Girl*).

42 Roland Barthes, quoted in Heath, op. cit., p. 117.

43 Roland Barthes, *Writing Degree Zero*, London 1967, pp. 37 ff.

10   *A perennial mode*

1 I have used Philip Vellacott's Penguin translation (1962).

2 See Vellacott's introduction, op. cit., p. 16.

3 Bruno Snell, *The Discovery of the Mind*, Oxford 1953, p. 109.
4 I disagree at this point with John Jones (see *Aristotle and Greek Tragedy*, Oxford 1962, pp. 111, 134–5), whose interpretations elsewhere I find very illuminating.
5 I use the most famous (or notorious) of Hegel's exquisite and outrageous puns.
6 This is what makes Auerbach's last chapter, on Virginia Woolf, the least satisfactory of the whole book.
7 Quoted from *Literary Language and its Public in Late Latin Antiquity and in the Middle Ages*, London, 1965, p. 7.
8 The task of literary history, writes Walter Benjamin, 'is not to present the works of literature in the context of their time, but to present the age that recognizes them—our age—within the context of the age in which they came into being' (*Illuminationen*, Frankfurt-am-Main 1961, p. 203, my own translation).
9 See Gombrich, op. cit., part ii, chap. 4.
10 Harry Levin, *The Gates of Horn*, New York 1966, p. 57.
11 Harry Levin, 'On the Dissemination of Realism', in *Proceedings of the Vth Congress of the International Comparative Literature Association*, Amsterdam 1969, p. 233.
12 Wittgenstein's motto to *Philosophical Investigations*, from Johann Nestroy: 'Überhaupt hat der Fortschritt das an sich, daß er viel größer ausschaut, als er wirklich ist' (*Der Schützling*, act IV, scene x).
13 Greenwood, op. cit., p. 94 (see note 21 on p. 188 above).
14 *Times Literary Supplement*, almost any week of the year.
15 Marx/Engels, *Über Kunst und Literatur*, ed. M. Kliem, Berlin 1967, p. 124–5; I quote from Peter Demetz, *Marx, Engels, and the Poets*, Chicago 1967, pp. 71–3 and note on p. 242, which contains details of dates of composition and publication (by Karl Kautsky in 1901). The *brouillon* was intended as part of the 'Introduction' to the *Critique of Political Economy*, but was suppressed ('or at least never published') by Marx, and replaced by the 'Preface' of 1859, from which I quote in note 17 below. These lines reflect, as Demetz points out (p. 71), the dilemma between the cultured German bourgeois with his traditional love of Greek antiquity and the materialist-theoretician and ideologist.
16 Karel Kosík, *Dialektika konkrétního*, Prague 1965, pp. 93–103, his italics.
17 Cf. Marx's 'Preface': 'The object-of-art [*Kunstgegenstand*], just like every other product, creates a public that is artistically minded and capable of enjoying beauty. Production therefore produces not only an object for a subject, but also a subject for an object.'
18 H. R. Jauß, *Literaturgeschichte als Provokation*, Frankfurt-am-Main 1970, p. 189.
19 Op. cit., pp. 200–1, where the term is attributed to Karl Mannheim and Karl Popper.
20 Kosík, op. cit., p. 97: 'Where is the boundary-line between an authentic and an inauthentic concretization of the work?'
21 Thus Georg Lukács condemns *Salammbô* because it is said to contain

'paradoxes which do not concern us and are artistic because they do not concern us' (*The Historical Novel*, Penguin 1962, p. 222). This supposed failure is said to be representative of 'the crisis of Bourgeois Realism', which in turn is explained by the assertion that 'For the countries of Western and Central Europe the Revolution of 1848 means a decisive alteration in class groupings and class attitudes to all important questions of social life' (p. 202). With regard to English history and literature at all events one is bound to ask, What crisis and what change? The argument of the book is hardly strengthened when, on p. 290, Lukács tells us that 'the historical novel' doesn't exist as a separate genre.

22 It is certainly not by virtue of his intermittent realism that Nietzsche is surely the most prophetic writer of the nineteenth century; in Lukács's terminology, of course, he figures as a proto-fascist.

23 In the introductory section of his essay on Goethe's *Elective Affinities*.

Index